The Experience and
Meaning of Work
in Women's Lives

The Experience and Meaning of Work in Women's Lives

Edited by

Hildreth Y. Grossman
Harvard Medical School

Nia Lane Chester
Boston University
Pine Manor College

LEA LAWRENCE ERLBAUM ASSOCIATES, PUBLISHERS
1990 Hillsdale, New Jersey   Hove and London

Lawrence Erlbaum Associates, Inc., Publishers
365 Broadway
Hillsdale, New Jersey 07642

Library of Congress Cataloging–in–Publication Data

The Experience and meaning of work in women's lives / Hildreth Y.
  Grossman and Nia Lane Chester, editors
      p. cm.
  Includes index.
  ISBN 0–8058–0246–0. — ISBN 0–8058–0247–9. (pbk.)
    1. Women—Employment—United States. 2. Work and family—United States.
I. Grossman, Hildreth Y. II. Chester, Nia Lane.
HD6095.E97 1990   89–16808
331.4'0973—dc20   CIP
Printed in the United States of America
10 9 8 7 6 5 4 3 2 1

To our mothers, with love and admiration

Contents

About the Contributors   ix

Acknowledgments   xiii

1 Introduction: Learning About Women and Their Work
Through Their Own Accounts
Nia Lane Chester and Hildreth Y. Grossman   1

2 Women's Experience of Power Over Others: Case Studies
of Psychotherapists and Professors
Hildreth Y. Grossman and Abigail J. Stewart   11

3 Women Supporting Women: Secretaries and Their Bosses
Virginia E. O'Leary and Jeannette Ickovics   35

4 The Pregnant Therapist: Professional and Personal Worlds
Intertwine
Hildreth Y. Grossman   57

5 Achievement Motivation and Employment Decisions:
Portraits of Women With Young Children
Nia Lane Chester   83

6   *Women's Employment Patterns and Midlife Well–Being*
        Jacquelyn B. James   103

7   *Divorce and Work Life Among Women Managers*
        Faye J. Crosby   121

8   *Crossing Boundaries Between Professional and Private Life*
        Judith Richter   143

9   *"Liberated to Work Like Dogs!": Labeling Black Women*
        and Their Work
        Cheryl Townsend Gilkes   165

10 *Work, Relationships, and Balance in the Lives of Gifted*
        Women
        Diane Tickton Schuster   189

11 *The Working Lives of Terman's Gifted Women*
        Carol Tomlinson–Keasey   213

12 *Blue–Collar Women: Paying the Price at Home*
        on the Job
        Jean Reith Schroedel   241

13 *Discovering the Meanings of Work*
        Abigail J. Stewart   261

        Author Index   273

        Subject Index   279

About the Contributors

Hildreth Y. Grossman is a psychotherapist in private practice in Brookline, Massachusetts. She also teaches and conducts research through the Lab in Social Psychiatry, Harvard Medical School. At present, she is continuing her research exploring the meaning and experience of work in women's lives and extending her study of women therapists. She lives with her husband, Richard, a psychologist, and their 4–year–old daughter, while her other three children are attending college.

Nia Lane Chester is an assistant professor of psychology at Pine Manor College in Chestnut Hill, Massachusetts, where she recently was awarded the Lindsey Professorship for excellence in teaching and research. She is also a research associate at Boston University. Her interests include stress and coping patterns in parents and children, and the role of work in the lives of contemporary women. She is currently working with colleagues on a book about the effects of divorce on families with children.

* * *

Faye Crosby is professor of psychology at Smith College. Her interests in the field of women and work are illustrated in her recent edited books, *Spouse, Parent, Worker* (1987) and *Affirmative Action in Perspective* (1985, with Fletcher Blanchard).

Cheryl Townsend Gilkes is associate professor of sociology and African–American Studies at Colby College. At present, she is writing a volume about African–American women and their community work, and studying religion, culture, and community, particularly concerning the Sanctified Church. An ordained clergywoman, she is an associate minister of the Union Baptist Church, Cambridge, MA.

Jeannette Ickovics recently completed her doctorate in applied social psychology at George Washington University. She is now a post–doctoral Fellow at Yale University, working on issues related to women's health. Her recent research includes a study of the health effects of underemployment for women.

Jacqueline James is a research associate at the Henry A. Murray Research Center of Radcliffe College. In addition to her work in women's studies, she is also examining life–span development and adaptation to aging. Her family life includes her husband, Sam, also a psychologist, and children, Ryan and Carrie.

Virginia O'Leary received her doctorate in social psychology from Wayne State University. She is the director of Radcliffe Conferences on Women in the Twenty–First Century and visiting scholar at Radcliffe College. She wrote *Toward Understanding Women* (1977), co–edited *Women, Gender and Social Psychology* (1985), and is writing a book about women working for and with women for Harvard Business Press in progress.

Judith Richter is a professor in the School of Management, Tel Aviv University, Tel Aviv, Israel. She completed her graduate studies in the United States where she received her doctorate from the Department of Psychology, Boston University. As a parent and professional, she lends her personal knowledge to her scholarship in her studies of the relationship between personal and work worlds.

Jean R. Schroedel is an assistant professor of political science at Yale University. She is the author of *Alone in a Crowd: Women in the Trades Tell Their Stories*. Her research interest in gender politics in the workplace is a direct result of her experiences as a bus driver, machinist, clerical worker, garment worker and grocery store "boxboy."

Diane Tickton Schuster is a research associate and teaches at The Center for Developmental Studies, The Claremont Graduate School, Claremont, California. She also teaches at California State University, Fullerton. Her current research focuses on the life–span development of gifted women and on transitions in the lives of young adults. In balancing her work and family life she is helped lovingly by her husband Jack and their two splendid daughters, Jordana (13) and Ariana (6).

Abigail J. Stewart is a professor of psychology in Women's Studies at the

University of Michigan at Ann Arbor. Her current research interests include families' and individuals' adaptations to transitions and change as well as methods for studying women's lives.

Carol Tomlinson–Keasey is a developmental psychologist whose research focuses on longitudinal studies. Most recently, she has been examing different facets of women's lives, asking how cognitive, emotional, and family factors in childhood contribute to adult functioning. Dr. Tomlinson–Keasey is a professor of psychology at the University of California, Riverside and is currently chairperson of the department.

Acknowledgments

A number of people have contributed to the creation of this book. We wish to thank each of our authors for their thoughtful accounts of women's work experiences. We are indebted as well to all the women who agreed to be interviewed for these projects, and who generously shared their experiences and feelings about their personal and work lives.

For serving as a catalyst in the inception of this book, we want to thank our friend Abby Stewart. We also are indebted to Annette Pringle for her help in finishing this project; her invaluable consultation on indexing brought order to an otherwise chaotic task.

In addition, each of us have individuals we would like to recognize for their direct and indirect contributions to this book.

For Hildy, Richard Bootzin has been a friend, mentor, and role model as a researcher. I am also grateful to Elliot Mishler who extended my research vision to include qualitative methodologies. I also want to thank my four children; Claire and David for their enthusiasm, support, and interest; Robin for what she has taught me about life; and Micaela for her exuberance and for inspiring me to study pregnant and postpartum therapists. I am also grateful to my parents for their support and belief in me. They would have been very proud of this book. Finally, a very special thanks goes to my husband, Richard who contributed in countless ways, both large and small. I am fortunate to have a loving partner in work and family.

For Nia, special thanks goes to the administration of Pine Manor College, and to my friend and colleague, Nancy White, for their enthusiastic and generous support of my involvement in this project. In recognition (and even appreciation) of the permeability of work and family boundaries, I am also grateful to my two terrific sons, Caben and Ian, and to Allan, my prime mover, for their love, enthusiasm, and patience.

Hildreth Y. Grossman
Nia Lane Chester

Chapter 1

Introduction:
Learning About Women and Their
Work Through Their Own Accounts

Nia Lane Chester
Pine Manor College

Hildreth Y. Grossman
Harvard Medical School

Current estimates are that 55% of all woman over the age of 16 are in the labor force, with about 70% at work in the 20–44 age range and 65% in the 45–54 age range (U.S. Department of Labor, 1986, Table A-4). Certainly many millions of woman participate in unpaid work in addition to, or instead of, their paying jobs. The majority of the nonpaying work involves nourishing and maintaining a stable family center for members (their husbands) and future members (their children) of the paid work force. The majority of women function in both capacities.

Due to the rapid expansion of women into all strata of the work force, and in particular in the social sciences, increasing interest and research has been devoted to women's work experiences. It has become clear from these studies that social scientists have relied predominantly on traditional models of work to understand women's experiences. These models, however, have been based on men's occupational experiences, which have been assumed to be the same for women. More recently, researchers and theorists from a variety of disciplines have begun to challenge earlier assumptions as inaccurate reflections of women workers' realities.

A majority of these newer studies have concentrated on the reasons for women's employment and career choices, including changes in economic, family and social conditions (Astin, 1984; Fitzgerald & Crites, 1980; Oppenheimer, 1982; Osipow, 1973, 1975). These studies suggest that women, contrary to traditional mythology, work for much the same reasons that men do: to earn a living and to function as productive and competent members of society. Other studies also provide some important insights into women's experiences within the workplace (i.e., Crosby, 1982; Fox & Hesse-Biber, 1984; Kanter, 1977). Many of them have begun to identify the patterns that typify working women's lives, and the many subtle and not so subtle ways in which institutional and societal barriers impinge upon the experiences and opportunities for working women.

Less attention has been given to the phenomenological experience of work for women; that is, studies that focus on how women view themselves as workers, how they experience their work, and the meaning they make of it in the context of the rest of their lives. The few studies that do take this approach (see e.g., Gerson, 1985; Ruddick & Daniels, 1977; Stratham, Miller, & Mauksch, 1988) confirm that only a direct examination of women's individual experiences clarifies the inaccuracies of earlier assumptions about their work lives.

One of the most obvious limitations to understanding the nature and meaning of work for women lies in the overly narrow definition of what constitutes *work*. Traditionally, social science has defined work as the production of goods and services that are of value to others (Fox & Hesse-Biber, 1984). With this definition as criterion, women should be viewed as involved in work throughout a good part of their waking hours, whether or not they are being paid. Nevertheless, women's work often has been taken less seriously than men's work, particularly when performed without pay. Even for women who do work in a paying job, their work, in contrast to that of men, has been considered less important, less central to their definition of self and personal identity, and less likely to reflect a genuine commitment. There are historical and social reasons behind such beliefs that we describe briefly in order to provide a context for exploring the experience and meaning of work in modern women's lives (see Anderson, 1988, for a detailed review).

A BRIEF HISTORY OF WOMEN'S WORK
IN THE UNITED STATES

During the Colonial period, women and men shared the work. Both were considered important and productive members of the family's and the community's economy. Because of the physical hardships of this frontier period, women's work was as essential and socially visible as men's (Matthaei, 1983).

Although the majority of women's work was devoted to the inner economy of the household, some served as nurses and midwives. In the more commercial economies, life was arduous for women, whose productive tasks included manufacturing fabric, sewing clothing, making candles and soap, and various other necessities for sale or trade (Ulrich, 1982). Making products at home provided a flexible economy for women, particularly during their childbearing and lactating years, when women had an average of eight children. This flexibility enabled her to meet her productive and "reproductive" responsibilities. This arduous life was compounded for Black women who not only faced similar productive and reproductive demands, but did so within the context of the bondage of slavery in the southern colonies.

In the Colonies, the law denied married women rights to property, income, or children separate from their husband's (Ryan, 1983). Some widows took over their husbands' businesses, yet most were impoverished during this period. Furthermore, by the end of the 18th century, widow's assets were vulnerable to their husband's debtors or to claims of adult male heirs (Salmon, 1979).

With the emergence of the Industrial Revolution in the early 19th century, factories took over the production of goods previously produced in the home. The resultant process intensified gender, race, and class stratifications (Anderson, 1988). Women's work became less visible (Cott, 1977) and centered around the home. The image of homemaker reflected the self-denying wife and mother who gratified the emotional needs of her family and promoted her husband's and children's realization of their abilities. The role of woman as caretaker came to be seen as a reflection of her natural abilities and duties, and as such, did not carry the same social value as work performed outside the home. Rather, she was the silent and invisible partner to the "self-made man" who was glorified in 19th-century America.

Many of the women who worked for wages by the end of the 19th century (only about 5%) maintained low visibility in that they continued to work within the home (Kessler-Harris, 1982). Home workers, whether single or married, actually were among the most impoverished members of the labor force. One alternative was for women to provide domestic work in other's homes in exchange for room and board rather than wages. These women also were exploited, and the work reinforced ethnic and racial patterns and stereotypes. Thus, Black women in the south, Irish immigrants in the north and west, and Chinese women in the west replaced native-born White women, which coincided with the social devaluation of domestic work.

Women's entry into textile mills during this period offered greater opportunities; however, they worked long hours with fewer chances for skill development or mobility, received lower wages, and experienced greater job vulnerability than men. In the latter part of the 19th century and the early part of the 20th century, single native-born White women gradually left domestic and agricultural work and attained clerical and retail jobs. They rose from 8% to 29% of the clerical and sales force between 1900 and 1940 (Davies, 1982). Black women, however, were limited primarily to segregated businesses or domestic work, and Hispanic women generally worked in agriculture in the Southwest.

Some women working in industries benefited from the union movement, yet they represented only 8% of the union membership by 1920. Moreover, they were not embraced as equals by male union members because they were seen as a threat to wages and men's jobs (Greenwald, 1980; Kessler-Harris, 1982; Milkman, 1979; Wertheimer, 1977). Where unions failed to provide needed improvement, women turned their efforts toward legislative reform for improving work conditions. Some researchers note that their gains in this area were based more on their rights as mothers than their rights as workers (Baer, 1978; Kessler-Harris, 1982; Nelson, 1984).

During the early part of the 20th century, women in the female-dominated professions had neither the power nor prestige of men in the male-dominated professions (Matthaei, 1983). In fact, during the Great Depression and the early recovery years, one solution to men's unemployment was to fire women holding jobs that were deemed suitable for men. Interestingly, women in female-dominated jobs found their jobs to be more secure.

During World War II, more women entered the labor force, many as replacements for men who served overseas, only to relinquish those jobs upon the return of the men at the war's end. The post-war period found increased consumer demands. This, coupled with women's varied work experiences, fostered women's desire to blend having a family with a paying job.

In recent years, particularly after the important Civil Rights legislation of the 1960s, women's work opportunities are improving, yet discriminatory practices and social pressures continue. Women still face limited employment opportunities in nontraditional areas (O'Farrell & Harlan, 1984; Rossiter, 1982), inadequate child care, and wage differentials, with women earning about 64% of what their male counterparts earn. Although there are growing numbers of women who are entering managerial and professional careers (for example, approximately 30% of the entering class of medical students are women; Grossman, Salt, Nadelson, & Notman, 1987), there are striking absences of women in positions of power and policymaking.

The fact remains that most women are concentrated in relatively few, relatively low-status occupations. In addition, employed women continue to do the bulk of the "home work," regardless of their status, hours, or pay (Baruch, Barnett, & Rivers, 1983).

WHY QUALITATIVE STUDIES?:
ON THE MEANING AND EXPERIENCE
OF WORK IN WOMEN'S LIVES

A number of studies have been conducted in the 1980s that begin to identify motives and patterns typifying working women's lives. Nevertheless, much of this research tends to rely on data generated through the government census bureau and social science research centers. Unfortunately, these large data sets are often used to imply that women's lot as workers has been improved greatly with regard to opportunities, conditions, and pay. Such conclusions can create a false optimism about women worker's experiences that can be particularly damaging for minorities, the poor and/or single parents. This is particularly problematic given that data produced through large survey polls are frequently the basis for policy decisions regarding how and where public money and energy are directed (Herman, 1988).

Research is needed, therefore, that looks for a deeper understanding of women workers' realities by including the meaning women make of their own experiences. It is this deeper understanding that has been called for by feminist researchers and other social scientists using qualitative methodologies.

In order to address this need, we have assembled the work of social scientists from various disciplines, whose investigations were based on qualitative methods and focused on women's work experiences. The research methods they used were varied and included individual interviews, open-ended questionnaires, archival data, group interviews, and other means dedicated to retaining the voices of the women workers who agreed to share their thoughts, ideas, and feelings. It was our intention to provide a forum for women to voice issues, raise questions, and share self-reflections about their experiences of work and the meaning they make of their work in the context of the rest of their lives. It was in this spirit that all of the chapters were written for this volume.

Work in Women's Lives

We have included the work of authors who explored the personal and work worlds of a broad spectrum of women with regard to age, race, marital status, educational background, work status, and individual talents. Given the range of women represented in this volume, it is not surprising that their experiences are varied; nevertheless, a number of common themes weave their separate stories together. Among the most salient are: (a) the need to expand traditional definitions of what constitutes "work"; (b) the fluid nature of boundaries between personal life and work life; (c) the importance of the relational aspects of their work; (d) issues related to the uses of power at work; (e) the role of work in the development of women's sense of self and personal identity; and (f) the degree to which women's work experience is colored by discrimination and sexism. Not all of these themes are represented in all of the chapters or by all women workers. They are sufficiently present, however, to interconnect women from diverse work experiences and personal circumstances.

For example, as the women talk about their work decisions and experiences, it is clear that their *own* definitions of work are much more encompassing of their activities than are traditional academic definitions. Only when we consider this broader context, defined by the women themselves, do we begin to understand what "work" means for the "enablers", "partners" and "mothers" presented by Tomlinson-Keasy, for whom work is construed as facilitating and supporting their husband's careers and their children's growth; how the meaning of a career as "mother" is construed and combined with other career aspirations as seen in the chapters by Chester, Grossman and James; how work for the women described by Gilkes must be understood in terms of their commitment, as professionals and activists, to the needs of the black community.

This broader context within which women experience "work" also helps to clarify why, for women, the boundaries between "work" and family seem so fluid. Given that many women, in fact, have more than one "occupation", they often are required to integrate and balance conflicting demands in ways which result in overflow from one boundary to the other (see e.g., Chester, chapter 5; Crosby, chapter 7; Grossman, chapter 4; James, chapter 6; Richter, chapter 8). The immediacy of this difficulty is reflected in the recent attention given by the media to the issue of a "mommy track": whether women who prefer to integrate their careers and family should be considered as on a separate track from women who chose to devote themselves to their careers (Ehrlich, 1989; Schwartz, 1989). It is interesting to note that in the various discussions of this topic, few have questioned whether focusing exclusively on a career, to the exclusion of other aspects of one's life, actually does produce the ideal worker.

Women also have been described as being less able than men to "compartmentalize" their home and work lives (Goode, 1960; Johnson & Johnson, 1980). In many cases, this observation has had a negative connotation, suggesting that women are deficient in this "skill." As Jessie Bernard (1975) cautioned, however, we must be careful not to be misled by research biases, particularly when it comes to labeling behavior. She notes that all too often the value-laden judgments in sex-role research reflect *male* biases. Thus, for example, the same behavior that could be called cooperative behavior among women is predominantly judged to be dependency. In the present discussion, compartmentalizing one's work life and family life has an implicit value of efficiency, seriousness, and single-mindedness that is highly regarded by males. An alternative evaluation of this behavior suggests that men who compartmentalize their lives often do so at the cost of compartmentalizing their emotions and distancing themselves from others. Grossman's account of pregnant therapists is a good example of how women's ability to draw upon their personal life experiences actually enhances their effectiveness in their professional work. Many of the studies in this volume, in fact, demonstrate that the issue of blending, balancing, integrating, and separating work and personal life is a central concern for women.

A related theme we observed across the chapters is the importance women place on the relational aspects of work. [Connections are important for women, whether it is between work and the family or between themselves and others within the work place.] The women in this book represent a variety of occupations and jobs, yet they put a comparable emphasis on the relational context of their work. The significance of this can help to explain some of the special abilities and sensitivities women bring to their work, as well as some of the stresses to which they are particularly vulnerable.

Several of the chapters, for example, focus on women's preference for nonhierarchical structures in the workplace, because hierarchical structures, by definition, promote inequality in relationships. Thus, women in positions of authority are more comfortable using their power to break down social barriers, to facilitate productive relationships by working *with* individuals rather than stressing their authority *over* them (e.g., Grossman, chapter 4; Grossman & Stewart, chapter 2; O'Leary & Ickovics, chapter 3). O'Leary and Ickovicks also consider the experience of women who work for women who are in positions of power but who are *not* in positions of authority themselves. These workers show a clear preference for bosses who use their power in nonauthoritarian ways. They also point out the dangers of working for women who try so hard to be nonhierarchical that they fail to communicate their directions and needs effectively.

The importance of the "relational context" for women has been acknowledged by a number of contemporary theorists and researchers (e.g., Gilligan, 1982; Miller, 1986). That this theme is also a significant aspect of women's work experience should not cause us to overlook the importance that work plays as a source of personal challenge, exploration, and development. A number of the chapters demonstrate the ways in which women's decisions about working and their experience of work reflect and contribute to their perceptions of self-worth and feelings of personal efficacy (see, e.g., Chester, chapter 5; James, chapter 6; Schuster, chapter 10; Tomlinson-Keasey, chapter 11). Indeed, a common position taken by women throughout the chapters is their commitment to doing their jobs well, and their discomfort when events in their personal life or within the work setting hinder their accomplishing this goal.

Finally, an important aspect of women's experience as workers that must not be overlooked is the degree to which sexism enters their work lives. In some sense, merely by working outside of the home, women are seen as violating social values and norms. The discrimination that they face occurs at all levels: societal (e.g., Gilkes, chapter 9; Schuster, chapter 10; Tomlinson-Keasey, chapter 11); institutional (e.g., Grossman, chapter 4; Grossman & Stewart, chapter 2; O'Leary & Ickovics, chapter 3; Schroedel, chapter 12); and personal (e.g., Chester, chapter 5; Schroedel, chapter 12). Subtle or not so subtle gender discrimination may be experienced through labeling, lowered expectations, lack of support, or overt harassment. Whatever form it takes, its recognition and eradication should be a central priority for a society concerned with enhancing the effectiveness and rights of all its members in the workforce.

REFERENCES

Anderson, K. (1988). A history of women's work in the United States. In A.H. Stromberg & S. Harkness (Eds.), *Women working: Theories and facts in perspective,* (pp. 25–41). Mountain View, CA: Mayfield.

Astin, H.S. (1984). The meaning of work in women's lives: A sociopsychological model of career choice and work behavior. *The Counseling Psychologist, 12,* 117–126.

Baer, J. (1978). *The chains of protection: The judicial response to women's labor legislation.* Westport, CT: Greenwood Press.

Baruch, G., Barnett, R., & Rivers, C. (1983). *Lifeprints.* New York: McGraw-Hill.

Bernard, J. (1975). *Women, wives, mothers: Values and options.* Chicago, IL: Aldine.

Cott, N. (1977). *The bonds of motherhood: "Women's sphere" in New England, 1780–1835.* New Haven, CT: Yale University Press.

Crosby, F. (1982). *Relative deprivation and working women.* New York: Oxford University Press.

Davies, M.W. (1982). *Women's place is at the typewriter: Office work and office workers.* Philadelphia: Temple University Press.

Ehrlich, E. (1989, March 20). The mommy track: Coping with career and kids in corporate America. *Business Week,* pp. 126–134.

Fitzgerald, L.F., & Crites, J.O. (1980). Toward a career psychology of women: What do we know? What do we need to know? *Journal of Counseling Psychology, 27,* 44–62.

Fox, M., & Hesse-Biber, S. (1984). *Women at work.* Palo Alto, CA: Mayfield.

Gerson, K. (1985). *Hard times: How women decide about work, career and motherhood.* Berkeley, CA: University of California Press.

Gilligan, C. (1982). *In a different voice.* Cambridge, MA: Harvard University Press.

Goode, W. (1960). Theory of role strain. *American Sociological Review, 25*, 483–496.

Greenwald, M. (1980). *Women, war, and work: The impact of World War I on women workers in the United States.* Westport, CT: Greenwood Press.

Grossman, H.Y., Salt, P., Nadelson, C., & Notman, M. (1987). Coping resources and health responses among men and women medical students. *Social Science and Medicine, 25*, 1057–1062.

Herman, A. (1988). Forward. In A. Stratham, E.M. Miller, & H.O. Mauksch (Eds.), *The worth of women's work* (pp. ix–xi). Albany: State University of New York Press.

Johnson, C., & Johnson, F. (1980). Parenthood, marriage and careers: Situational constraints and role strain. In F. Pepitone-Rockwell (Ed.), *Dual-career couples* (pp. 143–161). Beverly Hills, CA: Sage.

Kanter, R. (1977). *Men and women of the corporation.* New York: Basic Books.

Kessler-Harris, A. (1982). *Out to work: A history of wage-earning women in the United States.* New York: Oxford University Press.

Matthaei, J. (1983). *An economic history of women in America: Women's work, the sexual division of labor and the development of capitalism.* New York: Schocken.

Milkman, R. (1979). Women's work and the economic crisis: Some lessons from the Great Depression. In N.F. Cott & E.H. Pleck (Eds.), *A heritage of her own* (pp. 507–541). New York: Simon & Schuster.

Miller, J.B. (1986). *Toward a new psychology of women.* Boston: Beacon Press.

Nelson, B.J. (1984). Women's poverty and women's citizenship: Some political consequences of economic marginality. *Signs, 10*, 209–231.

O'Farrell, B., & Harlan, S.L. (1984). Job integration strategies: Today's programs and tomorrow's needs. In B.F. Reskin (Ed.), *Sex segregation in the workplace: Trends, explanations, remedies* (pp. 267–291). Washington, DC: National Academy Press.

Oppenheimer, V.K. (1982). *Work and family: A study in social demography.* New York: Academic Press.

Osipow, S.H. (1973). *Theories of career development.* New York: Appleton-Century-Crofts.

Rossiter, M. (1982). *Women scientists in America: Struggles and strategies to 1970.* Baltimore, MD: Johns Hopkins Press.

Ruddick, S., & Daniels, P. (1977). *Working it out.* New York: Pantheon Books.

Ryan, M. (1983). *Womanhood in America: From colonial times to the present (3d ed.).* New York: Watts.

Salmon, M. (1979). Equality or submersion? Feme covert status in early Pennsylvania. In C.R. Berkin & M.B. Norton (Eds.), *Women of America: A history* (pp. 92–113). Boston: Houghton Mifflin.

Schwartz, F. (1989, January/February). Management women and the new facts of life. *Harvard Business Review,* pp. 65–76.

Stratham, A., Miller, E.M., & Mauksch, H.O. (Eds.). (1988). The worth of women's work. Albany: State University of New York Press.

Ulrich, L.T. (1982). *Good wives: Image and reality in the lives of women in northern New England, 1650–1750.* New York: Knopf.

U.S. Department of Labor. Bureau of Statistics, (1986, January). *Employment and earnings.* Washington, DC: Anthor.

Wertheimer, B. (1977). *We were there: The story of women in America.* New York: Pantheon.

Chapter 2

Women's Experience of Power
Over Others: Case Studies
of Psychotherapists and Professors

Hildreth Y. Grossman
Harvard Medical School

Abigail J. Stewart
University of Michigan

In recent years there has been an enormous increase in research on women's work lives. Most investigations have focused on issues unique to the experience of women workers such as sex discrimination (Crosby, 1982; Fox & Hesse-Biber, 1984; Kahn & Robbins, 1985), sexual harassment (Brewer & Berk, 1982), and dual responsibility for child care and provider roles in the family (Rapoport & Rapoport, 1978; Voydanoff, 1984). Much less research has examined the meaning or inner experience of work for women (see, however, Veroff, Douvan, & Kulka, 1981 for some empirical analysis, as well as Ruddick & Daniels, 1977, for some first-person accounts). The purpose of this study was to explore a particular aspect of the experience of women in careers involving socially sanctioned power over others (specifically, professors and psychotherapists).

The Meaning of Work

There is nearly as little research exploring the meaning or inner experience of work for men as for women (see Osherson, 1980, for an exception). Traditionally, most research on men's work lives has focused on predictors of career success, occupational and social class mobility, and productivity (Duncan, Featherman, & Duncan, 1972; Treiman, 1975, 1977). The role of status or prestige—within one's occupation or within the society as a whole—has been a dominant preoccupation in that research. It has generally been assumed that the importance of status and prestige in men's occupational lives lies in the

fact that status and prestige are simply shorthand expressions of a man's capacity to wield power, command resources, and spend money (Winter, 1973),
and thus the primary motivations for men's work.

In contrast, it has been widely assumed that the purposes of work for
women are social contact, avoidance of boredom, earning supplementary
income for their families, and personal self-expression, although many
women must be employed in order to support themselves and their
families. Moreover, there has long been evidence that even in the absence of
dire financial necessity, money is an important motive for mothers' employment (see Crosby, 1982). It is, then, generally assumed that prestige, status
and wealth have little importance in women's motivation for work.

Research exploring aspects of power more directly (e.g., research on
leadership and power motivation), however, has indicated very few, if any,
sex differences in the tendency to be interested in power (McAdams, 1985;
Stewart & Chester, 1982; Winter, 1988; Winter & Barenbaum, 1985). Although there is some suggestion that women may prefer different power
strategies than men do (Falbo, 1977; Falbo & Peplau, 1980; Peplau & Gordon, 1985; Veroff, 1982; Winter & Barenbaum, 1985), there is little evidence
that women are actually less interested in power than are men.

It has also been suggested that women are less comfortable with having
power than are men, because power holding is inconsistent with the traditional female sex role (Miller, 1982). Thus, it may be difficult to persuade
women to discuss their experience of their own power openly; in fact, it may
be difficult for women to acknowledge their experience in this area to themselves (see Miller, 1986). By examining the meaning of work experiences for
women in careers defined by the fact of power over others, we hoped to explore some of the ways in which power may be important and problematic
in women's work, at least where it is explicitly sanctioned.

The Experience of Power

Theoretical and empirical discussions of power have emphasized the multidi-
mensionality of power (Bass, 1981; French & Raven, 1959; Winter, 1973). According to most definitions, however, interpersonal or social power is one
person's capacity to affect the behavior of another (see Winter, 1973, chapter
1). Power roles legitimate such power relations, conferring the right and responsibility for this capacity on individuals who occupy the role. Nevertheless, power may be formal or informal; sanctioned or unsanctioned; physical
or symbolic; direct or covert; interpersonal or institutional, and so on.

Discussions of the inner experience of power holders (which are more
rare than discussions of the external features of power relationships and interactions) tend to emphasize the sensation of *strength* (McClelland, 1975)
and *domination* (Sampson, 1965). Thus, the phenomenology of power hold-

and *domination* (Sampson, 1965). Thus, the phenomenology of power holding and power wielding has been conceptualized in rather narrow ways as based in an inner experience of personal (sometimes physical) vitality and superiority.

This connection between strength and power highlights the incompatibility of the female sex role and power, because weakness, helplessness, and vulnerability are central to most definitions of "femininity" or the "female sex role" (see Spence & Sawin, 1985). At most, according to traditional sex roles, women may be possessed of indirect power (the power behind the throne), veiled power (an iron fist in a velvet glove), or spiritual power. In fact, many negative stereotypes attend the directly, or overtly, powerful woman (castrating, cold; see Kanter, 1977). Further, Kranichfeld (1987) has recently shown that sex-role norms have served to obscure women's real power within the family, because power has been defined not only as strength, but as residing at the "macro" level, or at least outside the family.

There is one arena in which power is acceptable for women, and has at least some positive connotations: motherhood. Although "real" mothers are often experienced differently, ideal mothers are viewed as wise, pragmatic, loving, self-sacrificing, and fair (see Chodorow, 1978; Chodorow & Contratto, 1982; Dinnerstein, 1976; Trebilcot, 1984). They are powerful, but merciful and tender. Their goal, moreover, is ultimately to relinquish their power, as the children attain adulthood. Thus, their mandate is to empower others.

Traditionally, the high-status occupations to which women have had relatively greater access have been the "helping professions." Perhaps this is because these careers are defined, like motherhood, in terms of circumscribed interpersonal power. Thus, helping professionals (social service workers, teachers, doctors, nurses, therapists) are expected to be caring, fair, wise, pragmatic and self-sacrificing, too. Moreover, their goal—like that of mothers—is the renunciation of their power over any given individual client, patient, or student, as a result of their effective performance of their role (helping or teaching; see Miller, 1986, on "temporary inequality"). In addition, there are powerful norms demanding that the helping role take precedence in most situations (thus, doctors and nurses are expected to care for sick and injured persons, wherever they are). Moreover, there are strict rules of moral and ethical conduct governing the relations between the helper and the helped. In some professions (e.g., psychoanalysis), there has been an extensive and explicit consideration of the ways to limit and channel the power of the helper, for the benefit of the patient (Freud, 1912/1958a, 1913/1958b; Heller, 1985; Kaschak, 1981; Tennov, 1976). In short, the power of the helping professional is defined, delimited, and prescribed. It does not have the quality of exhilaration, personal aggrandizement, or individual initiative characteristic of other powerful occupations (e.g., political office-holding or "captains of industry").

Women's Experience of Power

There is little fully developed theory available to help define the important issues involved in women's experience of themselves in a work role that involves having authority, influence, and impact on others (as a helping professional). Most of the theorists who have explored the issue of women and power have focused on aspects of the mothering role (Dinnerstein, 1976; Janeway, 1980), or women's deep involvement in relationships (Miller, 1986), or both. All of these theorists assume that there may be some special features of women's experience of power (in contrast with men's), deriving from their unique social experience of low social status and extensive socialization in interpersonal skills and the importance of relationships (Janeway, 1980; Miller, 1982). Some consistent themes emerge from these theorists' writings, which have not always emerged from the more traditional literature on power per se.

First, power is viewed in these writings as inherently *relational*. Thus, power is experienced within the context of a human relationship that has many other significant elements or dimensions. Moreover, because relationships endure over time, the power relationship (like the entire relationship) shifts and changes over time. Thus, power is dynamic, or a *process*, rather than static or definitional. In addition, because power is contextualized as one feature of significant human relationships, it is closely linked with the rest of one's experience of oneself as a social being. Thus, power has consequences for one's *identity* as an acceptable, lovable, and loving human being. Because power is viewed, in all of these writings, as inseparably tied to women's emotional connections with other people, it has great potential to evoke *anxiety, ambivalence,* and *conflict.*

A number of issues are not clear, however. For example, in a clearly defined social relationship, how central are affective and identity issues to women's experience of power? How much do women's anxieties as power holders derive from relational issues and how much from other issues (e.g., fear of loss of power—generally considered a more "male" concern). And perhaps most mysteriously, how and how much can women possibly enjoy their own power if it is so intricately linked to anxiety and the risk of loss of identity?

Strategy of This Study

Our goal was to explore how women in relatively high-status helping professions experienced their own power in their work lives.

Psychotherapists and university professors were chosen for study because they held positions of socially sanctioned, legitimate power that were, nevertheless, not too inconsistent with the traditional female role (because they involve helping or empowering others). Because there has been little research in this area, our purpose was not theory testing; instead, we aimed both to accumulate some descriptive information, and to facilitate the development of theory. We adopted a design involving intensive interviewing of a small number of women drawn from two helping professions. This multiple-case study technique allows us to compare different individuals' experience in detail, in order to identify (as in this case) commonalities, or (in principle) differences (Rosenwald, 1988).

Although many interesting themes emerged in these interviews, our focus here is on the ways in which these women discussed—directly and indirectly—their experience of power in their professional activities. We examined the texts for references to the themes proposed by Miller (1982) as central to women's experience of power. In addition, we examined the texts of the interviews for discussions of other aspects of power not captured by themes derived from Miller's analysis. We hoped to extend, develop or revise our understanding of women's experience of power, as a result of these analyses.

METHODS

Participants

In a multiple-case study, "we are guided by the quest for good examples—cases which reveal the inner structure of a social phenomenon or developmental process clearly and distinctively. We select participants opportunistically rather than randomly, giving preference to those who are candid, fluent, reflective, and different from each other" (Rosenwald, 1988, pp. 259–260). For this study, six professional women (three psychotherapists and three psychology professors) were interviewed. All were from within the Boston area. The group of psychotherapists included one psychiatrist, one psychologist, and one social worker, all of whom were affiliated with training institutions and had private practices. We interviewed psychology professors exclusively so that they would be comparable to the psychotherapists in terms of their familiarity with psychological issues and processes. We limited our sample to women who were married, professionally active, and had small children.

Procedure

We explained to each participant that our study was of the professional
and personal experiences of women therapists (or professors). Each participant agreed to meet for two hour-long interviews at 1- to 2-week inter-
vals, in which they would tell their own stories. All interviews were
tape-recorded and subsequently were transcribed. We used interview
methods such as those described by Oakley (1981) and others (see Mishler,
1986, for a discussion of the research interview) who see the interview
emerge in the context of the relationship between the interviewer and interviewee. Oakley (1981), for example, provided a feminist methodological perspective to interviewing; she viewed her interviewees as
collaborators rather than as "subjects" in the research. In this study, we
proceeded with this perspective in mind, not only because of our general
agreement with the feminist perspective, but also because all of our participants clearly had the professional expetise to contribute to the work as
colleagues. Further, the interviews were conducted by us, a psychotherapist and psychology professor who were approximately the same age
and career attainment as the interviewees. Our intent was to minimize
self-presentations issues by having each woman interviewed by someone
who shared her profession and could be seen as a peer. Thus, we conceptualized our interviews as coming closer to a conversation between peers.
Despite this effort, there still remains some inequality in the structure of an
interview because the questions were primarily one-sided. As one professor noted, "After my initial interview with you I realized that I'm just
dying to know, what are your answers to these questions?"

We structured our interviews with open-ended questions in order to in-
vite active participation from each of the women. We began with comparable semi-structured interview schedules for therapists and professors
that addressed 15 areas of concerns (e.g., description of themselves as
therapists or professors; influences of work life on personal life and vice
versa; what is most satisfying and most unsatisfying about their work;
types of patients or students or types of situations that are particularly difficult to work with, including how she handles patients' or students' expressions of anger, sadness, sexual or other difficult feelings; description of
professional development at the present time). We encouraged participants
not to be bound exclusively to the questions we raised. Rather, we encouraged them to include whatever thoughts, vignettes, concerns or questions that occurred to them that would be helpful to better understand their
work experiences.

The second interview was particularly useful for a number of reasons.
First, we were able to generate new questions that arose from our listening
to the audiotapes and reading the transcriptions of participants' first inter-

views. On occasion, some women addressed aspects of a particular area of concern that had not occurred to us as we constructed our interview schedule. For example, when we asked about difficult emotions that were expressed by either patients or students, we included in our probes sadness, anger, and sexual feelings. On a number of occasions women mentioned guilt as a difficult emotion; we therefore integrated a probe for this emotion in subsequent interviews if it was not raised spontaneously. We also used the second interview to complete unanswered questions, and to directly ask about and test our ideas about power for women therapists or professors. Finally, we provided a copy of our results and conclusions to each of the participants to give them an opportunity to comment on any aspect of our interpretations. In fact, of the six participants, three did not provide any direct feedback, one indicated general approval of our interpretations, and two expressed enthusiastic endorsement of them.

Strategy for Data Analysis

The focus of our analyses was on the theme of power, although we are aware that there are clearly a number of other themes that are present and of importance and interest for these groups of women. There are numerous definitions of power (see Janeway, 1980; Winter, 1973); however, for our working definition of *power* in this chapter we combined important elements from several definitions, and thus arrived at "the perceived, experienced or demonstrated capacity to produce an effect on others. This includes individuals, institutions or social systems." Thus, we considered power as an interpersonal construct that included the realms of cognition, affect, or behavior.

We coded responses to the questions from our interview schedule for power themes. The questions were constructed on a theoretical basis for their potential to tap various issues, conflicts, or threats regarding power. All questions were written to be comparable for therapists and professors in form, although it was not possible to make them identical. They were intended, however, to address the same type of underlying material. We applied a thematic analysis of the data using two general strategies. First, we examined the text for dimensions of power outlined by Miller (1982), and then we reexamined the transcripts for themes of power that emerged directly from the material. The process and results of these analyses are described in detail here.

Identification of Power Themes

We initially examined our transcripts for themes of power along the dimensions outlined by Miller (1982) to see whether they were expressed by our sample of women. Miller described dimensions of power that are difficult for women who are in a position of, or face being in a position of, power. She developed her notions about the special concerns women have, based on her clinical observations and discussions with women across a broad class of professions and employment categories. In her discussion of women and power she proposed that there is a cultural norm against women having, using, or needing power. Thus, the preservation of this myth has resulted in women feeling more comfortable with seeing themselves as inadequate than powerful. She suggested that although perceiving one's self as inadequate is hardly ideal, it does not produce the conflict over a feminine self-image that being powerful does: "the use of our powers with some efficacy, and even worse, with freedom, zest and joy feels as if it will destroy a core sense of identity" (p. 4). Moreover, according to Miller, when women confront power they also face the following fears:

1. Power and Selfishness: "A woman's using self-determined power for herself is equivalent to selfishness, for she is not enhancing the power of others" (p. 4).

2. Power and Destructiveness: "A woman's using self-determined power for herself is equivalent to destructiveness, for such power inevitably will totally disrupt an entire surrounding context" (pp. 4,5).

3. Power and Abandonment: "A woman's use of power may precipitate attack and abandonment" (p. 5).

   She also discussed two additional issues as related to each of these themes that we coded for in our interviews; themes of power and inadequacy, and power and identity.

4. Power and Inadequacy: "For many women it is more comfortable to feel inadequate. Terrible as that can be, it is still better than to feel powerful, if power makes you feel destructive" (p. 4).

5. Power and Identity: "The use of our powers with some efficacy, and even worse, with freedom, zest and joy feels as if it will destroy a core sense of identity" (p. 4).

We independently coded our interviews for each of the dimensions Miller identified, by noting whether each theme was present to a strong degree, was moderately present, or was weak or absent, for each therapist and professor. In addition to coding for their occurrence, we noted the content of the episode that illustrated the theme. Examples are presented in the Results section along with the frequency of their occurrence.

Emergent Themes

We also coded power themes that emerged in the transcripts whenever accounts contained descriptions of issues related to power not captured by Miller's dimensions. These included experiences of comfort or pleasure in being in a position of power, powerful, or exercising power; conflicts around having or using power; wishes to be more powerful, or envy of the use or comfort with using power. Themes were identified within the written transcriptions of therapists and professors by each of us independently. We recorded themes only when there was agreement that they represented an aspect of power. The emergent themes from one interview were cross-checked as themes in the next interview. In this way we were able to identify themes that were common among therapists and professors, as well as those that were unique to one interviewee. Details of the themes we identified and their frequency of occurrence are presented in the next section.

RESULTS

Dimensions of Power

We coded the transcripts of therapists and professors for the dimensions of power that Miller (1982) suggested pose difficulties for women in general. Each of the three dimensions described by Miller was coded whenever a woman therapist or professor described herself as having difficulty with power and (a) selfishness, (b) destructiveness, and (c) abandonment. The following are examples of each of the dimensions from both therapists and professors, along with the frequency of their occurrence.

Power and Selfishness

This theme was observed in the transcripts of all three therapists, but it never appeared in a strong or straightforward way. For example, in regard to raising fees, one therapist stated:

> It's for people who contest for any reason, you know. I feel bad, is this a hardship on them?....You know, it's a lot of money; so that it's much easier in a group to do that than if you are alone in a private practice. It really changes it. I mean you do it as a part of a group, not just you individually. The place is raising the fees, not just you individually.

Although this is somewhat indirect, it seems that this therapist is most uncomfortable with the feeling that raising the fee may be seen as an action taken for her personal benefit. She feels it is less selfish if it can be seen as a group action. This indirect relationship of power and selfishness as mediated by guilt can also be observed in the example given here for the professor.

All three professors expressed this theme, two of them fairly directly. One professor described how she felt about finding time for her writing:

> People were always coming to the door, and I was trying to get writing done...I do have moments, almost sinful to me, it is almost sinful gratification of spending long hours by myself without interruptions. I love Saturday and Sunday here at the office.

Although this theme does not always involve exercising power *over* others, it does involve having the power to *exclude* or *ignore* others who have demands to make.

Power and Destructiveness

We coded all three therapists as describing this theme in a direct manner, two of them quite strongly. For example, one therapist indicated in discussing a suicidal patient, "the stakes seemed pretty high. I didn't want to overreact."

All three professors showed evidence of this concern, but their preoccupation with it ranged from quite weak to quite strong. As one of the professors who was most concerned about it asserted, in discussing a student who was angry about a grade:

> Well I recognize that their whole ego defense system has been terribly challenged, which is why they're here; that they're not at their best; that I have managed, as good as my motives may have been, to really hurt this person and I've probably lowered their self-esteem. So I try to be gentle.

Power and Abandonment

Two therapists clearly showed concerns along this dimension, one of them quite strongly, whereas the third showed only a very weak expression of this theme. One therapist expressed concerns about being abandoned, in the context of her planning to take a leave to have a baby, when she said "I don't want to come back to nothing."

All three of the professors described experiences along this dimension, but for one of them the issue appeared only weakly. One professor reported:

> I've had circumstances where a student dropped the course on the spot because of the feedback I gave. She was just so furious....She had rewritten the paper once. There were still enormous problems with it. She came into class. I gave them out on the spot. She looked at it. She slammed it down. She walked out of class. I never saw her again. That was the worst possible outcome.

Other Themes Drawn From Miller

Miller stated that women placed in the role of being a powerholder could suffer feelings of inadequacy and damage to her feminine self-image when she anticipates using, or exercises her power. Although she did not offer these concerns as separate dimensions, they do seem to be serious and costly repercussions of holding and exercising power. The dimensions of feelings of inadequacy and damaged self-image along with the dimensions of selfishness, abandonment, and destructiveness are distinct issues, however, they also are interrelated in some fashion. We proceeded to code our interviews of women therapists and professors for dimensions of power that reflected feelings of inadequacy or concerns about self-image. As with the other three dimensions, as we coded Miller's themes we found examples of each in our groups of women therapists and professors. We often found them, however, embedded in the context of other themes. For example, we found the concern about power and selfishness reported for the professor to be in the context of feelings of inadequacy. Therefore, we present in the text the example that best represents each individual dimension; however, it is on occasion at the expense of the primary meaning of the vignette being narrated.

Power and Inadequacy. This theme appeared to be very weak for all three therapists, with one showing only slightly more concern about this issue than the others. This therapist related the following:

> You deal with people with [depression] all of the time, but I think, with borderline patients, its really life and death and helplessness-helpless as kind of a steady fare. It gets difficult because you get so, you know, they make you feel that way.

In contrast to the therapists, all of the professors expressed rather strong concerns about inadequacy and focused primarily on evaluating students. A professor described her experience this way:

> I find it harder when students are in serious difficulty, when students are suicidal, a woman who's been raped. I find it scary because the students are more genuinely needy, and I'm never sure whether I'm gonna be able to come through the way they need, and I really worry about that. I may take more responsibility than I should, but my sense is that I'm the one they've come to, and they hope and are counting on my helping so I really do worry about it. So when it works out okay, then I feel terrific about it, but they're certainly more unnerving. I hate to see students in real pain and not feel very helpful. Even though I know that it is the reality, I'm not helpful myself, I can't, I don't have the clinical skills, so I can't start really taking care of them myself. And, I do panic.

Power and Loss of Identity.   This theme appeared to be a weak or non-existent theme for therapists and professors. One therapist may have touched on this concern when she explained the following:

> You get, in a certain way, I don't know if inured is the right word, but I remember when I was first starting out, it wasn't nearly so easy. I mean, you know, the identification was much stronger; the comparison, constantly comparing, you know, whatever you were learning about. You were that diagnosis for the month, whatever that was. So I think you sort of develop, and it's not so much distance, but it's not so personal. You don't take it so personally.

In contrast, one of the professors did say the following:

> I feel I get too emotionally involved. I mean, look at me now. I have this dream of myself as someone who's calm and measured and graceful. I think I'm much too affective. I wish I could be a little bit more calm, quiet. I start out always with these students trying, but I do get very emotionally involved.

Nevertheless, it is not clear that even in this example that loss of identity is at risk.

Emergent Themes

In our analysis of the interviews with women therapists and professors, we identified six Emergent Power Themes; three reflected satisfactions associated with power and three reflected strains or stresses associated with power. It is interesting that the satisfactions and the strains seem quite closely related to one another, perhaps, opposite sides of the coin of the same preoccupations or concerns.

We note here the frequency of occurrence of each of the emergent themes as well as examples of the form that they took in the interview. The themes bear a relationship to one another, and therefore they are not separate factors. Thus, the boundaries between emergent themes are not absolute. In addition, the themes of satisfaction and themes of strain appear to be dynamically, or even dialectically linked in ways we review in the Discussion section.

Themes of Satisfaction Associated With Power

1. *Power in the form of nurturance is experienced as very rewarding.* This theme was present to a moderate or strong extent for all therapists and all professors. Power over patients or students is seen primarily as life-giving, vitalizing, and helping, and that power is used is a benevolent way. Power, therefore is experienced in positive ways when it can be felt as nuturance.

For example, one therapist said:

My image [of a therapist] would be of a kind old woman who would listen to the patient...thinking that people come to their own understandings and figure out more things than they think they can....So that's my image, I suppose someone who lets the other person be themselves and grow up and get some confidence.

One professor noted:

That pleasure was tremendous...to feel that I was giving her ideas that she found interesting...feeling that I had made some kind of a difference, and that she—that I had contributed to her intellectual growth. And the other thing, sort of along with that, is to feel that I made someone feel better about themselves—recognize that they have skills that they might not have acknowledged.

2. *The goal of power is to maintain or strive for equality, mutuality, and symmetry.* This was coded as a moderate concern for all of the therapists and all of the professors. Hierarchical structure in relationships is reduced or eliminated by facilitating, empowering and fostering others. This is also accomplished by controlling, exerting authority, and setting limits. Thus, the therapist or professor desires to be on equal footing, without patients or students in a "one-down" or "one-up" position.

One therapist expressed this by saying:

I have a commitment to seeing people at affordable fees, being a practice where people could, a larger range of people could come, working class as well as professional people. So, my fees go pretty low. One way that I've tried to deal with that is to raise the top fee and not always raise the bottom fee....When I think about doing therapy, it may be that I more think about the issues that people bring in and what people's reality is. The therapy helps empower them to deal with that.

Similarly, a professor stated the following:

What I just plain enjoy the most is when a student comes to me with a strong interest of their own, even if it's not mine, and their excitement and their interest has taken it a certain way, and I can demystify a few things, and help them unsnarl a few things, and be a sounding board, and function that way....The student that I love the best in my teaching career does not seem to know what she's doing, or have plans for what to do with her life. So I've been able to bring her into the research project where she performed spectacularly, beyond any reasonable expectation, both in conceptualizing the issues, helping me devise questionnaires and interview schedules, and just in plain old nitty gritty getting things done—getting to the right place....In fact, I have a colleague here, so that there is a joy, both that it's wonderful to work with her, and also that I'm giving her something to put on her vita, and I'm telling her what are you doing and what are you thinking of doing? I guess I like to see myself in that role of sounding board, support figure.

3. *Power can be enjoyable (even exhilarating) even when it is not nurturant, if it is a clear, fully legitimated aspect of the role of therapist or professor;* that is, if it is unchallenged, or appreciated by others (also if used to correct a wrong or injustice, or to restore situations that are out of control). This theme showed considerable variability among therapists, with one displaying strong satisfaction in this area and the other two showing a weak or nonapparent concern for this theme. In contrast, this theme emerged to a moderate degree for all three professors.

For example, one therapist indicated that: "Dealing with people who are either very violent or crazy, I've always kind of thrived on that...I like people who are sick and who I can give medication to and do therapy with...I don't do group work or couples work. I don't like it. It just seemed like too much of a social thing rather than therapy."

One professor recounted the following example of enjoying power that included the following conflict:

I had one cheating incident, blatant, this past semester in the spring, which in a way I did not experience any of the negative emotions I thought I would. In fact I got a kick out of part of it. The exhilarating part was that I did not have to remain too long in suspense whether it was plagiarism...[I] found the published article, which it was, verbatim, from the title to concluding paragraph. So that was sort of exhilarating....Just a little piece of detective work. I felt great, and I felt no qualms whatever about pushing it to the limit. I didn't lose sleep over the notion of taking action and going to the dean.

This professor also expressed another example of her exhilaration with her power when she said:

One thing I do like is feeling center stage. Feeling that I have the audience in the palm of my hand, that I'm being entertaining, but I also like very much an interactive situation even when I'm in a large lecture; kind of a group. And I'm really much more stimulated if something is coming back to me.

Themes of Strains and Stresses Associated With Power

1. *Nurturance must be limited for the powerholder's sake (because of conflicts over feeling she must be infinitely able and available to help) and for the sake of others (to prevent her from being coercive, controlling or destructive).* All therapists and all professors were coded as expressing this theme to at least a moderate degree.

Thus, one therapist said:

To be a good therapist I have to have enough empathy and compassion for [patients], but not get so involved that I think I have to take it home with me, or it's my doing that they are having the troubles that they are. There is a certain amount of distance that you have to cultivate, and humility in realizing that there is only so much that you can do, and satisfaction with your own life outside of that.

As an example of the need to limit nurturance for the sake of the patient, one therapist said:

[in therapy] there is all the nurturing and support which...I'm not big on giving a lot of feedback in therapy to most of my patients because that's not what I feel is helpful. It's not guidance or counseling...I give support or approbation but more by bringing it up and talking about it. I'm very reluctant to say "boy that's great" or along those lines because I think sometimes it seems condescending. They don't know if you really mean it, and I think it's more respectful to note it and talk about it and just by your interest show that it is something to pay attention to than going overboard.

A professor articulated the need to limit nurturance for her own protection when she offered:

I think I'm more self-protective than I used to be and I think I have seen myself as highly un-self-protective, highly giving and selfless toward the students in contradistinction to some unnamed "other" group, giving margins of time, emotional energy and stuff, and I think I'm beginning to say, well, enough is enough. So, maybe I'm beginning to become more like my vision of what the generic teacher is like.

The concern, however, can be to limit risk of being inadvertently harmful to students when she noted:

I think of [being a professor] as a role model for young people. I see it as someone in a pivotal position to convey information on impressionable, and after all, eighteen year olds make up their minds to be dentists or architects or bus drivers on the basis of such incredibly limited knowledge and strange haphazard events. I mean that's the thing that gets to me. Just any chance remark, misinterpreted or interpreted incorrectly or overheard or not heard, you know changes a lot. And I think that teachers are, even in this day and age, accorded some respect by young people, by students. You know, another thing of teaching, I get the shivers sometimes at the way some of my lectures come back to me. Some of the ways that people have interpreted things that I've said. I think I've got to be more careful in some ways because things are going to be interpreted and, not that this happens all the time, but, just very impressionable minds you're talking about, and people who are on the verge of making very important decisions. So I see it as potentially and often inadvertently a powerful position to be in.

Clearly, then, power for this individual involves a responsibility for even unintended effects of one's actions—a responsibility which is burdensome.

2. *Hierarchical power relationships can interfere with symmetrical personal relationships, and can lead to anger, aggression, envy and exaggerated admiration, and therefore are to be avoided.* In addition, hierarchical relationships can produce painful feelings (e.g., envy) and unattractive behaviors (e.g., attempts to manipulate) in patients and students. When seen outside the domain of nurturance, hierarchical power relationships can intimidate patients and students, and knowing this can be uncomfortable for women therapists and professors. All six therapists and professors were coded for revealing this theme in at least a moderate form.

One therapist discussed this theme in terms of discomfort with a patient's envy of her.

People who are envious, on a personal level, being married, having a family. I find that uncomfortable. The competition related to that, you know, uh, the patient's feelings. Yea, I'm comfortable with patients who talk about, say wishing that I was their mother, and so on. I feel comfortable with that.

In a very different expression of discomfort with assymetrical relationships, one professor suggested that student's efforts to manipulate her were problematic consequences of her authority.

I guess I most dislike when I feel students trying to manipulate me, when I feel they may be lying to me, or a student who's been caught cheating, and comes in and tries to get away with it, shows no guilt, and expects you to tell them it's okay to do it. They really annoy me.

3. *Challenges to authority are perceived as personally threatening to the therapist or professor (i.e., ingratitude, open expressions of sexuality, overt or passive expressions of anger, accusations, complaints).* Such expressions can produce anxiety over competence, or adequacy. Two therapists and all three professors showed at least moderate concerns of this type.

Thus, one therapist said:

I guess it would depend on what I felt [a patient's sexual feeling about her] was meaning for him, or how he was using it. I feel that male sexuality has a kind of aggressive component, and I think it, if I thought there was an aggressive component, it might be more threatening to me.

A professor explained her feelings stating that:

When people come and wanna know why you took 3 points off, and when you explain to them why, they look at you and say, "yes, but why did you take 3 points off?" Yeah, people who come in and bitch about a grade, and there have been occasional times when I look at it and I've made a mistake, but mostly not. You explain, it isn't easy that they're complaining, although that makes me feel anxious, and then when you explain it to them they say in a hostile tone, but clearly didn't hear a word you said, "but so I don't see why you took off 3 points"...The whole grading process I think is fairly subjective, even though one tries not to be, and sometimes it's infuriating and sometimes I feel like I had to take a stance that I think I was justifiable in some way but that there's some way it's not, and I feel bad.

DISCUSSION

Detailed analyses of interviews with women psychotherapists and professors suggested that the themes of discomfort with power articulated by Miller are important aspects of these women's experience as powerholders. There were, however, other features of their experience not fully captured by Miller's analysis. These features included some more gratifying, even exhilarating experiences, as well as other painful, or problematic elements.

Themes Derived From Miller's Analysis of Women and Power

The three themes Miller suggested as negative associations with power for women are: selfishness, destructiveness, and abandonment. She found that women wielding power were particularly concerned with the fact that power may entail any or all of these consequences. In fact, we observed all three of the themes in the interviews with both psychotherapists and professors. A concern with appearing, or actually being, selfish was present, but only minimally and indirectly, in all six interviews. Concerns about the potential to do harm, or be destructive, also arose in all six interviews; however, in four of them it was a very strong worry. Finally, the abandonment theme could be identified in all six interviews as well, but it was more variable in intensity. It was only quite weakly and indirectly present in two, and in only two did it appear a very strong concern. Concerns about abandonment also tended to arise in somewhat complex ways, often overtly reflected in concerns about the therapist or professor abandoning or appearing to abandon the client or student (and thus being destructive or selfish), and then being abandoned in turn. In addition, some concerns about abandonment seemed to be in part a function of the structure of the professional relationship between therapists and clients, and teachers and students. Thus, the issue of abandonment appeared to arise in the context of therapists' and professors' wishes for symmetrical, rather than the actually

unequal, relationships with their clients and students. This issue is discussed in detail later.

Miller suggested that concerns about selfishness, destructiveness, and
abandonment both derive from and create even more threatening anxieties
about an individual's basic inadequacy and identity. Therefore, we sear-
ched the interviews for evidence of threats to identity, and experiences of
the self as inadequate in the power relationship. Concerns about inadequacy were prominent in all three of the professor interviews, specifically
arising most often in contexts of evaluation of students (grading, testing,
giving feedback), and student needs for clinical (as opposed to academic)
help. In contrast, the psychotherapists expressed little sense of inadequacy
in performing their role.

It is impossible to be certain about the source of this difference, but it may
be that differences in the two (generally similar) roles account for the difference. For example, the greater ambiguity in the role demands of the
professors may be a factor increasing their sense of inadequacy, although
not necessarily their actual performance. Psychotherapists operate within a
well-defined time and place (usually a 50-minute hour, in an office), and
certain patient behaviors (e.g., personal questions) are "off limits." Although therapists must "enforce" these limits individually, there is broad
consensus about their importance, and clients are taught to expect them. In
contrast, the precise limits of time and space in the professor–student
relationship are unclear. Although students have absolute access to professors in the classroom and office hours, they often expect to have access at
any other time (or place) they can find the professor. Thus, although
academic help is the major element mandated by the teacher–student
relationship, career counseling, personal advice, and information about
other services are often sought and sometimes seem appropriate. The lack
of clear boundaries to the teacher–student relationship, and therefore the
need to be "all things to all students" may render professors more vulnerable to a sense of inadequacy in fulfilling their expectations. In addition,
while therapists do behave in ways which clients perceive as painful, hostile, abandoning, and so forth, the explicit—and sole—purpose of psychotherapy is assisting the client. In contrast, the teacher–student relationship
does include an element of evaluation that is not necessarily aimed to
benefit the student (but may be designed to provide information about
comparative performance). Finally, it is possible that admission of feelings
of inadequacy is even more negatively sanctioned among psychotherapists
than among professors. Therapists are generally expected to meet some
standard of mental health, and must depend for their livelihood on referrals
of patients from one another. It may be, then, that the psychotherapists are
less willing to expose their feelings of inadequacy, rather than less likely to
have them.

The final issue raised by Miller as a danger associated with power for women is the risk of loss of identity. This theme was not directly or strongly reflected in any of the interviews with either therapists or professors. This is, perhaps, not surprising because all six women were experienced, and well-established in their professions. In addition, our sample may differ from the women Miller cited, because her examples were generally drawn from her clinical practice, a group for whom the issue of identity may be more salient. Occasionally, it seemed possible that concerns over protecting their identity indirectly motivated certain behaviors, although they were not expressed directly. For example, one therapist indicated that maintaining "distance" between herself and her clients was very important to her; it is possible, although by no means certain, that this distance was at least partly designed to preserve her identity. It should be noted, however, that to the extent that issues of identity were experienced as "on the line," for these women at all, it was the possible loss of *professional*, rather than sexual or personal, identity.

Several of the women did allude to a process of becoming comfortable with their roles, which suggested that some of the threats or anxieties they experienced had challenged their professional identities at earlier points in their careers. For example, one professor said:

> I can remember one time with a girl talking about how her boyfriend liked it [her paper] and I really let myself get sucked into an argument, and I was very ashamed of myself. It just seemed immature, it seemed like the sort of thing husbands and wives do, or brothers and sisters, and that has not happened in a long time.

More basic challenges to a central *personal* (vs. professional) identity were even rarer.

Overall, the themes Miller articulated clearly did characterize the experience of these women as powerholders to a degree. Nevertheless, some additional aspects of their experience in their roles seemed important and not fully captured by these themes (perhaps because these themes arose in the course of psychotherapy, a context that may tend to "pull" for material involving conflict).

Emergent Power Themes

The most important feature of the women's experience of themselves as powerholders not captured by the themes derived from Miller's analysis was their pleasure in and enjoyment of their power. All six of the women described the power relationship, and the experience of powerholding, as providing deep personal satisfactions and pleasures for them. These satisfactions were not unambivalent, and each of them carried a countervailing risk; nevertheless, the gratifications were real.

Three separate types of gratification could be discriminated, although they certainly also overlapped. First, and most clearly, all of the therapists and all of the professors described their capacity to nurture, support or help their clients and students as an important positive feature of their role. This pleasure in nurturance was experienced most strongly, although, when it took place in a context in which the client or student could be viewed as approaching equality and mutuality with the therapist or professor. On the one hand, both professors and therapists avoided being controlled or "put down" by their students or clients; more surprising, however, they also sought to avoid controlling or putting down their "partner." Thus *empowering* nurturance—resulting in the termination of the unequal power relationship—was experienced as the most gratifying; and the gratification of nurturance was weakened, even destroyed, if the power relationship felt too unequal, too hierarchical, or too permanent. Finally (and also related to the other two themes), these women felt strong and confident when they took actions in their roles that felt fully legitimated by the role. Thus, prescribing drugs for very disturbed patients, exposing plagiarism in students, lecturing to a large classroom of students were experienced as satisfying, sometimes even exhilarating.

Each of these gratifications was also associated with strains or tensions in the power roles. For example, all of the professors and therapists described a sense that their roles demanded nearly infinite nurturance, and that they were forced to protect themselves and their clients and students by setting limits to it. In some cases women reported that constant demands for nurturance at home and at work eroded their capacity to provide it; in other cases women indicated that the demands for nurturance at work were infinite, in principle, and therefore had to be limited. Finally, some women expressed a concern about providing excessive "nurturance"—nurturance that weakens, or creates dependency in the other. In all cases, then, these women experienced nurturance as potentially destructive to themselves or others. In this case, then, the danger of being destructive (identified by Miller) is tied to one of the principle gratifications associated with power; the gratification is only present when the danger is not great.

A second area of strain or tension for these women was the non-nurturant aspects of the "helping" relationship. To be in a relationship in which one can "nurture" or "help" is also to be in a relationship in which one may be manipulated, envied, resented, hated, and unrealistically admired. The painful feelings and unattractive behaviors sometimes elicited in clients and students by their experience as *recipients* of nurturance were difficult for these women to tolerate. Thus, some of the affective and behavioral concomitants of the nurturant relationship, *not directly related to nurturance* but resulting from it, were sources of discomfort and pain for both professors and therapists.

Finally, challenges to their authority were experienced by five of the six women as *personally* threatening; thus, they responded to challenges with anxiety about their competence, or adequacy, and concerns about losing not only their power, but also their relationship with the student or client. This aspect of these women's experience is closely related to Miller's notion that power is associated both with concerns about adequacy and abandonment for women. However, this association was most evident in our interviews in the context of direct challenges to the woman's authority by a client or student. Such challenges were not frequent, and therefore were not a central aspect of these women's experience as powerholders. However, the satisfaction associated with confident exercise of legitimate power on behalf of another were seriously jeopardized by expressions of dissatisfaction or anger on the part of the client or student. In this sense, it is clear that for these women power is profoundly *relational;* if the partner in the power relationship questions the professor or therapist's competence, or motives, or commitment, there can be little or no pleasure in the exercise of power.

CONCLUSION

It is evident that the principle gratifications experienced in the context of these helping professions (legitimate authority, nurturance, and empowerment) were relational, and carried with them analogical strains. It is both the depth and strength of these women's pleasure in their power relations, and the intimate connection between the pleasures and the pains, that seemed not fully captured by the themes derived from Miller's analysis. Nevertheless, most of the painful aspects of these women's experiences were captured at least to some degree by the Miller themes.

The themes identified here may be aspects of all experiences of power; they may not be unique to women or to individuals in helping situations at all. The normative requirement of helping, and the context of a relationship which must extend over time, seem factors likely to make a difference. It is impossible even to begin to draw such conclusions in the absence of other phenomenological data about the experience of power. The gathering of such data—from women in other kinds of power roles, and from men— should be an important priority for students of power, and of the meaning and experience of work.

ACKNOWLEDGMENT

We are grateful to our six interviewees for their candor, interest, and support throughout this project. In addition, we are grateful to Richard Grossman, George Rosenwald, Joanne Veroff, Joseph Veroff, and David Winter for helpful comments on the chapter.

REFERENCES

Bass, B. M. (1981). *Stogdill's handbook of leadership.* New York: The Free Press.

Brewer, M. B., & Berk, R. A. (Eds.). (1982). Beyond nine to five: Sexual harassment on the job. *Journal of Social Issues, 41*(4).

Chodorow, N. (1978). *The reproduction of mothering.* Berkeley CA: University of California Press.

Chodorow, N., & Contratto, S. (1982). The fantasy of the perfect mother. In B. Thorne (Ed.) *Rethinking the family* (pp. 54–75). New York: Longman.

Crosby, F. J. (1982). *Relative deprivation and working women.* New York: Oxford University Press.

Dinnerstein, D. (1976). *The mermaid and the minotaur.* New York: Harper & Row.

Duncan, O. D., Featherman, D. L., & Duncan, B. (1972). *Socioeconomic background and achievement.* New York: Seminar Press.

Falbo, T. (1977). Relationship between sex, sex role, and social influence. *Psychology of Women Quarterly, 2*, 62–72.

Falbo, T., & Peplau, L. A. (1980). Power strategies in intimate relationships. *Journal of Personality and Social Psychology, 38*, 618–628.

Fox, M. F., & Hesse-Biber, S. (1984). *Women at work.* Palo Alto, CA: Mayfield.

French, J.R.P., & Raven, B. (1959). The bases of social power. In D. Cartwright (Ed.), *Studies in social power* (pp. 150–167). Ann Arbor, MI: Research Center for Group Dynamics, University of Michigan.

Freud, S. (1958a). Recommendations to physicians practising psychoanalysis. In J. Strachey (Ed.), *The standard edition of the complete psychological works of Sigmund Freud* (pp. 109–120). London: Hogarth Press. (Originally published 1912).

Freud, S. (1958b). On beginning the treatment (Further recommendations on the technique of psycho-analysis I). In J. Strachey (Ed.), *The standard edition of the complete psychological works of Sigmund Freud.* (pp. 121–144). London: Hogarth Press. (Originally published 1913).

Heller, D. (1985). *Power in psychotherapeutic practice.* New York: Human Sciences Press.

Janeway, E. (1980). *The powers of the weak.* New York: Alfred A. Knopf.

Kahn, E. D., & Robbins, L. (Eds.). (1985). Sex discrimination in academe. *Journal of Social Issues, 41*(4), 135–154.

Kanter, R. (1977). Some effects of proportions in group life: Skewed sex ratios and responses to token women. *American Journal of Sociology, 82*, 965–990.

Kaschak, E. (1981). Feminist psychotherapy: The first decade. In S. Cox (Ed.), *Female psychology: The emerging self* (pp. 387–401). New York: St. Martin's Press.

Kranichfeld, M. L. (1987). Rethinking family power. *Journal of Family Issues, 8*, 42–56.

McAdams, D. P. (1985). *Power, intimacy, and the life story.* Homewood IL: Dorsey Press.

McClelland, D. C. (1975). *Power: The inner experience.* New York: Irvington.

Miller, J. B. (1982). *Women in power* (work in progress No. 82-01). Wellesley, MA: Wellesley College, Stone Center for Developmental Services and Studies.

Miller, J. B. (1986). *Toward a new psychology of women.* Boston: Beacon Press.

Mishler, E.G. (1986). *Research interviewing: Context and narrative.* Cambridge, MA: Harvard University Press.

Oakley, A. (1981). Interviewing women: a contradiction in terms. In H. Roberts (Ed.), *Doing feminist research* (pp. 30–61). London: Routledge & Kegan Paul.

Osherson, S. (1980). *Holding on or letting go.* New York: The Free Press.

Peplau, L. A., & Gordon, S. L. (1985). Women and men in love: Gender differences in close heterosexual relationships. In V. E. O'Leary, R. K. Unger, & B. S. Wallston (Eds.), *Women, gender, and social psychology* (pp. 257–291). Hillsdale NJ: Laurence Erlbaum Associates.

Rapoport, R., & Rapoport, R. (Eds.). (1978). *Working couples.* New York: Harper.

Rosenwald, G. C. (1988). A theory of multiple-case research. *Journal of Personality, 56*, 239–264.

Ruddick, S., & Daniels, P. (Eds.). (1977). *Working it out.* New York: Pantheon Books.

Sampson, R. V. (1965). *The pornography of power.* New York: Random House (Vintage Books).

Spence, J. T., & Sawin, L. L. (1985). Images of masculinity and femininity: A reconceptualization. In V. E. O'Leary, R. K. Unger, & B. S. Wallston (Eds.), *Women, gender, and social psychology* (pp. 35–66). Hillsdale NJ: Laurence Erlbaum Associates.

Stewart, A. J., & Chester, N. L. (1982). Sex differences in human social motives: Achievement, affiliation, and power. In A. J. Stewart (Ed.) *Motivation and society* (pp. 172–218). San Francisco: Jossey-Bass.

Tennov, D. (1976). *Psychotherapy: The hazardous cure.* Garden City, NY: Anchor Press/Doubleday.

Trebilcot, J. (Ed.). (1984). *Mothering: Essays in feminist theory.* Totowa NJ: Rowman & Allanheld.

Treiman, D. J. (1975). Problems of concept and measurement in the comparative study of occupational mobility. *Social Science Research, 4*, 183–230.

Treiman, D. J. (1977). *Occupational prestige in comparative perspective.* New York: Academic Press.

Veroff, J. (1982). Assertive motivations: Achievement versus power. In A.J. Stewart (Ed.), *Motivation and society* (pp. 99–132). San Francisco, CA: Jossey-Bass.

Veroff, J., Douvan, E., & Kulka, J. (1981). *The inner American.* New York: Basic Books.

Voydanoff, P. (1984). *Work and family.* Palo Alto CA: Mayfield.

Winter, D. G. (1973). *The power motive.* New York: The Free Press.

Winter, D. G. (1988). The power motive in women—and men. *Journal of Personality and Social Psychology, 54*, 510–519.

Winter, D. G., & Barenbaum, N. B. (1985). Responsibility and the power motive in women and men. In A. J. Stewart & M. B. Lykes (Eds.), *Gender and personality* (pp. 247–267). Durham, NC: Duke University Press.

Chapter 3

Women Supporting Women: Secretaries and Their Bosses

Virginia E. O'Leary
Radcliffe College

Jeannette R. Ickovics
Yale University

Sigourney Weaver's portrayal of Katherine Parker, the "boss from hell" in the film *Working Girl* has rekindled the debate about the difficulties that torment women who work for women. At the heart of the debate lies the stereotypic view of the woman boss as someone for whom no one, man or woman, wants to work (cf. Bowman, Wortney, & Greyser, 1965; Ferber, Huber, & Spitze, 1979; Kahn & Crosby, 1985; Sutton & Moore, 1985). Fueling the debate are a number of recent trade books such as *Women versus Women: The Uncivil Business War* (Madden, 1987), *Woman to Woman: From Sabotage to Support* (Briles, 1987), *Success and Betrayal: The Crisis of Women in Corporate America* (Hardesty & Jacobs, 1986), and *How to Work for a Woman Boss* (Bern, 1987). The latter details "over 280 coping strategies that will help you to adjust to this new phenomenon in the workplace" (p. 3). The book contains seven self-administered questionnaires designed to assist those who work for women bosses to identify their bosses' management styles as "non-listeners, power brokers, non-management managers, or hesitant decision makers, etc." Clearly the underlying premise is that working for a woman is problematic, a situation with which one must learn to cope. The depiction of women in positions of status and power as problematic is pervasive. Is it accurate? Several studies conducted to examine the relationship between women bosses and their secretaries suggest that it is not (Ickovics & O'-Leary, 1988; O'Leary & Ickovics, 1987; Stratham, 1986).

Today, women work for women in a variety of capacities, as administrative aids, deputy directors, vice presidents, and associates. However, one of the most prevalent working relationships between women who work for women is that of secretary and boss. Indeed, almost one third of all women employed by either women or men, work as secretaries, according to a 1987 report by the National Commission on Working Women. However, research on working women has focused on college graduates, professional, and middle-class women, resulting in a dearth of research on the "average" or "typical" working woman: the secretary. We know that secretaries are often overqualified for their jobs (Burris, 1983; Majchrzak & Gutek, 1977), experience moderate to high burnout (Nagy, 1985), are relatively dissatisfied compared to women and men in higher status jobs (Golding, Resnick, & Crosby, 1983), and suffer significantly higher levels of coronary heart disease than other working women (Haynes & Feinleib, 1980). However, we know little about their day-to-day work lives and their relationships with co-workers and bosses.

Further, although a reciprocal relationship between secretaries and bosses clearly exists, secretaries have rarely been queried about their perceptions of work-relevant factors (for exceptions see Gupta, Jenkins, & Beehr, 1983; Ickovics & O'Leary, 1988; Kanter, 1977; O'Leary & Ickovics, 1987; Stratham, 1986). With the exception of some research on supervisory leadership and satisfaction with supervisors, most research on sex and status in the workplace has been uni-directional. It has focused on the evaluation of subordinates by superiors—with researchers looking for the effects of sex and status on these evaluations (Hollander, 1985). There has been relatively little research investigating the perceptions and evaluations of bosses by their subordinates.

This study was designed to begin to fill these gaps in the literature. Twenty-three female secretaries employed in an academic setting were interviewed. Each was asked about a variety of aspects of her job and the job environment, her boss, and her relationships with both boss and co-workers. This sample was unique in that bosses and secretaries alike were women. As we see here, the information we gathered on women supporting women did not confirm the current popular depiction of women as "bosses from hell," nor did we find unlimited competition, cattiness, or betrayal.

We hope we have been honest and objective in our presentation of the information that these women shared with us. Wherever possible, we have permitted them to speak for themselves: all quotations (unless otherwise referenced) come directly from the respondents themselves. We have simply combined the information in a logical and coherent manner.

In order to acquaint the reader with the basic demographic characteristics of the sample, we begin by describing the secretaries themselves and their jobs. We then go on to examine the relationships between the secretaries and the women for and with whom they work. Within the context of these boss and peer relationships, we explore issues of cooperation and competition, intimacy and friendship, and competence and sensitivity. Secretaries' perceptions of their bosses' management styles, task- versus person-oriented or instrumental versus expressive, are emphasized, as well as the secretaries' perceptions of the manner in which their bosses use power. Finally, the nature of the work environment is considered from a "community" perspective. Where possible, corroborative data from other empirical studies are used comparatively, and the interview findings are discussed in terms of contemporary organizational theory.

THE SECRETARIES

Participants in the current study were women employed at a prestigious women's academic institution. This institution employs 104 individuals; of these, 28 women work in clerical and support positions for women supervisors. All of these staff assistants were contacted and asked to participate in the study. Twenty-three (82%) agreed. All of the workers held similar low level staff jobs; however, they worked in a variety of small offices, ranging from 3 to 14 employees. In these offices they were exposed to diverse work situations with diverse co-worker and supervisory experience.

The women ranged in age from 19 to 58, with an average age of 32. Thirteen were age 30 or younger. Two of the women were Hispanic, one was Black, and the remaining 20 were White. The highest degree obtained by a majority of study participants was a college degree ($n = 20$); of the remaining three, two had Masters' degree, and one had a high school degree. Six were married (five had children, who ranged in age from 3 to 36); one was in a committed lesbian relationship, and three others were self-reported lesbians. The remaining 13 were heterosexual, some of whom were involved in monogamous relationships.

Five of the respondents were in their first job following completion of college or after a year of graduate school. Ten had previously worked in other secretarial jobs or as "temporaries." Three had been employed as writers or editors before assuming their current positions; another three came from different nonsecretarial jobs. Two had re-entered the work force after their children were grown. The length of time each had been employed in her current position ranged from 1 week to 11 years. More than half of the sample (13 of 23) had been in their jobs for 1 year or less.

Most reported that they had high expectations for the future. Some thought they would stay in their current positions for a while, but most saw their present situation as temporary. They were "biding their time," until they could return to school or until the right job came along. Their aspirations ranged from travel consultant, through architect and psychologist, to college president.

THE JOBS

All respondents were classified by the personnel department as either "Staff Assistant I" or "Staff Assistant II." Annual salaries ranged from $14,330 to $23,550. More than one half of the secretaries we interviewed were making under the salary mid-point of $16,940.

According to the job description published by the personnel office, these positions entailed the performance of a variety of "noncomplex or moderately complex" support duties for an administrative unit. This includes day-to-day clerical, financial, record keeping or processing duties; gathering data and assisting in the preparation of reports; and, acting as liaison between the institution and the general public, providing information in their particular areas of responsibility. Typing and word processing, oversight of other support staff and personnel, and "performing job-related duties as required" rounded out the job description on record. The educational requirement stipulated for these positions was high school graduate or equivalent, preferably with business training beyond high school and 1 or 2 years of office or related experience.

The secretaries in our sample were better educated and/or more experienced than their job descriptions stipulated. As previously mentioned, all but one respondent had at least a college degree. Two-thirds of the women reported that they had responsibilities beyond those described as traditionally clerical. Some indicated that they engage in research and report writing, others do bookkeeping and other forms of financial accounting. Other duties included office management, such as ordering supplies and coordinating social functions. These tasks are generally in line with the formal job description, and they match the self-reports of secretaries' office tasks in another recent study (Kagan & Malveaux, 1986). Not everyone saw herself as "a secretary," although the duties delineated in the job description for Staff Assistant are clearly those of secretary, clerical worker or lower-level administrative assistant.

Even though it is difficult to characterize the secretaries' job descriptions and job tasks as stimulating or challenging, almost all of the women we talked to said that they played an important role in the overall success of their offices. They saw their work as "crucial" to day-to-day functioning. "I know very well that without the clerical staff places tend to fall apart," observed one woman. Some suggested that if they were not there, office functioning would be disrupted. One woman said, "If I don't answer phones and make appointments, no one will." Another reflected, "If I were to leave the office, there would be panic for about a month because I do all the bill writing, have all the people to call at my fingertips, and know where to get things done." As one person put it, "My work is necessary, but not meaningful."Even though most of the women interviewed reported that they had "a voice" in the decisions made in their offices, they viewed that voice as minor and wondered if their ideas were afforded real respect. One secretary noted, "Sometimes, I get the feeling that they don't give you the respect you deserve....I know I'm capable of making some of the decisions and making adequate suggestions." She also found it difficult to evaluate how seriously her suggestions were taken: "I don't really know [if they listen to me], they are still going to do what they want to do. Sometimes they look at me as though I have two heads." Many reported that their contributions were "undervalued" and "unappreciated."

Two-thirds of the women we interviewed felt that they were "overqualified" for their jobs. Some used education as their criteria, others used experience. "I feel overqualified in that even though you have to have certain organizational skills—someone who does not have working experience would not be able to do this job—there's not enough real challenge or reward for someone who has more experience like I feel I do." Another reported, "I feel overqualified because I have different goals for myself and I wasn't expecting to be doing this." One college graduate indicated that she was "embarrassed" to admit how she earned her living.

A common complaint (15 of 23) was that their jobs provided few opportunities to learn new things. Of those who did report they had acquired new skills, those skills were almost entirely technical (i.e., word processing, computers). Only 3 of 23 women in the study considered themselves to have any opportunity for advancement. The majority described their jobs as "temporary" or as a "stepping stone." "You have to leave here to get anywhere," said one secretary, "so you might as well do a good job while you're here." Another stated, "Everyone in this office knows that it is going to be a stepping stone, that they will go on to do something better."Not surprisingly, these women reported that the least satisfying aspect of their overall work experience was the secretarial job itself. Low pay, lack of prestige, little challenge, tasks characterized by repetition and tedium, and the dead-end nature of their positions were the negative factors these women attributed to the secretarial role. Despite these negatives, for the majority of the secretaries there was an overwhelming sense of satisfaction with their overall work experience. Their satisfaction with work was defined by the relationships they enjoyed with the people, almost exclusively women, with whom they interacted: their bosses, their co-workers, and the scholars in residence. Indeed, when asked to identify the single most satisfying aspect of their work, the answer was *relationships*.

THE RELATIONSHIPS

Despite the plethora of popular literature on women's working relationships, little is empirically known about the quality and the dynamics of these relationships (see O'Leary, 1988, for a review). Contrary to some of the early literature suggesting that women's relationships in the workplace are negative and unhealthy (Goldberg, 1968; for a review see Nieva & Gutek, 1981; Staines, Travis, & Jayerante, 1973), more recent evidence seems to suggest that these relationships can be positive and productive (O'Leary & Ickovics, 1987; Slade, 1984). The current study strongly supports this positive view: The women in our sample like working for and with other women.

All of the respondents reported that they got along at least moderately well with co-workers and supervisors. Many rated these relationships "very good" or "excellent." "I think the relationships are the reason I like this job and intend to stay, even though on a lot of levels I am dissatisfied. I feel the people are all worth it," said one woman. Another described the relational aspects of work as "crucial" to her sense of satisfaction, even more important than money. "If I wanted to make more money I could be working at a high-tech firm 15 miles away; those jobs are there. But I care much more about this one and about the people I work with—they're worth it." In the words of a third secretary, "The relationships keep me going. Relationships are 90–95%: that makes the job."

The significance of relationships is so great that when they are troubled (i.e., a co-worker with a negative attitude or a boss in a bad mood), the respondents say they "absorb it" and it affects them adversely. "If everybody around me has a bad attitude...then I find it impossible to work with those people after a certain point." Another stated:

> I find it difficult to work in situations where I don't have respect for the people I work with, or they don't have respect for me. It makes a tremendous difference: you spend more of your life working and with these people than you do with anybody else.

Only 4 of the 23 respondents indicated that their feelings about their jobs were independent of their feelings about their co-workers.

Competition in the Workplace, or Lack Thereof. In spite of the great number of contemporary writings depicting competitive women "backstabbing their way to the top" (Petersen, 1988, p. A1), we found little evidence that sisterhood stops at the office door. As Lipman-Blumen (1988) recently observed, "women hold the title for collaborative, contributory, and mentoring behavior" (pp. 24–25). In our sample, 20 out of 23 of the women interviewed reported that there was "absolutely" no competition at work. When asked whether there were feelings of competition in the workplace, the "no" was both immediate and unequivocal. In the overwhelming majority of cases, respondents indicated that there was "definitely cooperation" and that they "never sensed competition." One woman described the office relationships as characterized by "immense loyalty," another labeled the climate as one reflecting "team spirit."

Among the plausible explanations for the lack of competition reported is the clear delineation between the roles of director and support staff. In a series of interviews conducted with young women in a cooperative program training to be secretaries, O'Leary (1987) asked about their reactions when they found themselves assigned to a woman boss for a week. The criteria they used to evaluate women bosses were distinctly different than those they used to evaluate men. They reported making immediate judgments about the women—negative judgments based on feelings of competition when the boss resembled them too closely in age, experience (or lack thereof) and appearance. When the woman boss was clearly older, more experienced, or looked the part of boss (i.e., was professionally groomed and attired), that is when her role was clearly delineated, the secretaries-in-training were more positively disposed and were less likely to report feelings of competition.

An alternative explanation for the absence of competition is the lack of any expectation for advancement (Kanter, 1977). This is illustrated by a comment from one secretary:

[There is] the feeling that we aren't going anywhere. This job is not as important as a career. It's nothing worth creating a negative relationship over. It's just a job, which is very different from a sense of a profession and a need to climb.

These two factors are interrelated in the view of one woman who noted, "Most of the roles are very defined. There is not any sense that anyone would be moving up or trying to show up another person in order to look better than anyone else." Another woman observed that "there is no competition because no one wants my job."

The role separation between women was stronger for secretaries and bosses than for secretaries and co-workers. It did not seem to occur to anyone that they might be competitive with their bosses; their bosses held an edge, both in terms of education and experience. "I am not in a position to compete with my boss—for anything," said one secretary.

Many of the secretaries we spoke with reported that everyone "works together to get the job done," "to reach the office goals." Apparently this extends to the basic "office-keeping" tasks such as photocopying, sharpening pencils, and making coffee. These were important issues to many of the respondents. They were very aware of the "demeaning" quality of these tasks, and when possible, they were grateful to be spared these responsibilities. For example, one secretary told the story of being asked to sharpen her bosses pencils. After she politely refused, she ordered her boss an electric pencil sharpener. She reported that this was an isolated incident; both boss and secretary now sharpen their own pencils. In another office, "coffee" was an issue. The division of labor is such that the first one in makes the coffee; when the pot runs out, the person who pours the last cup makes a fresh pot. Cleaning the coffee pot at the end of the day, etcetera, is done by whomever has "KP" duty, an undesirable assignment that is rotated weekly.

Most of the secretaries viewed this cooperation and community spirit as beneficial, although one woman remarked that sometimes they spend so much energy being nice to each other that job tasks do not get done. In her ideal work world "you don't have to be so super-careful about feelings if it's pretty clear what the objective is in terms of getting something done." Another commented, "Because we're all so personal, sometimes it's hard to be matter of fact about things." Contrary to what might be expected, this spirit of cooperation was not based on intimacy of association as much as a more bounded sense of community.

Work and Friendship May Not Mix. Only one third ($n = 8$) of the secretaries characterized their relationships with their co-workers as "friendships." An additional six suggested their relationships with others were friendly in that they talked and went to lunch together but did not share confidences. The remainder reported that they kept their personal and professional lives separate. Older women were more likely than younger ones to deem such separation appropriate. This was especially true for those older women with children, who felt they had more in common with one another than with their younger peers. One woman reported:

> Another lady in the office is about my age and I get along with her fine because we have a lot of things in common. The other two girls are a lot younger than I am. Maybe it's because they are still single and don't have the same problems I deal with, sometimes they don't understand when I need flexibility. I don't know, they seem to be insensitive to the ladies.

Presumably for her, the distinction between "girls" and "ladies" was one based on age and parental status. This theme was echoed by another woman, who when asked if she shared personal concerns with her co-workers, replied, "No, because I'm the only woman in the office who is a wife and mother."

Some of the respondents did consider their bosses as friends. One secretary said, "you wouldn't even consider her a director, because she's so much like us; you know, we talk to her like a friend. She's the Director, your supervisor, but she's a lot easier. And she'll join right in with us, whatever we're saying." Although the majority of respondents liked and respected their supervisors, there was a certain personal distance due to what was deemed "an appropriate relationship" between secretary and boss. The relationships among women were defined, in part, by perceptions of their similarities and differences (O'Leary, 1988). The age-based disparity between younger and older co-workers seemed to be magnified by the role-based disparity between secretaries and their bosses.

THE BOSSES

In a reference handbook for secretaries, entitled *How to Be a Top Secretary,* Delano (1954) addressed the uniqueness of the secretary–boss relationship. She stated that "there are some elements which transcend the ordinary employer-employee relationships (p. viii). Kanter (1977) too has examined this relationship, concluding:

> The secretary–boss relationship is the most striking instance of the retention of patrimony within the bureaucracy. Fewer bureaucratic "safeguards" apply here than in any other part of the system. When bosses make demands at their own discretion and arbitrarily; choose secretaries on grounds that enhance their own personal status rather than meeting organizational efficiency tests; expect personal service with limits negotiated privately; exact loyalty; and make the secretary a part of their private retinue, moving when they move— then the relationship has elements of patrimony....Secretaries are bound to bosses in ways that were largely unregulated by roles of the larger system and that made the relationship a highly personalized one. (pp. 73–74)

Kanter (1977) also suggested that one important aspect of the social organization of the relationship was "status contingency (the fact that secretaries, primarily, and bosses, secondarily, derived status in relation to the other)" (p. 74). The existence of these interdependent roles renders each party reliant on the other for satisfaction of workplace goals. To understand the complexity of these relationships, one must understand the interpersonal dynamics.

When asked what they "liked most" about their supervisors, all of the respondents were able to generate at least one characteristic. Most mentioned their bosses' sensitivity, kindness, patience, and ease of relating. One woman described her boss as the "nicest person I have ever met." One secretary found her boss' "genuine interest and desire for people to get along and to make things work" admirable. Said another secretary, "I have a really good relationship with my supervisor. It's one of the things that's kept me working here so long."

A great number of respondents also characterized their bosses as competent. They admired that quality. One secretary praised her boss' "intelligence, commitment to ideas and programs." Bosses' competence on the job was a characteristic mentioned frequently as a best-liked characteristic. For the respondents, the definition of job-related competence included providing encouragement to those they supervised, inspiring progress and teamwork, control, and serving as a role model.

Many characterized their bosses as sources of inspiration. In one woman's words, "I do like her idea of having things done right; [she's a] perfectionist, I like that. That's what inspires me to make sure that I do things right too." Several women described their bosses as "role models," and said they had ambitions to be like them.

Several of the secretaries liked the fact that their bosses were fair, equitable, and honest—hardly reminiscent of Weaver's "boss from hell." Other positive qualities mentioned by secretaries were sense of humor, lack of hostility, and provision of direction.

Other studies of female secretaries and their bosses provide evidence that women who work for women like both their bosses and their jobs. In one of the few empirical studies of secretaries' perceptions of their bosses that has been conducted, Stratham (1985) found that women supervisors, in contrast to men, were seen as more competent (e.g., more hard-working and thorough) and more considerate (e.g., more sensitive and appreciative) and more likely to treat their secretaries as equals and inquire about their career goals. Evidence of job competence and interpersonal sensitivity were further corroborated in our initial study of the relationship between women secretaries and bosses (O'Leary & Ickovics, 1987). Female bosses' positive interpersonal relations with their secretaries were maintained and fostered by behavioral commitments such as bringing them flowers, inquiring about their personal lives, expressing concern for them as individuals, treating them with consideration, and encouraging their best efforts. This may have culminated in a work environment congenial to the secretaries' enhanced performance. It is interesting to note that the interpersonal concern of women bosses was reciprocated by their secretaries, who were more likely to report discussing their personal lives with their bosses, complementing them, and acting sensitive to their needs compared to secretaries of men. Not surprisingly, in both studies, (O'Leary & Ickovics, 1987; Stratham, 1985) women who worked for women rated their bosses more positively than those who worked for men.

While women bosses are well-liked for a variety of reasons, they are not perfect (nor should perfection be expected). In addition to examining the positive qualities of female supervisors, we asked the respondents in this study what they "liked least" about their bosses. Three of the secretaries had no response. The remaining 20 often cited the *lack* of sensitivity or the *lack* of good managerial skills. When the most desirable boss characteristics, such as sensitivity and competence, were not descriptive of a particular boss, her secretary noted their absence with dismay.

Ambiguity of roles and lack of directness were among the things that the secretaries disliked about their women bosses. One woman said, "It's my job, I just want her to be straight with me. You know, just say 'please do this,' instead of being [so indirect]." Characteristic of this often-cited difficulty in giving direct instructions was the tendency of some bosses to say, "we need to do————," rather than to make a direct request, leaving the secretary to infer the "you" behind the "we." The difficulty in giving direct instructions was also manifested in other ways. One secretary observed that "[my boss] is so busy thanking me that she doesn't have time to tell me what to do." Another woman described her boss' failure to clearly articulate expectations as "a large source of personal upset" noting, "I care very much about doing this job well, but I find it hard to do it as well as expected if I don't know what I am expected to do."

Several secretaries characterized the emotional tone their bosses set as a negative contribution to the work setting. In the eyes of one, there was "an inordinate amount of emotional reactivity...due to the person in charge who tends to 'stress out rather than chill out'...[She] escalates or overreacts to everything, leading to a sense of running around tearing hair out when I don't think the problem merits that expenditure of emotional energy." Not surprisingly, she did not find this style "healthy, desirable or productive." Another woman commented that if she were the boss, she "would try to promote a little less emphasis on the interpersonal, keeping people at a bit more distance." She said she felt "too old to be treated so [intimately]." Although she did acknowledge that "men could be like that too" she thought "it might not permeate so much."

One of the characteristics of women's relationships with women in the workplace that most differentiates them from those found between men and women appears to be their affective intensity (O'Leary, 1988). O'Leary and Ickovics (1987), for example, found that although most of the women secretaries who worked for women business owners liked both their bosses and their jobs, those who did not were very negatively disposed toward them. The same kind of affective intensity marks girls' relationships with other girls during childhood and early adolescence, and may be an example of the "spill-over" of sex-role socialization into the workplace (Gutek, 1985).

Another common criticism was their bosses' overemphasis on detail. One young woman said, "I think [the office] runs effectively but it's with a great amount of effort, much more effort than I really think is necessary." Another woman indicated that her boss becomes involved in "a thousand, million details and [she] tends to make things more complicated, or at least leave them complicated, rather than streamlining them, because she gets very involved and does not have an overview...." A third noted that her boss "focuses too much on things that aren't important, she gets too involved in details that she shouldn't be involved with. She should allow other people to take care of things."

The difficulty that some of the women bosses were purported to experience in "letting go of the details" appears characteristic of the difficulties many women report in delegating responsibility. Indeed, Henning and Jardim (1977) suggested that this difficulty was one of the most significant factors preventing women workers from making a successful transition from middle to top management.

Interestingly, a good deal of the secretaries' criticism of their bosses centered on ways in which they failed to meet their secretaries' expectations either because they were not behaving enough like [male] bosses or because they were acting too much like women and therefore not maximizing the role distinction between themselves and those who worked for them.

Both good managerial skills and sensitivity were seen as vital. Lipman-Bluman's (1988) work on achieving styles suggests that the combination of tough and tender, direct and relational styles comprise the ideal "connective" leader, a leader who "integrates and creatively revitalizes (masculine) individualism with a crucial female perspective, that is, seeing the world as a system of interconnected, uniquely important parts, rather than independent, competitive and isolated entities" (p. 4). Stratham (1986), too, found that women supervisors were both task- and people-oriented (i.e., *both* instrumental and expressive)—contrary to the traditional/stereotypical dichotomy. According to recent conceptualizations of successful management, the "best" managers are "connective leaders," both task- and people-oriented, both competent managers and sensitive leaders (Kanter, 1983). Given these seemingly contradictory requirements, we were interested in examining how the secretaries in this study perceived their bosses' power.

Power of Responsibility. To date, most of the research available on women's relationships with women in the workplace has focused on the vertical dimensions of work. Although rarely explicitly addressed, all of the research on this topic touches on questions of women and power. Because we were interested in learning more about how women perceive other women who have power, we asked our respondents a number of questions regarding this issue. For example, we asked each secretary how her woman boss handled the power her position as director afforded her. Most of the secretaries reported that their bosses do not wield power; they are not "power-hungry" or abusive. In fact, rather than speak of power, these secretaries discussed their bosses' orientation as fair, responsible and communicative team players. One secretary noted, "She's very much a team-player, and not into power at all. If anything, she kind of uses her power as a protection: she protects our department against everybody else....You get the feeling she stands between you and everyone else." Yet another mentioned her boss' promotion of teamwork and described her use of power as "judicious," in a way that is "fair." Other terms used to describe their bosses' use of power included "beautifully," "gracefully," and "humbly."

Many secretaries reported that their bosses use power constructively to accomplish things: "power as a responsibility not a force of dominance." One secretary said:

> The women I work with tend to take their confidence and power from themselves and from their work, not from their titles or their positions of being dominant over someone else. That to me is a much easier and more effective way to work.

In the words of another secretary "most of the supervisors I work with are confident enough of themselves that they don't need to wield power in any way." Many of the respondents described their bosses as "concerned with getting things done" rather than with power.

"Responsibility" was used repeatedly as a synonym for power; many of the secretaries insisted that this was a preferable term, emphasizing their bosses disinterest in power, per se. Several writers have suggested that women powerholders are also more likely to see their own positions in terms of increased responsibility than men powerholders, who see their ability to influence others as their due (Bardwick, 1977; Grossman & Stewart, this volume; Kayden, 1989).

The term *power* appeared to have a negative connotation in the eyes of our respondents. When asked to discuss their bosses' power, they frequently hesitated to describe their bosses as powerful. Yet they did acknowledge that their bosses exerted influence, and insisted that this influence was exerted in a benign fashion through the "power" of communication. Several of the secretaries described their bosses as willing to "take the time to explain anything." In response to the question—How does your boss handle power?—one woman mentioned that her boss was "open to questions," while another reported that her boss was always willing to "tell you what you need to know." Another secretary indicated, "We all have a voice, but then she makes the final decision." Clearly, open communication between boss and secretary was a characteristic highly valued by the respondents. When it was present they commented favorably about it. Among those women who had women bosses who did not provide open lines of communication, its absence was a source of contention.

A number of secretaries criticized their bosses for not exerting enough direct power or influence. However, the precise definition of *power* and *authority* were difficult to discern. "I think she doesn't assert her authority enough" commented one secretary, but the exact behavior to which she referred remains elusive. Another woman observed:

> I don't think she handles it [power] very well. If I had her job, I would defi-
> nitely try to be more organized and make distinctions between professional
> and personal....I think I would want it to be close and comfortable but I think
> it is necessary to draw some kind of line, to not try to be friends on the same
> level.

Interestingly, three persons did not attribute any power to their women bosses, even though they held the title "director." In one case the lack of power was seen as a result of the institution's entanglement in red tape.

> I don't think they have much power; they don't have a lot of say....It's not like
> having your own business where you make your own decisions. She has to
> take everything to her boss for approval; her boss takes it on up the line. There
> is a tremendous amount of red tape that one has to go through. I find it very
> frustrating. I think it must be very frustrating for her. So she doesn't really
> have a lot of power. I don't think of her as very powerful.

Another secretary, commenting on her boss' difficulty exerting power within this administrative structure gives her boss the benefit of the doubt: "I think she does the best that she can do—given these constraints."

Even though the respondents did not describe their bosses as "power-ful," half of them indicated that they themselves wanted power. Most of the secretaries answered the question "how would you wield power" in the context of how their bosses do or do not. When asked what they would do if they had it, they said they would "use power wisely." It seemed that they thought they could learn from their bosses' strengths and weaknesses in order to improve their own performance. They would adopt their bosses' styles when they were effective, including their styles of open communica-tion and sensitivity, and would compensate for their bosses' weaknesses where they occurred. For instance, those secretaries who thought their bos-ses were too personally involved said they would be "more distant." Others who felt that their bosses were too ambiguous when giving task instruc-tions said that they would be "more direct."

It has been demonstrated that effort acquires differential meaning when it is exerted by women versus men (O'Leary & Hansen, 1985). It may be that power also has different connotations, in the eyes of both perceivers and powerholders, depending on the sex of the person wielding it. Certainly there is ample evidence to suggest that identical behaviors performed by women versus men in the workplace are ascribed different labels (e.g., bitchy vs. assertive).

It has frequently been suggested in the popular literature that women are less inclined than men to be willing to accept or to feel comfortable assuming positions of power because of their concern with maintaining interpersonal harmony. Consistent with this suggestion, some of the secretaries did report that their women bosses had difficulty maintaining a clear line between their professional and personal relationships with the women who worked for them. The criteria upon which that distinction should be based are not clear. What is too personal in the eyes of one individual may be appropriately personal in the eyes of another. According to one person:

> There is more respect for personal concerns in the workplace [here]. Women are more tolerant of bringing up these issues. I think this is important and appropriate [when you are working with the same people every day]. Women are more interested, or at least they feign interest; with men, it [the interest] is more perfunctory.

Of those individuals who said they did not want power, or were not yet ready for it, most did not want the additional responsibility of "taking the office home with them." Two people mentioned that they wanted respect, not power. Apparently the "p" word is troublesome for many women. On the other hand, the secretary who had the lowest level of education, when asked how she would feel about having the power her boss has, replied, "Oh lord, I want more power than that!"

THE COMMUNITY

Many of the respondents characterized their female-dominated environment as unique. They were aware that being in a workplace that was almost exclusively female and the respect and prestige that their institution held was unusual. Although for most, the sense of community was an unmitigated plus, others had reservations. Although many took their jobs because they wanted to work within a female-dominated institution, for some (5 out of 23), the absence of men in the workplace was seen as "unnatural," "not like normal society." They reported that they would prefer to work in a mixed-sex environment. Regardless, nearly everyone agreed that this was the "best of a women's environment." Immediate responses to the question what is it like being in a predominantly female environment included "wonderful," "fun," "interesting," "different," "refreshing," "I love it."

This workplace environment was characterized by caring, cooperation, comfort, and sensitivity to one another's needs. One woman noted that "women are more understanding about any issue. Some have worked as secretaries before, some worked in offices with a big hierarchy, so maybe that had an understanding of what I was going through." The support to which the respondents repeatedly referred was not just a "good feeling" but rather manifested itself in instrumental ways during times of need.

> It seems like everybody is very sensitive to others' needs especially in terms of health. Everybody pats each other on the back and says "go home if you're sick." Also there are a lot of people who have family concerns, and the women here are just more sensitive to one another's needs.

Another woman reported:

> There's more understanding about personal issues because we've all been in the situation at one time or another—be it family illness or a family crisis or an emotional problem—people [here] are much more understanding. I think there's a sense of sameness which isn't to say that we're not all different but there's still something about it that makes it the same.

This sense of sameness, in part, led a number of women to discuss their workplace and co-workers metaphorically as "a community." However, the concept of community was still too impersonal for several other women who described their co-workers "like a built in family." In fact, said one woman, "We even have a house [to work in], and it's pretty and it's quiet." Another woman suggested that her boss was "like both a mother and a father" to her subordinates.

A number of the women indicated their appreciation of the environment as one that placed a high premium on women, their interests, and their concerns. Many came to work here, and stay despite the lack of challenge and low pay, because of this commitment to women's issues. Some characterized the environment as "openly feminist," although they did not articulate the meaning they attached to the term. Several mentioned the "feminist vision" that this institution claims within its formal objectives. On the other hand, for at least one respondent, it was not feminist enough. "I thought [this institution] totally supported women, but I realized it doesn't work that way. You have to sort of fit their mold to get attention. They're not really open."

Many women observed that there was an atmosphere of "tolerance." In fact, several women were pleased to report that they felt comfortable as open self-identified lesbians in this environment. As summed up by one secretary:

> One of the things I find most satisfying is being in an environment where there are people who accept diversity and come from diverse backgrounds them-

selves. Something that I really like about it is that I am a lesbian and this is an environment where I can be "out." That's really important to me. I know I wouldn't have that in some other environment.

Several women, discussing the comfort and ease with which their co-workers interact, used stereotypically female examples to illustrate their point. For instance, one woman, noting the comfort with which she and her co-workers related on many levels, said, "We're feminists—we all know that we're feminists—but we can still talk about red nail polish." Another woman, also reflecting on the comfort she feels in her work community, discusses the lack of importance of making a fashion statement when working almost exclusively with women: "With men, sometimes you are always trying to make an impression or something....With other women, I don't really care what they think, because they know that I'm a good person. They don't really care about my outfit." A third woman said, "I feel generally when women are in a single-sex environment, their guard is down, and it is a more relaxed and caring atmosphere. It is much more supportive. It's actually a relief, coming to work and being with all women."

Many praised the ready availability of "wonderful women role models," and several mentioned their pleasure at having the opportunity to see women in decision-making positions first hand. One woman talked about the positive impact this has had on her: "I think I've become much stronger as a person because I've just had so many good role models....This has just been wonderful, the women aren't afraid of being direct and upfront with each other. It has encouraged me to take on more control." Many frequently re-affirmed their own commitment to women's issues during the course of the interviews.

Interestingly, many of the secretaries mentioned that they were forced to pay an "initiation fee" when they entered the community. Several reflected on the "lack of warmth in the welcome" they received. Three respondents reported that when they first began working, they felt "alienated" from their co-workers. They felt "a sense of tension" and found their new work environment a "hard place to break into." Fortunately, after the first several weeks, tensions eased, and they felt comfortable and welcome. Regretfully, those who had characterized their own first weeks as difficult, admitted (unsolicited) that they did not go out of their way to make it easier for new employees when they arrived.

SUMMARY AND CONCLUSIONS

Twenty-three female secretaries working for female bosses in an academic institution were interviewed. Each was asked about a variety of aspects of her job and the job environment, her boss and her relationships with boss and co-workers. These secretaries were engaged in a variety of administrative support duties ranging from typing and bookkeeping to research and report writing. Despite the many objectively negative aspects inherent in the secretaries' descriptions of their jobs (e.g., low pay and lack of opportunity for promotion, lack of prestige and challenge, limited decision-making power, tasks characterized by repetition, and limited opportunities for learning new skills), the majority of them were positively disposed toward their overall work experiences. This positive disposition was often defined in terms of interpersonal relationships, and characterized by cooperation, communication, support, and mutual respect.

The secretaries liked and admired their women bosses in large part because they exhibited both sensitivity and competence—characteristics of a successful manager. They criticized their women bosses if they were indirect with task instructions, too emotional, or over-emphasized detail. Secretaries reported that their bosses used power responsibly, communicated openly, and worked toward achieving office goals constructively. Many secretaries claimed that they would learn from their bosses' strengths and weaknesses in order to improve their own performance as leaders. Finally, for most, the sense of community in their female-dominated environment was seen as a benefit.

Several factors that may limit the generalizability of our findings should be noted. First, the study was conducted in a women's institution. Women who thought that working for other women would be unpleasant would not be likely to seek work in that environment. In addition, it may be that when women who work for women are unhappy with their situations, they are quick to find alternative employment.

A second factor that may limit the generalizability of this study is also related to its context. It should be recalled, that despite their dissatisfaction with both their jobs and their pay, the secretaries in our study report that they are happy with their positions because they find the relationships satisfying. Their reactions might have been different in a mixed-sex environment, where it has been found that women who work for women enjoy less status than women who work for men, and whose access to organizational rewards is limited by their (female) bosses' lower status positions in the organizational hierarchy (cf. Nieva & Gutek, 1981; Gupta et al., 1983; Kanter, 1977, 1983; O'Leary, 1988). In order to assess the extent to which this factor played a significant role in our findings, it would be necessary to replicate the study in a larger organization in which the proportion of women to men bosses was equal or favored men.

Third, the participants in our study were hand-picked by the bosses for whom they worked; as the offices were small (ranging in size from 3 to 14 persons), bosses did their own hiring. The match between the personalities and styles of the women bosses and their subordinates, therefore, may have been unusually good, and as a result, conducive to positive relations.

Finally, we think a word of caution about the interview results is in order. Although we allowed the women in our study to speak for themselves, we cannot help but wonder whether our choice of excerpts from those interviews was biased by our own perceptions. For example, the material that we found to be salient may have been based on our preconceived notions of what issues are important to women working with and for other women. During the course of conducting the interviews, we thought the majority of the secretaries had expressed concerns about their own ability to do their jobs. We found this reasonable as women's tendency to view themselves as imposters has been widely discussed. However, when we took a look at the actual number of women expressing this concern, it was minimal. That experience heightened our caution, and led us to try to quantitatively verify our qualitative findings. But in the end, no research is value-free.

An additional concern with findings based on interview data when each respondent has been interviewed only once, is the distinction between what Dash (1989) has termed the "adopted story" versus the "actual story." In Dash's investigative report of the factors that motivate young adolescents to have children, he found that the adopted story given to school counselors, irate parents, and investigative reporters about the reasons for adolescent pregnancy fell away only after the third or fourth interview with the same respondent. This occurred only after a "real" rapport between interviewer and interviewee had been established. Prior to that point, the adopted reasons given were the socially accepted (if not acceptable) reasons for the event, such as having gotten caught in a moment of passion, or not knowing enough about birth control. The actual reasons given were surprisingly different and reflected a desire for some accomplishment in a life that seemed rather bereft of opportunity to accomplish anything. Dash's (1989) findings highlight the need to question even those results that fit the cultural rhetoric best. In the case of our study, we may have evoked the best of feminist rhetoric when we asked about the relations among women in an institution dominated by them.

In spite of these cautions, it is clear that the widespread assumption about "problematic" relations between women bosses and their women subordinates must be re-examined in light of the evidence presented here. Surely, there are women bosses who might be characterized as "bosses from hell," but there are also women bosses who fit the description of "the nicest person I ever met." Like their male counterparts, women bosses represent a diverse array of personalities and management styles. There is no prototypic woman boss; some are better than others.

As Virginia Schein (cited in Slade, 1984) observed:

When both the boss and the secretary are women, there is the potential for an unusually productive relationship, as the woman boss may be less inclined to demean the role of another woman and more inclined to afford her respect and responsibility. However, the potential for an unusually unproductive relationship also exists if the woman boss is insecure and afraid of being identified as "one of the girls." (p. 26)

In our study, evidence supports the former situation where women's relationships could be identified as productive. This is in contrast to the weight of the anecdotal evidence that favors the latter explanation (i.e., unproductive relations; cf. Agins, 1986), and fits the commonly held stereotype of both women and men (Bowman et al., 1965; Rosen & Jerdee, 1974; Sutton & Moore, 1985; Kagan & Malveaux, 1986). It is only when women and men actually work for women that this stereotype breaks down (Feild & Caldwell, 1979; Ferber et al., 1979; Ickovics & O'Leary, 1988; Stratham, 1986).

Increasing numbers of women and men will have women bosses, as the demographic structure of the workplace shifts to accommodate a greater number of women and minority workers (Bureau of National Affairs, 1986; Workforce 2000, 1987). The fact that experience makes a difference by diminishing the negativity of attitudes expressed toward women bosses is encouraging (cf. Fiske & Taylor, 1984).

ACKNOWLEDGMENTS

The authors gratefully acknowledge the assistance of Pilar Olivo, who scheduled all of the interviews, and Janie Hoefler, who typed the transcripts in a timely manner. Special thanks must also be extended to the staff assistants who volunteered their time and who shared their work experiences with us openly. We hope that we have presented your stories clearly and that your voices are heard. For those of you who do not see yourselves as *secretaries*, we use this term for linguistic ease, and with the utmost respect for the crucial contributions that you make to your departments each and every day.

REFERENCES

Agins, T. (1986, March 23). The uneasy office. *The Wall Street Journal*, p. 13.
Bardwick, J.M. (1977). Some notes about power relationships between women. In A.G. Sargent (Ed.), *Beyond sex roles* (pp. 107–111). St. Paul, MN: West.
Bern, P. (1987). *How to work for a woman boss.* New York: Dodd, Mead.

Bowman, G., Wortney, B.N., & Greyser, S.H. (1965). Are women executives people? *Harvard Business Review, 43*, 14–28, 164–178.

Briles, J. (1987). *Woman to woman: From sabotage to support.* Far Hills, NJ: New Horizons Press.

Bureau of National Affairs. (1986). *Work and family: A changing dynamic* (Product Code No. 45 LDSR-37). Washington, DC: Author.

Burris, B.H. (1983). The human effects of underemployment. *Social Problems, 31*, 96–110.

Dash, L. (1989). *When children want children.* New York: William Morrow.

Delano, M. (1954). *How to be a top secretary.* Atlanta, GA: Tupper & Love.

Feild, H.S. & Caldwell, B.E. (1979). Sex of supervisor, sex of subordinate, and subordinate job satisfaction. *Psychology of Women Quarterly, 3*, 391–399.

Ferber, M., Huber, J., & Spitze, G. (1979). Preference for men as bosses and professionals. *Social Forces, 58*, 466–476.

Fiske, S.T., & Taylor, S.E. (1984). *Social cognition.* Reading, MA: Addison-Wesley.

Goldberg, P. (1968). Are women prejudiced against women? *Trans Action, 5*, 28–30.

Golding, J., Resnick, A., & Crosby, F. (1983). Work satisfaction as a function of gender and job status. *Psychology of Women Quarterly, 7*(3), 286–290.

Gupta, N., Jenkins, D., & Beehr, T.A. (1983). Employees gender, gender similarity, and supervisor-subordinate cross evaluations. *Psychology of Women Quarterly, 8*(2), 174–184.

Gutek, B.A. (1985). *Sex and the workplace.* San Francisco: Jossey-Bass.

Hardesty, S., & Jacobs, N. (1986). *Success and betrayal: The crisis of women in corporate America.* New York: Simon & Schuster.

Haynes, S.G., & Feinleib, M. (1980). Women, work and coronary heart disease: Prospective findings from the Framingham study. *American Journal of Public Health, 70*, 133–141.

Henning, M., & Jardim, A. (1977). *The managerial woman.* New York: Anchor Press/Doubleday.

Hollander, E.P. (1985). Leadership and power. In G. Lindzey & E. Aronson (Eds.), *The handbook of social psychology* (pp. 485–537). New York: Random House.

Ickovics, J.R., & O'Leary, V.E. (1988). *Expectations versus experience: When women prefer working for women.* Unpublished manuscript, George Washington University, Washington DC.

Kagan, J., & Malveaux, J. (1986, May). The uneasy alliance between boss and secretary. *Working woman,* pp. 105–109, 134, 138.

Kahn, W.A., & Crosby, F. (1985). Discriminating between attitudes and discriminatory behaviors: Change and stasis. In L. Larwood, A. Stromberg, & B.A. Gutek (Eds.), *Women and work: An annual review* (Vol. 1, pp. 215–238). Beverly Hills, CA: Sage.

Kanter, R.M. (1977). *Men and women of the corporation.* New York: Basic Books.

Kanter, R.M. (1983). *The change masters: Innovation for productivity in the American corporation.* New York: Simon & Schuster.

Kayden, X. (1989). *Surviving power.* New York: Simon & Schuster.

Lipman-Blumen, J. (1988, August). *Connective leadership: A female perspective for an interdependent world.* Invited Address, Division 35, American Psychological Association annual convention, Atlanta, GA.

Madden, T.R. (1987). *Women versus women: The uncivil business war.* Washington, DC: American Management Association.

Majchrzak, A., & Gutek, B.A. (1977, August). *Satisfactions and dissatisfactions of secretaries.* Paper presented at the open symposium on women, sponsored by Division 35, American Psychological Association annual convention, San Francisco, CA.

Nagy. S. (1985). Burnout and selected variables as components of occupational stress. *Psychological reports, 56*, 195–200.

National Commission on Working Women. (1987). *Secretaries and clerical workers; A fact sheet.* Available from the National Commission on Working Women, 2000 P Street, NW, Suite 508, Washington, DC 20036.

Nieva, V.F., & Gutek, B.A. (1981). *Women and work: A psychological perspective.* New York: Praeger.

O'Leary, V.E. (1987). [Secretarial students' perceptions of women and men bosses]. Unpublished data, Boston University.

O'Leary, V.E. (1988). Women's relationships with women in the workplace. In B.A. Gutek, L. Larwood, & A. Stromberg (Eds.), *Women and work: An annual review* (Vol. 3, pp. 189–214). Beverly Hills, CA: Sage.

O'Leary, V.E., & Hansen, R.D. (1985). Sex as an attributional fact. In T. Sonderegger (Ed.), *The Nebraska Symposium on Motivation* (Vol, 32, pp. 133–178). Lincoln, NE: University of Nebraska Press.

O'Leary, V.E., & Ickovics, J.R. (1987). *Who wants a woman boss? Only those who have one.* Washington, DC: George Washington University. (ERIC Document Reproduction Service No. ED 288174).

Petersen, K.S. (1988, December 30). Sisterhood vs. 'betrayal' at the office. *USA Today,* pp. 1A, 2A.

Rosen, B., & Jerdee, T.H. (1974). Influence of sex-role stereotypes on evaluations of male and female supervisory behavior. *Journal of Applied Psychology, 59*, 9–14.

Schein, V.E. (1975). Relationships between sex role stereotypes and management characteristics among female managers. *Journal of Applied Psychology, 60*, 340–344.

Slade, M. (1984, October 15). Relationships: Women and their secretaries. *New York Times,* p. 15.

Staines, G., Travis, C., & Jayerante, T.E. (1973). The queen bee syndrome. *Psychology Today, 7*(8), 55–60.

Stratham, A. (1985). *The gender role revisited: Differences in the management styles of women and men.* Unpublished manuscript, University of Wisconsin, Parkside, WI.

Stratham, A. (1986). *Women working for women: The manager and her secretary.* Unpublished manuscript, University of Wisconsin, Parkside, WI.

Sutton, S.D., & Moore, K.K. (1985). Probing options: Executive women—20 years later. *Harvard Business Review, 85*(5), 42–66.

Workforce 2000: Work and workers for the 21st Century. (1987). Indianapolis, IN: Hudson Institute. (Also available, U.S. Government Printing Office, Washington, DC).

Chapter 4

The Pregnant Therapist: Professional and Personal Worlds Intertwine

Hildreth Y. Grossman
Harvard Medical School

Pregnancy is a special and unique event that affects the personal and professional life of a therapist. The literature on pregnancy reveals that women may experience psychological, emotional, and cognitive changes (Davids, DeVault, & Talmadge, 1966; Lubin, Gardner, & Roth, 1975; Murai & Murai, 1975). Moreover, during this major transition in their development, women must cope with the changes that pregnancy introduces in their roles, relationships, priorities, and values (Ballou, 1978; Benedek, 1956; Breen, 1975, 1977; Entwisle & Doering, 1981). It is against this backdrop of physical, emotional, and psychological changes that this chapter explores how therapists experience their work during pregnancy and postpartum.

A cornerstone of the work of psychotherapists is the development of ongoing, consistent relationships with their patients (Pines, 1975). Yet, pregnancy appears to strain the capacities of therapists to remain consistently giving and available. As a result, therapists' views of themselves and their work may be affected significantly by their pregnancy. For example, pregnant therapists tend to feel self-absorbed and preoccupied with physical changes or thoughts about the baby (Balsam, 1975; Barbanel, 1980; Baum & Herring, 1975; Paluszny & Pozanski, 1971; Rubin, 1980), and experience feelings of greater vulnerability (Baum & Herring, 1975; Butts & Cavenar, 1979; Fenster, Phillips, & Rapoport, 1986; Kariv-Agnon, 1988; Lax, 1969; Nadelson, Notman, Arons, & Feldman, 1974; Naparstek, 1976; Schwartz, 1975). In contrast, pregnant therapists also seem to have a greater sensitivity toward patients (Kariv-Agnon, 1988; Nadelson et al., 1974). Moreover, they also are more apt to be self-disclosing and show a greater sense of relatedness toward patients (Barbanel, 1980; Fenster et al., 1986; Rubin, 1980; Schwartz, 1975). In addition, they also anticipate having difficulty in integrating dual roles of mother and therapist (Butts & Cavenar, 1979; Fenster et al., 1986; Nadelson et al., 1974; Naparstek, 1976; Schwartz, 1975). Concomitant with these changes is the pregnant therapist's wish to deny that there is anything different about her (Baum & Herring, 1975; Benedek, 1973; Kariv-Agnon, 1988; Lax, 1969; Paluszny & Pozanski, 1971)!

Most of the studies of pregnant therapists, however, are based on informal observations of colleagues or personal reminiscences by the author. Only two studies systematically interviewed pregnant therapists (Fenster, 1983; Kariv-Agnon, 1988) and only the former included a follow-up interview 6 months after their babies were born.

The present study examines the experience of women therapists during and following their transition to motherhood. The voices of the women who shared their experiences of this very intimate period of their lives were retained as much as possible through interviews and discussions among peers. In this way, these women directly revealed the wishes, conflicts, and discoveries about themselves and their work that emerged during their pregnancy and following the birth of their babies.

DATA COLLECTION

The Sample. Sixteen women were included in this study of women therapists' experiences of pregnancy and transition to motherhood. All were employed as professional psychotherapists at the time of their pregnancy; 9 were PhD psychologists and 6 were MSW social workers. Fourteen of the women were trained or had some supervision in psychodynamically oriented psychotherapy. Ten women had institutional or clinic affiliations (some in addition to part-time private practices) and 6 were employed in private or group practices in the greater Boston area at the time of their pregnancies. All but 3 were first-time mothers and were between the ages of 33 and 40 at the time of their pregnancy. Participants were recruited through the assistance of an obstetrician with a large practice. He announced the opportunity to participate in a research project involving pregnant therapists as well as the possibility of becoming a member of an ongoing group to discuss issues of professionalism and motherhood. The 16 participants in this study represent all of the obstetrical patients who were psychotherapists in the obstetrician's practice at the beginning of this project.

Procedure. The interview material was collected for the present study through individual interviews and through group interviews with women psychotherapists. The research strategy behind these open-ended and interactive interviews is illustrated best by Oakley's (1981) research position that stated "the goal of finding out about people through interviewing is best achieved when the relationship of interviewer and interviewee is non-hierarchical and when the interviewer is prepared to invest his or her own personal identity in the relationship" (p. 41). Thus, all participants knew that I was a psychotherapist, and the mother of a new baby, and a researcher. As with Oakley's research on transition to motherhood, my view was that because the world of the psychotherapist is a very private world and because of the intensely personal nature of pregnancy in therapists' lives, it would be more problematic and unnatural to assume a more distant and less personal stance with the women I was interviewing. Thus, all of the interviews were considered a joint construction of meaning and collaborative research effort.

This nontraditional perspective has received more attention in recent years (see Grossman & Stewart, this volume; Laslett & Rapoport, 1975; Mischler, 1986; Oakley, 1981). In their recent book on naturalistic inquiry, Lincoln and Guba (1985) also emphasized the importance of being sure that the context is thoroughly understood by the researcher because it is not possible to divorce meaning from its context. One way that they and other naturalists recommend accomplishing this is to become immersed in the culture that is to be studied. In the present research, my involvement as a member and observer of the culture of the pregnant therapist made it more likely that participants were sufficiently comfortable to provide as honest and distortion-free accounts as possible.

The major source of data for this study was from group interviews with two groups of psychotherapists who were pregnant and/or had recently become new mothers. The material was collected over a 12-month period for both groups. The first group began with eight members and the second group with four members and added a pregnant therapist member 3 months later. In addition, I served as an interviewer/participant in each of the groups. By the end of the first year, the first group retained 6 members and the second group three members. In the first group, one therapist dropped out because she already had one child, and another moved out of state. In each of the groups, the initial meeting began by asking the members to discuss their experience of being pregnant therapists. Over the course of the meetings, the focus of discussion shifted from pregnancy experiences to current concerns about being a therapist and a new mother.

Meeting as a group provided a means of interactive interviewing that was invaluable. Members were able to use their mutual experiences to clarify, intensify, and illustrate the complex situation of being a pregnant therapist. Participating in a group of peers enhanced their ability to be open about their experiences, and the interaction among these women contributed to a richer and more complete portrait. This method was viewed as a multiple case study approach in which each participant served to illustrate clearly and distinctively the social phenomenon and developmental process of women therapists in their transition to motherhood (see Grossman & Stewart, this volume, Rosenwald, 1988, for a more in-depth discussion).

The second source of data for this study was gathered from three therapists who were interviewed individually at two time periods. One of these therapists also participated in one of the groups. The individual interviews were indispensable for expanding upon, clarifying, and enriching the group interviews. Repeated interviewing offered tremendous benefits, such as providing an opportunity for participants to reflect upon, qualify, or add to information shared in the earlier interview. The second interview also afforded the occasion to discuss ideas about the research with the participant and receive feedback for validating these notions. As Rosenwald (1988) noted, "interviewing people over time can yield vivid demonstrations of a developmental process in which knowledge and knower move together" (p. 255).

The first interview was held during the last trimester of a therapist's pregnancy, and the second within the first 3 months postpartum. Each interview lasted approximately 1 hour. The first interview began with an open-ended, general question, "Tell me what your experience has been like being pregnant and a therapist." The purpose of this question was to allow the therapist as much flexibility as possible to define and describe her experience. Prompts were used to determine whether or not there were other aspects of this experience that she had not talked about. If they were not mentioned spontaneously, therapists were asked what it was like to tell their patients about their pregnancy, whether or not they had concerns about pregnancy symptoms, what patients had been the most difficult during this period, and how they were handling their forthcoming maternity leave. The second interview began by asking the therapist if there were any experiences of being a pregnant therapist which she had not mentioned in the first interview as well as to discuss her present experiences as a new mother and a therapist. The interview ended with sharing issues of research interest and asking for reactions. Each of the interviews were audiorecorded and transcribed for future data analysis.

A 3-year follow-up was held with all of the members of the first group and also with one of the therapists who had participated in an individual interview in order to discuss the results of this study and help to validate the findings.

DATA ANALYSIS

Once the individual and group interviews were transcribed, they were coded first for themes of power and nurturance (a more socially accepted form of power for women, see Grossman & Stewart, this volume) as they emerged directly from the material. The analyses began with these two important theoretical constructs that I hypothesized would be particularly salient for women therapists during pregnancy. There are numerous definitions of power (see Janeway, 1980; Winter, 1973). The working definition of *power* in this chapter was provided by Grossman and Stewart (this volume), "the perceived experience or demonstrated capacity to produce an effect on others. This includes individuals, institutions or social systems." The definition of *nurturance* is more consistently agreed upon and is essentially synonymous with caretaking or caring for another. Moreover, nurturance involves sustaining, developing, and fostering the well-being of another. Interviews of both groups and individuals then were examined for the emergence of additional themes. What follows here is a description of the themes of nurturance and power as well as other emergent themes of guilt, identity, and boundaries.

THEMES FROM INTERVIEWS WITH PREGNANT THERAPISTS

Nurturance: Unconditional Versus Conditional

Nurturance can be one of the central features of a therapist's work, and it is often what attracts people to the profession. Providing care clearly satisfies an important need of the patient. Caring for patients, however, also fulfills the therapist's need to nurture. Thus, a significant conflict emerges as pregnant therapists endeavor to apportion their nurturance among the patient, the baby and themselves. Because having a baby so completely gratifies and prioritizes a new mother's need to nurture, there is genuine concern among therapists that they be sensitive enough to the needs of their patients during this period. In showing her sensitivity to this issue, one therapist said:

> I sometimes think about how I would feel if I were in treatment with a therapist who was pregnant and I wonder how I would feel knowing that the therapist was having private experiences and sensations with her baby. I would feel threatened and left out, and I think that the awareness of that feeling keeps me from getting too involved with it because I feel that's not fair to my clients not to attend to them as much as I can at this point.

Many of the therapists who were interviewed attempted to ensure that their patients were well cared for before they took time for themselves and their babies. In many cases, they felt pressure to give even more than usual in order not to feel that they were depriving their patients of the nurturance they needed. For example, one therapist said:

> I feel like I've worked hard on sort of dealing with, the last six months or so with each aspect of each client, and if anything bent overboard to um you know to reach for their feelings and to deal with it, but I am so glad (laughs) its almost over because I am just, I've really had it. I want to take care of me, I'm tired now, and yet I feel like I can go with a good feeling because everybody is squared away and everyone's been taken care of.

Unfortunately, despite increased efforts to avoid depriving patients once the baby is born, many therapists reported that they felt they could not sufficiently nurture their family, their patients, and themselves at the same time. One therapist depicts this conflict clearly:

> I feel like I have to coordinate the baby's schedule, my schedule, the babysitter's schedule, my husband's schedule, and the client's schedule. I feel like in the past I've been very available. I feel very much less flexible now, and that no matter what I do I'm going to be set up to be depriving.

Despite being dedicated to their work, most therapists became ambivalent toward patients' demands for their nurturance during their pregnancy and maternity leave. Their commitment to "giving their all" at the office required counterbalanced giving to the baby. Therapists reported that during their pregnancy, and once they became new mothers, they also needed more time alone, away from patients. Many reported they were "less available" in some ways in the therapy, and were less flexible about changing appointment times or speaking on the telephone between sessions. These changes were not easy, because therapists wanted to remain as available and nurturant as possible. One therapist revealed:

> A part of me wants to just take three months for me. But, you know, I really care about them and I feel, I really don't feel that it's that big a deal to be available to them.

A group of women therapists concurred that it was particularly difficult to return to their practices after their maternity leaves to face some patients who expressed, either directly or indirectly, loss and rage at being abandoned. Several therapists said that their first inclination was to make it up to the patient. Yet, as they were trying to compensate or overcompensate for patients' losses, therapists resented patients' criticism and demands. For example:

> The first thing that I could relate to was the wish to do something. I mean I really needed to remind myself about articles that I'd read about what empathy really is. Gradually it dawned on me because with my baby I think that's all I am. I do things for her and I try to make them better, and I found myself with patients wanting to fix things for them.

Prior to having a baby, therapists viewed patients' anger as more benign or less noxious. After having a baby, however, many of the therapists reported a greater need to limit patients' rage (e.g., by deciding when a patient's verbal expressions become abusive) and behaviorally (e.g., having less flexibility in rescheduling visits).

There were positive effects of therapists' redefining nurturance and questioning how different their nurturance should be between their patients and their babies. One of the most consistent reactions of pregnant therapists was the wish to see their patients as less infantile and more adult. This change in therapists' attitudes frequently had positive consequences for patients who felt more empowered and received support for greater independence. The following examples illustrate some of the changes in therapists' perceptions:

> I am aware that I have been seeing patients as healthier than they are so as not to feel that they need more during pregnancy and after delivery.

> I have a baby now and when I didn't have a baby before I thought I could be a good mother to all of these other people. But now I am a good mother and it's sort of like I want them [clients] to be more grown up.

> I didn't feel any longer that I wanted to mother all of these patients, feeling like I was a real mother now. I didn't want to take care of all of them in the same way.

One aspect of nurturance, however, which is discomforting for some pregnant therapists is when they find themselves nurtured by their patients. Reversing roles contributes to therapists' feeling a loss of control and a heightened sense of vulnerability, as is described in the following example:

> [A 19-year-old male patient] has been doting on me, which I've had a lot of trouble with...[I'm] feeling too pampered, or the implication is that I can't do it myself, or treating me differently. Wondering if I can handle things. Before I was pregnant I was one of the few staff that was effective when he was acting

out. He could get pretty violent. A few times he called me Mom. He slipped.
And so now, it's very different.

In this example, the therapist reported that it was especially difficult to
tolerate their role reversal, because during the months of her pregnancy this
young man had matured physically. She confessed that it was easier to nurture him when he acted and looked like a little boy. Given his physical
maturity along with her pregnancy, the situation had obviously become
very different.

Power Versus Vulnerability

Women therapists enjoy the power inherent in their profession and express
concern about losing their power. In our society the role of "caretaker as
mother" is not as valued or seen as prestigious as that of "caretaker as
psychotherapist." Thus, most pregnant therapists were compelled to
reexamine their changing feelings about the relative value of mother versus
therapist. For some therapists, the possible loss of prestige and power intro-
duced a conflict in their transition to motherhood. The women therapists interviewed in this study were on the average in their mid-30s, with a career
established before the birth of their first child. Some who chose to cut back
on their careers after having their babies, however, felt these changes jeopardized their hold on the power and prestige they had acquired. For example, many of the therapists changed from full time to part time or
hospital and clinic practices to private practice. Surrendering an institutional affiliation while building a private practice and beginning a family was
felt by some as a loss of power, prestige, and legitimacy as a professional.
The following discussion portrays the concern of women therapists about
their loss of power and value in their transition to motherhood.

> Therapist A: The kinds of things I've been invested in are sort of being
> active or responsible or taking some position of power in the system. I
> know that I only thought about women whose research interests had
> to do with babies or development, I devalued that enormously and I
> thought, you know...it isn't real psychology. It's just um baby stuff,
> you know. And that never felt as valuable and as valued as what's
> work related. And that's the trouble that I'm having. To me running a
> unit or teaching was the kind of stuff that was valuable. Even having a
> full time private practice, I used to say, "You'll never catch me having
> a full time private practice. That's too passive for me." You know, I
> want to be involved in a university system or a hospital system. You
> know, fighting it out with the big boys kind of thing. And when I left
> my job, in which I was employed in a hospital, and I looked at private

practice, I had a horrible identity crisis, and the only thing that kind of eased it was the knowledge that I was in part preparing for being a mother and I thought, well, that's the reason. But I miss it terribly and I feel very cut off and I feel that I've put that on hold. I haven't really resolved that, and it still feels to me like that's the real stuff, and it's hard for me to think that a private practice is any more than, you know like keeping busy.

Therapist B: It's like this [motherhood] isn't enough of a challenge. (laughs)

Therapist C: This isn't enough power.

Pregnant therapists often have a strong need to feel in control because many aspects of pregnancy are essentially out of their control. For example, a pregnant therapist not only experiences her abdomen growing over the months of sitting with patients, but also many women encounter various symptoms of pregnancy (i.e., nausea or vomiting, fatigue, dizziness, or having her water break while going into labor) that can produce feelings of loss of control. Understandably, it can be very disconcerting when these symptoms occur while working with patients. One therapist in a group described her own worries about losing physical control:

I was worried about nausea I think because I was so nauseated throughout my pregnancy and a couple of times on the verge of throwing up with my patients that I sort of had this practice that I was prepared with what I should say if I had to ask them to leave. So I just figured that if my water broke I'd say, "Well I think we have to stop now."

The other therapists listened to this account and responded with knowing laughter about the anxiety these situations produce.

Concerns about loss of control, however, are not restricted to the physical domain. There are a number of ways in which pregnant therapists struggle with the need to be in control in their relationships with patients. For example, one of the earliest and most difficult situations in which control is an issue is how and when to tell patients about their pregnancy.

I was just ending my 3rd month. I had crossed the room to get to my desk and one [patient] said, "are you pregnant?" (laughs) I wanted to say, "no, I'm not pregnant." It's such an intrusion in my space.

All therapists give a great deal of attention to sharing the news of their pregnancy, although they may vary in their theoretical position as to whether or not to allow patients to notice the pregnancy, or whether to simply reveal this information at their own discretion. Thus, one therapist commented:

> I decided to tell people because I couldn't bear sitting there waiting for people to notice, and I didn't want to be preoccupied and I sort of wanted it under my own control.

Another therapist recounted how stressful it was for her when her pregnancy was announced in a general community meeting of patients and staff by the only patient she had informed of her pregnancy. She felt she had to share the news at this early date due to the patient's suicidal depression and need for early preparation for her leaving.

Another therapist described how her bosses actually usurped control over informing patients of her pregnancy by insisting that she wait until she was "beginning to show." She reported:

> I felt like even though I wasn't showing, two of us were walking into the setting every day. And I think the other side to that is feeling very frightened about the unknown. And so, to keep it private was painful for me. It seemed like being able to talk about it openly also gave me license to talk about the other things that I needed to talk about openly. But to have to keep it sort of a secret until this other person felt it was OK was very unnatural.

There is evidence that patients also face a dilemma about the public and private aspects of their therapist's life during her pregnancy. One therapist, for example, reported that after waiting for her patients to notice her pregnancy but getting no response, she informed them herself. She reported that patients said, "oh yea, I noticed" but felt that they could not say anything.

In contrast to this therapist's experience where patients did not want to be intrusive, another therapist related that one of her patients encouraged her to bring the baby along with her to their therapy sessions.

Pregnant therapists are more vulnerable in not being able to guard their private worlds from their public worlds. Therapists cannot hide their pregnancy from their patients in the way that it is possible to hide other life changes (i.e., a death in their family, marriage, or divorce). One therapist recalled her feelings at work after the break-up of a long-term relationship:

> I remember coming into work and I had been crying all night and I was just a wreck and I remember I didn't want to look at anybody. And yet, that was something I did not feel that people would necessarily have to know, or whatever. It was something I could just keep to myself. I remember one client said that I looked like kind of a wreck, or I looked upset, and I asked them how they felt about it (laughs). You know, I didn't have to deal with it. Yet being pregnant it's right there in the session, and it's getting bigger.

Thus, pregnant therapists are more vulnerable to public revelations of other aspects of their lives that were previously private. For example, they cannot deny that they are sexual people, or that they have a man in their lives. Consequently, they have no choice about keeping these intimate features private. One therapist explained:

> There was something that happened that really had to do with my personal life, but for the first time I really couldn't keep it as separate as I would normally.

During pregnancy, therapists also feel vulnerable to potential harm from patients, not only for themselves, but also for their babies. One therapist explained:

> I'm sitting there and a part of my dress is moving back and forth, and I'm thinking, great. You know sometimes the kid will be very active and I feel very protective of it and very vulnerable, and I don't, I really don't want to subject the child to their being able to attack it, or comment on it, and yet, it's in there in the sessions, so how can you not do that?

Some therapists also experienced vulnerability after their babies were born in terms of their patients' requests for information about their babies.

> One patient asked me what my baby's name was the first thing when I was back, and I did not want to talk about it. Somehow bringing her name into the session was something I was not prepared to do. It was hard. I had this very intense reaction. I answered it, I couldn't very well not answer it, but I just really became upset by that and upset by the intensity of doing that. Since then, a couple of other people have asked me and I've been very calm.

Vulnerability clearly intensifies when therapists actually encounter patients' murderous or destructive wishes toward the baby. Such expressions are tremendously difficult for pregnant and postpartum therapists to tolerate. Moreover, some pregnant therapists explained that they felt vulnerable to and overwhelmed by not only angry feelings, but also other strong feelings such as envy and anxiety. A common response was to protect themselves from feeling overwhelmed, at times, by discouraging rather than encouraging patients to express their strong feelings.

Therapists who worked in settings where physical violence was possible worried more about putting themselves and their babies in jeopardy. One pregnant therapist described this exchange with a violent adolescent inpatient:

> I didn't know how strong he was. The only fantasy I had was that he could be physical and that the baby would be hurt. I very rarely think in terms of me

getting hurt. I wasn't thinking of myself. That's been an ongoing thing. I felt physically vulnerable. I mean I'm a pretty big woman and I'm strong and have felt very fragile physically since I've been pregnant.

Pregnant therapists also feel vulnerable to the behavior and attitudes of colleagues. Many of the women therapists reported that during their pregnancy they felt uneasy about how they were perceived and treated by their colleagues. One therapist noted how shocked she was when two of her male colleagues showed unprofessional conduct by having "no qualms about coming up and patting my belly and saying, 'Oh, getting bigger.' And I think they felt very free to do that and didn't think that there was anything wrong with that."

In some cases, pregnant therapists were confronted directly by devaluing reactions of colleagues that challenged previously held perceptions of their competence. One therapist revealed that in addition to having to tolerate disrespectful "size jokes" from staff members as it got closer to her delivery date, colleagues inferred that her pregnancy would interfere with her ability to do her work. She admitted how hurtful this was for her because she took so much pride in her work and identified herself as an effective therapist. The following discussion among therapists shows, surprisingly, that anger, sadism, and denial were present among co-workers.

Therapist A: I'm kind of angry in a way that things aren't changing....There is a way in which there is this view that if you're pregnant you can't possibly be competent.

Therapist B: I wonder how that jives with giving a pregnant woman more and more work. It's sadistic.

Therapist C: Yea it's hostile.

Therapist A: Or there is a way in which it proves, you set up a situation in which you're bound to fail and you fail. Then you've proved your point. They can't handle what you can't handle. They're pregnant and not competent.

Therapist C: There's also a sense of denial, I mean I was assigned new patients two months before I was due!

In some cases, pregnant therapists' heightened experiences of vulnerability promoted even greater sensitivity to patients' vulnerability. A pregnant therapist learns that in becoming a mother she is not only vulnerable to hurt from her patients, but also she could be potentially hurtful to her patients. Thus, most therapists felt a heightened sensitivity, during and following their pregnancy, not to be inadvertently insulting or rejecting, or behave in a way to make patients feel unseen. Moreover, many therapists reported that the very actions that contributed to their own feelings of powerlessness and vulnerability had a parallel effect on their patients (i.e., insensitivity to the feelings of others, abandonment, actions, or statements that are critical or denote worthlessness). Some therapists shared their experiences:

> I began to wonder afterwards if I wasn't telling her [I was pregnant] because I knew how devastating it would be. It was her major issue. It was just one loss after another.

> I felt terribly responsible [that I had been preoccupied], and I felt that I had been somehow off center and missed something.

Another therapist worried that in returning to work after her maternity leave she would have a "happy glow about herself," which she would be unable to hide from her patients. She was afraid that this "glow" would heighten her patients' feelings of competition and fears of not receiving enough.

When therapists become new mothers, they also become vulnerable to having to depend on others to care for their babies in order to be responsible to their patients. As such, their husbands or child-care people may interfere with therapists' ability to be reliable to their patients. This situation is similar to that of the majority of other professional women who assume the major responsibility for the children. Because of the unique nature of the ongoing relationship between a therapist and her patient, and her commitment to be there to provide care, therapists who are new mothers have special anxieties about last minute difficulties in child-care arrangements. For example:

> In terms of the work, it occurred to me at some point that if our child-care didn't work out I was stuck. There I was home alone. No neighbors around. Patients arriving at the door and nothing to do.

Guilt: Responsibility/Reliability
Versus Selfishness/Abandonment

Another major theme emerging from the therapists' dialogue was the guilt they experienced when they became the object of their patients' envy. The therapists interviewed agreed that they tended to feel guilty when they experienced themselves as having so much in contrast to many of their patients' deprivation. This was particularly true in cases where their patients were not married and wanted to be, or were having infertility problems, or were having a threatening health problem, or had lost a loved one. For example, one therapist who was treating a family in which the mother developed uterine cancer noted:

> I feel so guilty. You know here I am starting my family and, um, you know, being excited and being happy and um, these people are dealing with a tremendous tragedy.

Another therapist worried about telling a patient of her own pregnancy because the patient had been undergoing infertility treatments for years without success. She admitted, "I was just dreading telling this woman. I was just feeling like she was absolutely going to hate me."

It was striking to note that therapists reported their guilt was greatest when they were envied for their personal life rather than their professional life, as this therapist notes:

> I was fairly anxious about telling people [I was pregnant] and I wound up telling people because they didn't notice....Initially I was dealing with I guess a mixture of feeling anxious about being the object of envy to my female patients who are single...So I had some anxiety about dealing with people's anger and envy...I felt that this represented some kind of moving on, you know, my moving on even further in terms of going where a number of my patients are trying to go. And I am much more aware of comparing myself with my patients and feeling both guilt and glee that things were working out this way for me. So I found myself postponing telling because I was uncomfortable with it. And I also wanted to wait until I had my amnio because I just felt too vulnerable at the thought of having to deal with that in a public way [if anything happened to the baby]....So the amnio was both, I could rationalize well, I want to make sure everything is OK, but in addition to that I had anxiety about just dealing with my patients around my having something good in my life.

In a group discussion of personal guilt, one of the therapists realized that as a result of her guilt feelings she had allowed too much verbal abuse from one of her patients who frequently wished aloud that the therapist's baby would die. In contrast to the therapist's happiness with her growing family, her patient had been abused physically throughout her childhood, and currently had no loving relationships in her life. This disparity gave rise to the therapist's enormous guilt feelings. In turn, she responded by giving the patient virtually unchecked permission to express all of her hateful feelings. The therapist was surprised by her own reactions, and said, "I've always been clear with her in other areas about what constitutes abuse, so why did I not do it this time?" Clearly, her guilt had prevented her from taking the steps she needed to limit her patient's abusive behavior.

Another common source of guilt feelings among pregnant therapists is their worry about abandoning patients. In preparing for her maternity leave, one therapist described trying to cope with not abandoning patients while still allowing for her own needs:

> So I basically, I don't feel that I can refer them to somebody else for three months and say, you know, talk to this other person. On the other hand, I don't feel that I can be as available to them, and I've said both of these things to them....That has just been the worst in terms of feeling torn.

Pregnant therapists describe feeling guilty for forsaking patients' needs in order to care for themselves and their babies. Thus, they report feeling uneasy and guilty for abandoning patients for reasons that feel selfish.

In addition, many therapists felt threatened that their patients would either abandon them emotionally, or prematurely terminate their treatment. The following therapist's guilt was in reaction to some of her patients' abandoning her by dropping out of treatment during her pregnancy without giving her an opportunity to compensate them for being unavailable herself during her maternity leave:

> I felt guilty about taking so much time [maternity leave] and they don't give you a chance to make it up to them. [I felt] I'm back now. I'm back. I'll make it up to you and we can work it through and it will be great for you to understand all of your feelings about it, and basically they'd say "screw off" [by leaving].

Therapists also felt guilty when they felt they abandoned their babies in order to care for their patients. This discussion illustrates how therapists feel torn between two people who need their care.

Therapist A: Underneath it all I feel somewhat torn, somewhat of a low down guilt. I don't feel guilty, intellectually, but there is some aspect that's not the same as it used to be.

Therapist B: When I'm at the office, although it is somewhat easier, I'm thinking is he alright? Is he giving the baby-sitter a hard time? Is he crying? You know, is every thing OK at home? And it's there in the back of my mind.

Therapist A: It's always there.

Therapist C: I can't block it out. It really is there, and feeling guilty if I get home and he's fussy.

Therapist A: I think it's living with that, knowing that there is always going to be a piece of it that's going to be caught up and involved; that's never going to go away and it's very hard to adjust to.

Therapist D: I've had fantasies about giving up my practice and becoming a full-time mother, but I know it really isn't...

Wanting to be less responsible also produced feelings of guilt. A number
of pregnant therapists reported feeling guilty for wanting to take on less,
and guilty for not being able to take care of everything. These were difficult
experiences for women who were used to "giving their all."

One pregnant therapist who was working a demanding schedule of over
30 hours of clinical work a week admitted that despite this rigorous
schedule, "I'm feeling guilty about not wanting to take on more things."
Another therapist claimed that although she needed more time for herself
and with her husband before the baby was born, she felt "guilty if I'm not on
top of everything."

Changing Identity (Personal and Professional): Changing Style and Theory

Professional and personal identity is in a constant state of flux during
therapists' transition to motherhood. Pregnant and postpartum therapists
exert great effort to try to integrate the roles of therapist and mother. Theirs
is also a quest for self-definition and self-worth as evidenced by the ways
that many of the women changed essential aspects of their work during this
period. For example, most of the women interviewed left full-time private
and hospital practices for part-time private practices. Many found this a
dramatic change that prompted a reexamination of their careers and their
sources of identity. Because the therapists interviewed had spent their adult
lives developing their careers, a major feature of their identity was as
professional therapists. The following therapists illustrate some of these
concerns:

I've been such a good mother to all of these people, and now I really want to be
a good mother to my baby. Also my career has been my life, my self-esteem,
my identity. How I get good feelings. It's been very important to me.

It has been a big concern to me and I guess my fear, or perhaps it's my wish,
that I'm going to be very involved in being a mother and that my work life is
going to be less important to me.

[Changing from a full-time to a part-time practice is] as major or almost as
major as having the baby. I had always worked, you know 80 hours a week,
and all of a sudden I had a fifteen hour, maybe if I was lucky, practice. I just
didn't know who I was.

The quest and validation of self-worth are important parts of the process of redefining one's identity. Many of the therapists were questioning the relative value of motherhood and their work as therapists. One significant issue they faced was whether the standards to be used as the basis of these values reflect male's or female's values. The following illustrates some of the tensions the women experienced among identity, roles, and values in work and personal life.

> [Having recently returned to work after maternity leave] I realized last night that I'm getting worse in a sense. I said to my husband that I feel like I'm not going anywhere with my life. I got hysterical because the laundry wasn't put away! (laughter) My whole life feels like it's off center. I can't decide whether I should take the time to take notes after a session or rush home to the baby to see if he's alright. I feel so split all of the time. Nothing that I do somehow feels quite right. It's hard to find a way to integrate it all.

> It's a very male orientation that working and being valued and being valuable in the workplace has to do with the amount of time you put in. But it still feels to me that I'm putzing around and I'm not particularly serious if I'm only working half time.

One of the areas in which there was strong agreement among the therapists was that their pregnancy contributed significantly to a change in style and manner of practicing. For some, these changes developed into a change in theory about what is curative in the therapeutic relationship. The essential change centered around the therapist "becoming more real," being perceived less as a machine by her patients, and using her self more in her work. The therapists interviewed at a 3-year follow-up agreed that this process of change evolved not in a premeditated fashion, but rather from the discovery that being more present in a personal way not only was *not* damaging to patients, but rather was beneficial for the majority of them. Thus, over time, most therapists reported being more comfortable with personal questions, and found that they shifted away from a more distant, self-protective therapeutic stance to a more vulnerable one. It is crucial to note that this was a gradual shift that resulted from therapists' feeling that they had no choice other than to be more real with their patients. This engendered a lot of conflict for some therapists whose training and theoretical orientation mandated that a good therapist be neutral and private about her personal life. Changes in style of practice and/or changes in personal theory of therapy, therefore, directly resulted from various experiences of pregnant therapists. One therapist, for example, expressed surprise at the positive results of being more "real" with her patients.

> I feel more like a real person. I feel more present as a real person as their therapist. I feel a little bit more known and instead of that feeling threatening, and that it might not help the work, it has actually felt very conducive.

Another therapist explained:

In some ways it's felt like a relief. Somehow I felt it was like a confirmation
about myself. Having it [the pregnancy] be public with my patients and myself that I was married and sexual felt, I don't know whether I felt proud or I
felt more adult, but it wasn't too uncomfortable....I should just say one other
experience that I had that I didn't expect and that is that even though I tend to
be a more distant therapist and don't easily talk about myself, I found that
once I did tell people that I was pregnant, I found myself very responsive to
answering their questions, and that surprised me and I don't entirely understand that.

Thus, pregnancy and transition to motherhood has important and positive effects on some therapists' theoretical and personal stance in the
therapeutic situation. Consider the following:

It [the pregnancy] made me start thinking of the differences between male and
female therapists, and sort of the making of a woman therapist in a sense that
going through these events with patients and having to deal with them, how
has that changed me as a therapist? And not just reacting to a crisis situation,
but how has that made me more flexible and more open, and how much can I
use myself in sharing things about me judiciously in the therapy and that men
do not have to face those things and don't have to deal with them ever? I think
I use myself much much more, and I think it is very good. I mean I'm very glad
that I did. I don't think that I do any less work, in the sense that I'm using it
therapeutically, but I think that I feel much more effective. It's kind of like driving a motorcycle I mean either you drive the motorcycle or you also use your
body to help steer it and control it. And it's with this sense that I'm viscerally
involved and to use parts of me more non-verbally. I think once getting
through that uncertainness about it, it leaves you that much more room to do
it intentionally.

Another therapist elaborated on this issue in a group discussion by
saying that her patients also noticed a change in their relationship after she
had her baby. One of her women patients, who had two children of her own,
described the change in their relationship as moving from a strictly professional one at all times to feeling more like a "kaffee klatch" with a friend, or
two mothers sitting together. Another therapist in the group responded:

It gives you more range, because there is a way of doing it and I think, and I
probably wouldn't be caught dead saying this two years ago, but it can be very
useful with patients where you don't have to turn it into a "kaffee-klatch" but
you can really change the nature of the relationship in a way where, and who
cares exactly what the transference is like or how you analyze it, but where a

patient feels involved and that you're there with them and that you're understanding them and seeing them.

The first therapist agreed and noted that she really did understand more about child-care arrangements, and that when a mother of young children said that she wasn't able to make a therapy appointment because her child-care arrangements fell through at the last minute, she wasn't so quick to interpret this as resistance on the part of the patient. Another therapist revealed that she came to realize that her patients' questions were natural and positive rather than pathological. She said:

What I really was not prepared for was the number of people afterwards, women, who wanted to see pictures. Wanted to see the baby. And when I looked at it with them, it wasn't inappropriately intrusive or anything too crazy, but this feeling that they had gone through it with me. Here we had spent all of this time talking about three people in the room, and about people having dreams. You know it was me and this woman and here was this shadowy person walking by our side and things like that. All of this time I had spent helping them recognize how much they felt there was another person sitting in the room with them. Then all of a sudden I come back and that person's gone. For them it was a loss. You're saying all of a sudden, the message was that you're saying that this is a private event, that you're not going to share with me, and this is you, and basically, what do you mean? I've watched it grow for nine months. What do you mean a private event? I've been a part of it. And I had to recognize that that was very real and it was not just this kind of inappropriate wanting to climb into my lap, but it was a real issue for them. And I decided to bring in a picture framed and leave it on my desk, and if people asked about it then it would be there.

These are the kinds of insights that contributed to therapists' feeling that their work had grown in a positive manner. These kinds of insights also fostered important expansions in theoretical perspectives for many of the therapists, although not without struggle for some.

Fluctuating Boundaries: Setting and Resetting Limits

During pregnancy, boundaries are in flux within the therapist as well as in her relationship with her patients and colleagues. Some therapists, for example, experienced difficulties in keeping various aspects of their work lives and their private lives separate. For example:

I've been having dreams that my patients are coming to my house or that there was a bottle of baby formula in the safety deposit box....It's my professional self and my child caring and married self all mushed together. It's so intense.

Several of the therapists returned to work in private practices where their offices were in their homes. Although some reported that this was the best of all possible worlds, to have their work so close to the baby, others found it more difficult to separate the two worlds of mother and therapist, as this therapist revealed:

> It almost would be easier if I left for the whole day because then, psychologically, I'm fine and I'm not thinking about him until I return. This way I see several patients and I come back, it's at home. So I'm in and out, which in some ways is better for him, but for me it's harder.

Another issue that challenged the boundaries between therapist and patient was when patients offered therapists gifts. Although this is not a problem for some therapists, it is a practice that is strongly discouraged by others on theoretical grounds. During her maternity leave, one therapist described her quandary over whether or not to accept a gift for the baby from one of her patients. This dilemma was complicated further by the patient's wish to bring the gift to the therapist's home. Even though the therapist's office was in her home, this situation posed a breach of the usual boundaries of the therapeutic situation for this therapist. She described her inner struggle to redefine boundaries this way:

> [The patient] wanted to bring him a gift, and she didn't say, "could I come by?" She said, "when would be a good time for me to come by to drop off a gift?" I'd seen her for six or seven years, and you know I thought she'd be really offended and really hurt if I made her go through the office to give him a gift. Yea, it changes all of my thinking. It is really important to be sensitive to that. I expected gifts, and I'd never accepted gifts. But I feel like it is really different. I think it's really insulting otherwise. I mean it's crazy otherwise, someone's really offended, and there's no therapeutic gain.

Pregnant therapists, thus, face a dilemma over whether to be more protective of their private life or whether to make it more accessible.

DISCUSSION

Through systematic analyses of the individual interviews and group discussions with pregnant and postpartum therapists, five themes emerged as major sources of conflict; nurturance, power, guilt, identity, and limits/boundaries. The women therapists in this study directed tremendous amounts of emotional and intellectual energy toward resolving these conflicts while maintaining their commitment to caring for their patients.

The conflict over *nurturance* emerged as an important theme in this study. The struggle around nurturance resulted from contradictory personal expectations either to be all giving, or restricting. Pregnant therapists were dedicated to making sure that their patients' needs would be taken care of before taking maternity leave; often they overcompensated by working harder than ever to accomplish this. Once their babies were born, however, demands from baby, family members, and patients made it increasingly clear that the therapists needed to limit and redistribute their nurturance. As a result, some therapists always felt they were depriving someone, including themselves. Anticipating multiple demands for their care, pregnant therapists felt more ambivalent about "giving their all" at the office. Moreover, in light of their efforts to satisfy everyone, pregnant and postpartum therapists grew to resent patients' criticisms about not getting enough.

As pregnant therapists prepared to become "real mothers" to their own babies, they were forced to reconsider their relationship with their patients, a relationship that has been likened to a surrogate parent (Fenster, 1983), or a "good enough mother" (Winnicott, 1963). In our culture, motherhood has become idealized such that mothers are seen as devoted exclusively to nurturing and caring for their babies (Leifer, 1980), as the only one who can meet the needs of a baby (Chodorow & Contratto, 1982), and as not having a life independent of her child. This societal ideal is applicable to the role of therapists as well as mothers. Thus, therapists, who also are products of our culture, struggled with trying to be an "ideal mother" to both her patients and new baby.

As therapists coped by restricting and redefining their nurturance, there were beneficial results. For example, a number of therapists reported referring patients for supplementary treatments, such as biofeedback, relaxation training, and other anxiety management measures. These measures were recommended in order to help assure therapists that their patients would have added means to care for themselves during the therapist's pregnancy and maternity leave. Although these treatments might not have been considered previously, they appeared to have useful effects and helped to empower patients.

Finally, some pregnant therapists experienced conflict over being in situations where patients reversed roles and offered to nurture them. This role reversal appeared to threaten the more equal and symmetrical relationships that women therapists prefer with their patients (Grossman & Stewart, this volume).

The theme of *power* was a related and pronounced area of conflict for pregnant therapists. Consistent with previous findings (Grossman & Stewart, this volume), the women in this sample expressed pleasure in having power and prestige. During their pregnancy, however, some therapists were anxious about losing the power and status afforded them through their work. Because pregnant women and mothers of young children are not regarded with the prestige and respect in our society (see Chodorow & Contratto, 1980) as therapists, the anticipated role of mother offered much less visible power than that of psychotherapist. Thus, the potential loss of power and prestige was a major concern for a number of therapists.

Pregnant therapists also expressed concerns about losing control physically and emotionally while being with their patients. Thus, as Krainchfeld (1987) maintained, "any woman who is pregnant, nursing or caring for a newborn infant is in the process of learning powerful lessons about relinquishing control over body, time, and her identity at a fundamental level" (p. 47). Therapists, therefore, not only had to grapple with changes in body, emotions, and sense of herself, but also to deal with these changes while sitting with their patients. In addition, pregnant therapists felt vulnerable as a result of losing control over what is public and private in their lives, including their sexuality and the presence of a love relationship. Previously this information would be disclosed only at the therapist's discretion. Now there was no hiding them.

Another significant issue for pregnant and postpartum therapists was *guilt*. A prominent source of guilt was patients' envy, particularly of therapists' personal life. Expressions of envy, particularly by patients who had neither spouse, family, or close and loving relationships stimulated therapists' feelings of guilt for having so much—perhaps too much. Miller (1982) argued that women are very uncomfortable with power because it makes them feel selfish. Although Stewart and I (Grossman & Stewart, this volume) found little evidence of women therapists feeling selfish, pregnancy makes this a viable concern.

Therapists also felt guilty about separations in which they felt they were abandoning their patients for their babies, and later, abandoning their babies for their patients. As Gilligan (1984) noted, women experience a great sense of responsibility through connections with others. Moreover, Miller (1976) added that "for many women, the threat of disruption of an affiliation is perceived not only as just a loss of a relationship, but as something closer to a total loss of self" (p. 83). It is this latter concern that emerged as another important theme in this study; the process of *changing and integrating personal and professional identity*.

Throughout their pregnancies, and after their babies were born, therapists experienced a changing sense of themselves both personally and professionally. Because many therapists said they derived their self-esteem and identity from their career, they wondered how motherhood would affect their sense of self. Those women who chose the profession of psychotherapy for its more "masculine" components (i.e., power and influence, prestige, and independence), struggled with the perceived loss of value in the eyes of colleagues. They worried about being devalued as a result of assuming the less socially prestigious role of motherhood, changing from full-time work at a prestigious institution to part-time work in private practice, and perhaps from being unable to deny the realities of pregnancy and have things "business as usual" (Baum & Herring, 1975; Benedek, 1973; Kariv-Agnon, 1988; Lax, 1969; Nadelson et al., 1974; Paluszny & Pozanski, 1971).

One important change reported by all of the therapists in this study was that their style of working changed as a function of their pregnancy; specifically, they became more "real" with their patients. This finding is consistent with reports from other research (see Fenster et al., 1983). The therapists in the present study noted that the process of becoming more "real" was a gradual one that, for many of them, emerged under circumstances where they felt no choice other than to be candid and less reserved. Some therapists, particularly those with more psychoanalytic training, reported feeling uncomfortable at first, but, over time reported feeling relief and comfort in being flexible about sharing personal information. All agreed that pregnancy had changed them as therapists, and offered an opportunity that distinguished them from male therapists who, other than in rare circumstances, would never find themselves in situations where important aspects of their private life were as apparent. Seven of the women were reinterviewed at a 3-year follow-up described a lasting change in their work; ranging from changes in technique to fundamental philosophical changes. In all cases, the pregnancy was seen as having a positive influence on the therapist's personal and professional development.

A final theme that emerged in this study was the experience of *fluctuating boundaries*. Perhaps as an aspect of grappling with their personal and professional identities, pregnant therapists faced setting and resetting comfortable limits between their public and private world without being destructive toward patients, themselves, or their babies.

CONCLUSION

The overall experience of pregnancy and becoming a new mother was captured in a group discussion among women therapists. It was clear how significant their pregnancy was, not only for them personally, but also for their work. It was interesting to reflect back over the entire process of their transition to motherhood, recalling their struggles with boundaries, conflicts over telling patients about their pregnancies, the demands for nurturance, and challenges to their personal and professional identities. Ironically, there was a common sentiment among the therapists that once their pregnancies were over, and their babies were old enough for them to return to work, they missed having their babies with them in the therapy hour. Even more profound was the disappointment in starting work with new patients, since they didn't know about this recent and important experience in their therapist's life. This final note was very moving, and was sounded in sharp contrast with therapist's initial reactions in their pregnancy, when the baby's presence was unsettling for both the therapist and her patients.

Without the direct conversations with therapists during their pregnancies and after their babies were born, we would have no way of knowing and understanding the enormity of this experience in women's personal and work lives.

ACKNOWLEDGMENTS

I wish to express my appreciation to the women therapists who contributed their experiences and insights so generously to this project. I also want to acknowledge Ronald Marcus, Richard Grossman, Dewie Weiner, and Nia Chester for their invaluable input at various stages of this research.

REFERENCES

Ballou, J. (1978). *The psychology of pregnancy*. Lexington, MA: Lexington Books.

Balsam, R. (1975). The pregnant therapist: In R. Balsam (Ed.) *On becoming a psychotherapist* (pp. 265–288). Boston: Little, Brown.

Barbanel, L. (1980). The therapist's pregnancy. In B.L. Blum (Ed.) *Psychological aspects of pregnancy, birthing, and bonding* (pp. 232–246). New York: Human Sciences Press.

Baum, E., & Herring. C. (1975). The pregnant psychotherapist in training. *American Journal of Psychiatry, 132*, 419–423.

Benedek, T. (1956). The fourth world of the pregnant therapist. *Journal of the American Psychoanalytic Association, 4*, 389–427.

Breen, D. (1975). *The birth of a first child: Towards an understanding of femininity*. London: Tavistock.

Breen, D. (1977). Some of the differences between group and individual therapy in connection with the therapist's pregnancy. *International Journal of Group Psychotherapy, 26*, 149–162.

Butts, N., & Cavenar, J. (1979). Colleagues' responses to the pregnant psychiatric resident. *American Journal of Psychiatry, 136*, 1587–1589.

Chodorow, N., & Contratto, S. (1982). The fantasy of the perfect mother. In B. Thorne (Ed.), *Rethinking the family* (pp. 54–75). New York: Longman.

Davids, A., DeVault, S., & Talmadge, M. (1966). Psychological study of emotional factors in pregnancy. *Psychosomatic Medicine, 23*, 93–103.

Entwisle, D., & Doering, S. (1981). *The first birth: A family turning point*. Baltimore, MD: Johns Hopkins University Press.

Fenster, S. (1983). Intrusion in the analytic space: Pregnancy of the psychoanalytic therapist. *Dissertation Abstracts International.* (University Microfilms No. 83-17, 555)

Fenster, S., Phillips, S., & Rapoport, E. (1986). *The therapist's pregnancy: Intrusion in the analytic space.* Hillsdale, NJ: The Analytic Press.

Gilligan, C. (1984). *In a different voice.* Cambridge, MA: Harvard University Press.

Janeway, E. (1980). *The powers of the weak.* New York: Alfred A. Knopf.

Kariv-Agnon, E. (1988). *The pregnant therapist: The effect of pregnancy on one's experience as a psychotherapist.* Unpublished doctoral dissertation, Massachusetts School of Professional Psychology, Newton, MA.

Krainchfeld, M.L. (1987). Rethinking family power. *Journal of Family Issues, 8,* 42–56.

Laslett, B., & Rapoport, R. (1975). Collaborative interviewing and interactive research. *Journal of Marriage and the Family,* 968–977.

Lax, R.F. (1969). Some considerations about transference and countertransference manifestations evoked by the analyst's pregnancy. *International Journal of Psychoanalysis, 50,* 363–372.

Leifer, M. (1980). *Psychological effect of motherhood: A study of first pregnancy.* New York: Praeger.

Lincoln, Y.S., & Guba, E.G. (1985). *Naturalistic inquiry.* Beverly Hills, CA: Sage.

Lubin, B., Gardner, S., & Roth, A. (1975). Mood and somatic symptoms during pregnancy. *Psychosomatic Medicine, 37,* 136–146.

Miller, J.B. (1986). *Toward a new psychology of women.* Boston: Beacon Press.

Miller, J.B. (1982). *Women in power.* (Work in progress No. 92-01) Wellesley, MA: Wellesley College, Stone Center for Developmental Services and Studies.

Mischler, E.G. (1986). *Research interviewing: Context and narrative.* Cambridge, MA: Harvard University Press.

Murai, N., & Murai, N. (1975). A study of moods in pregnant women. *Tohiku Psychological Folia, 34,* 10–16.

Nadelson, C., Notman, M., Arons, E., & Feldman, J. (1974). The Pregnant Therapist. *American Journal of Psychiatry, 39,* 235–237.

Naparstek, B. (1976). Treatment guidelines for the pregnant therapist. *Psychiatric Opinion, 13,* 20–25.

Oakley, A. (1981). Interviewing women: A contradiction in terms. In H. Roberts (Ed.), *Doing feminist research* (pp. 30–61). London: Routledge & Kegan Paul.

Paluszny, M., & Pozanski, E. (1971). Reactions of patients during the pregnancy of the psychotherapist. *Child Psychiatry and Human Development, 4,* 266–274.

Pines, D. (1975). Pregnancy and motherhood: Interaction between fantasy and reality. *British Journal of Medical Psychology, 45,* 333–343.

Rosenwald, G.C. (1988). A theory of multiple-case research. *Journal of Personality, 56,* 239–264.

Rubin, C. (1980). Notes from a pregnant therapist. *Social Work, 25,* 210–214.

Schwartz, M. (1975, January). Casework implications of a worker's pregnancy. *Social Casework,* pp. 27–34.

Winnicott, D.W. (1963). Dependence in infant-care, in child-care, and in the psychoanalytic setting. *International Journal of Psychoanalysis, 44,* 339–344.

Winter, D. (1973). *The power motive.* New York: The Free Press.

Chapter 5

Achievement Motivation and Employment Decisions: Portraits of Women With Young Children

Nia Lane Chester
Pine Manor College

A majority of the mothers of young children now enter the labor force by the time at least one of their children is 12 months old (U.S. Bureau of Labor Statistics Census, 1987). Work patterns among these women tend to be varied. Some return full time, and remain full time; others return full time, only to cut back their hours in response to institutional or psychological constraints or family demands. Many return on a part-time basis, but to positions that offer little in the way of financial security or career development. A number of factors have been found to affect the employment patterns of women during the early childbearing years, including education, length, and type of employment before having children (Shaw, 1986); husband's attitudes, income, and type of job (Winter, Stewart, & McClelland, 1977); women's childhood perceptions of their own mother's experience (Gerson, 1985); and women's own attitudes toward the feasibility and desirability of combining paid employment with the rearing of young children (Eccles, 1985; Nieva & Gutek, 1981). The impact of social and attitudinal constraints is thus well documented. Yet none of the studies investigating these factors tell us much about women's own perceptions and experiences regarding the desirability of combining employment and parenthood.

Gerson's study is one of the few that attempts to document, through primarily retrospective interviews, the dynamics of women's efforts to respond to the realities of the workplace and the family (Gerson, 1985). Gerson concluded that the hard choices women make "are more likely to reflect the mix of structural constraint and opportunities available to them when critical life decisions are made" (p. 201) than to represent aspects of individual personalities. Her portraits effectively demonstrate the very real difficulties encountered by most mothers trying to reenter the work force with young children. However, in an important discussion of women's "achievement related decisions," Eccles (1987) reminded us that we need to examine more carefully the meaning of achievement from the woman's perspective, particularly when exploring the "problem" of women's occupational patterns. Although women are indeed constrained by social and personal situations, they still experience themselves as making their own decisions and choices. Values and attitudes, as well as individual dispositions, importantly affect how women perceive and respond to the complicated and often seemingly contradictory demands of mothering and employment.

Within the literature on motivation, for example, a number of studies demonstrate that motives may affect the way individuals experience and behave within social roles. One perspective defines motives in the tradition of Murray (1938) and McClelland (1980, 1984) as relatively specific tendencies to be sensitive to and attracted by particular situations. Motives can affect an individual's interpretation of events as well. Thus, differences in motive dispositions may influence the ways in which individuals perceive and respond to the same role demands (Veroff & Feld, 1975). The need for achievement, for example, defined as the need to compete successfully with an internal or external standard of excellence, has long been associated with job performance in men, particularly in those situations where the individual experiences moderate challenge, is given feedback about performance, has the opportunity to advance, and is allowed to function in a relatively autonomous manner (Atkinson, 1981; McClelland, 1980). Such an orientation is thus likely to predict successful performance and/or satisfaction with one's performance in the workplace only under particular circumstances.

A thorough review of the empirical literature reveals no differences between men and women with regard to the presence and intensity of the achievement motive (Stewart & Chester, 1982). There is some evidence, however, that the areas in which the motive is most likely to be expressed may be different for men and women, due partly to differences in social norms regarding gender-appropriate arenas for achievement. For example, Veroff (1982) found in a national sample that need for achievement was associated with work-satisfaction variables in men, but to concerns about competence in parenting among women. Jenkins (1987) found need-for-achievement scores assessed in college senior women predicted their labor force participation 14 years later; this was particularly the case in areas such

as teaching which satisfied their achievement needs but were also normative for women. In addition, Stewart (1980) demonstrated further complexities in the relationship between need for achievement, career pattern, and gender roles, finding that need for achievement predicted career persistence in a longitudinal sample of childless women but not within a sample of women with children.

These studies suggest that the need-for-achievement motive is most likely to be relevant in roles that are considered "norm appropriate." Current labor force patterns suggest that combining parenting and outside employment has become normative for contemporary women. The achievement motive, therefore, may significantly affect the way the complex demands of combining mother and worker roles are perceived and dealt with, both with regard to decisions about whether and when to reenter the labor force, and with regard to the way role combination is experienced. There is some evidence that high need-for-achievement mothers are less confident of their parenting skills during their children's infancy, when feedback regarding the consequences of their actions as parents is less clearcut than when their children are older and more able to verbalize their needs (Chester, 1988; Veroff, 1982). As a result, early infancy may be particularly frustrating to these mothers, who may then be more likely to seek an early return to jobs outside the home. On the other hand, the logistical and psychological pressures of employment while parenting an infant may be equally stressful for women high in the achievement motive if they cannot work out a system in which they feel they are doing both jobs (i.e., home and family) in a way that measures up to their standards.

To some extent, the success of any mother's efforts to work outside the home will depend on external variables (i.e., status within the organization, flexibility regarding hours, availability of day care, attitude of spouse, and so forth). Nevertheless, information about personality attributes, such as individual motive levels, may also lend important and legitimate insights into the different ways mothers react to the demands of dual roles. The study reported on here represents an effort to explore the relationship of a particular motive, the need for achievement, to individual women's experience of their decisions regarding employment during their children's early years. For this purpose, case material was analyzed from a sample of mothers who provided information about their lives over a period of 7 years following the birth of their first child. Although the association between the need for achievement and work pattern provided a context for this study, the central goal was to look within individual cases for evidence of how this particular motive affected these mother's plans, expectations, and experiences regarding role combination.

Sample and Procedures

In 1977, 40 couples from the Greater Boston area who had recently had their first child participated in a study of new parenthood. Originally recruited through newspaper ads, 20 of the new mothers who responded to the first set of questionnaires participated in three follow-ups: when their first child was around 9 months old, again when he or she was around 3 years old, and finally, in 1984, when the first child was around 7 years old. Subjects completed questionnaires at each time that contained open- and close-ended questions about their past and current employment; the effect of having children on their work; their satisfaction with themselves, their marriages, and their lifestyles; their experiences as parents; and their hopes and plans for the future. The subjects participated in an in-home interview at the third data collection, and also wrote stories at the first and third data collections to four standard picture cues, which were scored for need for achievement using a method adapted by Winter (in press) from Atkinson's original system (Atkinson, 1958).

Group Characteristics

The subjects in this study were White and lower middle to middle class. The average age at the time of the birth of the first child was 26, with a range of 19 to 32. Most had had at least some college education, although few had attended prestigious institutions. One third of the sample had a second child by the time the first child was 3; another third had a second child by the time the first child was 7 (the remaining group was divided equally among those who had a third child and those who had only one child). All but one of the women had been employed before they became mothers. At the first data collection, all expressed the expectation that they would probably be employed outside the home once their children were in school.

As it turned out, one third of the sample returned to work by the time their first child was 1; two thirds were working by the time the first child was 3 (this included several women who had had a second child by this time). Two thirds of the sample were also working when their first child was 7, although these were not necessarily the same people who had been employed at the earlier data collection. Some women who had returned to work earlier had dropped out of the work force by the time their first child was 7, and some had entered the work force at this point for the first time. Most of the women were employed in fields and positions traditional for women, as secretaries, clerks, nurses, teachers, and librarians. Two taught at the college level. This was, then, a fairly representative group of women, reflecting current norms regarding the appropriateness of mothers entering the work force (as well as the financial necessity of doing so). The variability among their work patterns attests to the continuing difficulty of remaining consistently in the work force while parenting young children, as well as to the variety of personal solutions to the dilemma.

INDIVIDUAL DIFFERENCES:
ACHIEVEMENT AND ROLE COMBINATION

In this sample, 53% of the mothers with high need-for-achievement scores at the first data collection were employed before their first child's first birthday, as compared to 26% of the mothers with lower need for achievement scores. They were also more likely than those with lower need for achievement scores to be employed by the time their first child was in school (70% as compared to 44%). These percentages suggest that there is some tendency in women with high achievement motive scores to be drawn early on to lifestyles combining parenting and outside employment.

An effort was thus made to better understand how mothers characterized by differences in achievement motive levels experienced the early years of parenthood, particularly with regard to their feelings about and experiences with employment during this period. To this end, subjects were categorized according to whether their need for achievement scores were consistently high or consistently low over the 3-year period, relative to the sample as a whole, based on median splits of the two sets of achievement scores. I then read over the protocols of the women who were either above the median at both times or below the median at both times, to see whether over the 7-year period there were differences in their perceptions and experiences regarding parenting and outside employment. I was particularly interested in seeing whether women characterized by relatively high levels of achievement motive perceived the potential difficulties and satisfactions of role combination when their children were young differently than did women with relatively lower need-for-achievement scores.

I have selected five women to describe here, three whose scores were consistently above the median and two whose scores were consistently below. All five had at least some college education but came from working-class or lower middle-class families. All were employed before their first child was born, and indicated in their first questionnaire, if they were not already working outside the home, that they intended to return to work at least by the time their children were in school. These five women thus share a number of characteristics, but, as we see, their actual choices, and their reactions to these choices, varied. They are not meant to illustrate all possible cases. Each was selected, however, because the themes and reactions in her questionnaire struck me as occurring often enough in the sample to be representative of a particular orientation to the dilemmas posed by role combination. Although environmental factors clearly play a role in their perceptions and decisions, knowledge of the difference in their motive levels contributes to a richer understanding of the differences in the way they experienced and reacted to their employment experiences and decisions.

HIGH NEED FOR ACHIEVEMENT SCORES:
IN PURSUIT OF HAVING IT ALL AT THE SAME TIME

Three women were chosen as representative of those mothers whose need for achievement scores were above the median at both time periods. Their perceptions and decisions, although reflecting to some degree their own unique circumstances, seem also to reflect the sort of themes one might expect among individuals with this orientation (i.e., enjoyment of challenge, pursuit of opportunities for individual accomplishment, frustration with situations not offering immediate and concrete feedback regarding performance). As we see, however, each experiences the satisfaction of her achievement needs in different ways.

Sandy: High Achievement Orientation
and Consistent Employment

Sandy's need for achievement scores were well above the median at both times that motives were measured. Sandy first participated in this study at age 30, shortly after the birth of her only child. She had married at age 22, moving directly from her parents' house into an apartment with her husband. It was the first time she had been away from home. Her father was a security guard, her mother a nurse. Although her mother was at home for most of Sandy's childhood and adolescence, she told Sandy that she had gone right back to work after Sandy was born, but had quit a year later when Sandy called the babysitter "Mommy." Her mother then stayed at home until Sandy was 17, returned to work part time for financial reasons, and eventually quit because of what Sandy described as a "deep depression."

Sandy started working as a research clerk with a large government agency in 1974, and continued in this capacity for the next several years, completing her bachelor's degree in the process. She enjoyed her work and gradually was given more responsibility over the selection of samples, editing of questionnaires, and working out of coding systems. She described her husband, an electronics technician, as very supportive of her working during the first years of marriage.

The birth of their child, Thomas, occurred after several years of their trying to conceive. In fact, Sandy said she had finally decided she did not want children and was at first "very distressed" to learn that she was pregnant. "To my great surprise," she said in the first questionnaire, "I enjoy being a mother. I'm amazed at the love I have for this child—it's the most immense love I've ever had."

At the same time, she remained committed to her job. She returned to work 2 months after the baby's birth, "the *only* person," she commented, "in the history of this organization to come back after having a baby." In each of the questionnaires she alluded to the difficulty of combining work and motherhood. She received very little support from others during this early period. She identified returning to work as early as she did as a source of conflict with both her mother and her father. She thought that now that they had a child, her husband would really prefer an "old-fashioned wife who would stay home and take care of things." Nor did she perceive her work environment as particularly supportive, "My bosses," she said when her baby was 10 months old, "still don't believe, after 8 months, that I won't decide to stay home as a full-time mother."

In spite of the lack of support from others, she persisted in her job, having placed Thomas in family day care. She enjoyed her unique status at work, even though things might have been easier if other mothers before her had socialized her bosses regarding working mothers. She perceived the difficulties involved in combining work and parenting to be challenges. In the first questionnaire, when she had been back at work for 8 months, she described the effect of having a child on her sense of self as a positive one, but particularly in the context of also continuing her job; "I've expanded who I am," she said. "I see myself as a mother, which is very important to me, but I also know I can manage and juggle a lot more than I ever thought."

By the time of the second interview, when Thomas was 3, Sandy had been promoted to a supervisory position, and had applied to and been accepted in a government-sponsored job-training program that would allow her to take courses in research and statistics. This gave her, in her words, "the credentials to get the pay appropriate to what I was doing." By the time Thomas was 6, she had completed the program and was enjoying her job immensely. "As my experience grows," she said, "so does my capacity for problem solving, and so does my competence and confidence."

Looking back over the 6 years since Thomas's birth, Sandy's observations are full of references to the familiar problems of working mothers: wishing she had more time to be with her child, wishing she had more energy, hating having to decide whether Thomas was sick enough for her to stay home when she had something important at work to do. Yet she construes these strains as defining a challenge, the meeting of which being an important source of satisfaction. Indeed, she defines herself as thriving on such challenge. When asked what advice she would give to parents expecting their first child, she said, "I'd tell a woman who was involved in education, or career, or volunteer work that she cared about, not to give it up. I'd be less happy and not as good a mother or a wife if I'd given it up when I didn't want to." She went on to say that her job was in fact so important to her that if she was asked which came first, job or family, she was not sure how she would answer.]

A number of situational factors weighed against Sandy remaining as consistently in her job as she did. She had not completed a college degree when she began her job. The position was initially a clerical one, without an automatic promotional ladder. Her family was not supportive of her working. Yet she was clear about her needs and prevailed in a lifestyle that was difficult, but intrinsically satisfying to her. Her statements are full of themes reflecting the reactions associated with the achievement motive: enjoyment of challenge, of doing something unique, of setting clear and specific goals for herself and of meeting those goals.]

Nancy: High Achievement Motive, Varied Work Pattern

Nancy also had high need-for-achievement scores and returned to the labor force relatively soon after her first child was born (at 12 months). However, she found it harder than Sandy to find a way to combine full-time work and parenting in a way that was satisfying to her.

Nancy worked as a clinical nurse until her baby was born, at which time she took a year's leave of absence. She found the transition from work to home to be a "drastic" one, particularly after working 60 hours a week in the highly pressured position of supervisory nurse in a critical care unit. Getting used to the larger amount of free time, as well as to the "endless routine tasks that keep needing to get redone" was particularly hard. Yet she also derived a great deal of satisfaction from being involved in her daughter's development. "When you see accomplishments, when you see her moving on and upward, you get a feeling of accomplishment that you did have something to do with it. With all the hours put in you do really feel like—of course it's her own personal development too—but you feel like you really are sort of collaborating in her achievements." Here, Nancy describes mothering itself as part of her achievement domain, in contrast to Sandy, who was more likely to define the juggling aspect of this period in terms of achievement satisfactions. Their differing emphases remind us that achievement satisfaction, at least for women, can be found in a variety of contexts, as well as in different aspects of the same context.

By the time the baby was 12 months old, Nancy made the decision to return to work on a part-time basis, starting with 1 day a week. "I can't afford to stay out any longer and keep up in the field," she said. She found leaving her child harder than she thought she would. "I became extremely anxious about finding the right babysitter," she commented, "to the point that I went through three sitters in 6 months. I finally realized that it really was separation anxiety on my part, and then I found someone I really liked or maybe I just got more comfortable with the idea that Sharon could survive without me for a day." Nancy also noted that one of the things she particularly liked about her job was the responsibility she had for making important decisions quickly, which she felt she did very well. Interestingly, she described what she didn't like about herself as a mother as being her inability to make decisions quickly about what was the best thing to do, particularly in situations about "things I'd not been confronted with before—which was most of them, since I hadn't had any experience with babies. It was annoying to me," she said, "because often things would work out later on anyway, regardless of what I did." This observation points out an interesting dilemma that mothers who are high in the achievement motive may have. Decisions regarding children's needs and behaviors, particular early on, are made without much previous experience or concrete clues as to what is the best decision to make, unlike decisions made in the workplace, which at least in Nancy's case, rely on more clearcut information and elicit more immediate and specific feedback.

By the time Sharon was 3, Nancy had increased her outside work to 20 hours a week. She felt that in many ways she was working more effectively because she was devoting herself to her job more intently during the hours that she was there, in order to get as much accomplished as possible. At the same time, her part-time status was frustrating to her because it did not allow enough time for the degree of professional involvement and status she wanted. Equally importantly, it did not give her the authority to set her own schedule, and she often found herself working hours that she felt conflicted with her family's needs. At this point, she made plans to go to graduate school, which she felt would be an important step both in terms of professional development and in terms of enabling her to find a comfortable balance between family and work-related needs. "I'll come out a nurse practitioner, or some allied animal," she explained. "I hope I get accepted into primary care, at which time I will go from the land of the dead to the land of the living, where we work regular hours. They'd be more consistent with Sharon's hours in school, and my husband's hours. Also, for my own independence—having been a supervisor, I would like to be more independent." When asked about the effect she thought becoming a full-time nurse practitioner would have on her family, she replied, "Well, obviously I'm going to need some more help, though Doug and I have always shared some things. Sharon will be in a regular nursery school program by then, which will help." When asked how she thought her family would adjust to the change, she said, with a chuckle, "I guess they'll become more independent. They'll be weaned. The 31-year-old and the 3 1/2-year-old will be weaned. That's about it, in a nutshell."

Five years later Nancy had completed her graduate work and was a nursing supervisor in an urban teaching hospital. Her daughter was now 7 and in second grade. Nancy and her husband were hoping to have more children, although they had not been successful as yet. Nancy was working a 40-hour week, leaving the house at 7 a.m., and returning at 5 p.m. She enjoyed her work very much, particularly with regard to the opportunities it gave her for "autonomy, responsibility, professional and personal growth, and at times the need to get away from home." Yet it did not give her the flexibility she had hoped for to respond to her family's needs, and to satisfy her own needs to be with her family. She felt that the hours away from home were "excessive"; it was almost impossible to give as much time and involvement to each of the two arenas of her life—home and work—as she would like. At this point, Nancy had decided to leave her position in 4 months time, and to reduce her hours to half what they had been. The decision to do this, she said, was her own and she looked forward to spending more time with her husband and daughter. "A 50–50 arrangement, or I guess I should say a 100%–100% arrangement just doesn't work," she commented, "at least not the way my profession is structured. I just can't get to where I feel like I'm giving my best to both, where I can accomplish what I want in both. I think for the time being, part-time work is the closest I can come, where I can come closest to quality in both." Yet when asked to describe what she hoped her life would be like in 10 years, she mentioned returning to full-time work, one or two more children, a happy marriage, and days with more hours in them.

Louise: High Achievement Motive, Alternatives to Paid Employment

Both Sandy and Nancy's statements reflect themes associated with individuals with strong achievement motive orientations. Both took pride in being able to juggle two roles, both valued efficiency and autonomy. Both felt that combining roles was the most fulfilling lifestyle for them, although Nancy had a more difficult time finding a way to function in both roles in a way that met her standards for each. Although these two case studies are representative of those women with high need-for-achievement scores who returned to work, some women with relatively high need-for-achievement scores did not return to work right away, demonstrating again that motive orientations can be satisfied in a variety of ways.

Louise illustrates the case of a woman whose need-for-achievement scores remained consistently high over the 7-year period, but who did not seek employment outside the home during that time. Louise's father was an ophthalmologist, her mother a housewife. After receiving a degree from a local university, Louise began working at an advertising agency, eventually becoming a senior media planner in charge of several major accounts. Although she had married while in college, Louise worked for 5 years before having her first child. In the first questionnaire, Louise mentioned her hopes to return to work "in a few years," and noted that her desire to go back to work, and/or to go to graduate school were major areas of conflict between herself and her own mother. In the second questionnaire, 9 months later, Louise noted that one effect of having a baby was to eliminate her career for the time being. She had begun to join some social service organizations, however, and to get involved in community affairs. Her view of her future in 10 years included another child, working outside the home, and perhaps getting a graduate degree in business. Two years after this questionnaire, she had had a second child, and said she was feeling much more satisfied with her life.

During her first child's infancy, Louise expressed concerns similar to many of the other mothers with high need-for-achievement scores. "What I found difficult with the first child," she said, "was all the free time I had, if you can believe it. I really prefer being busy. And at the same time, when the baby was awake it was hard, because I realize now I was afraid of the baby. I wanted to be the perfect mother and I was so afraid of doing something wrong. And of course he was colicky and lots of times there really wasn't much I could do about it. That was really hard for me to accept, I kept thinking there must be something wrong with me if I couldn't solve his unhappiness." She was feeling much more comfortable with the infancy of the second child. "I'm also feeling much less dependent now," she added. "Obviously I have a lot to do to take care of the two kids, even though my husband helps a lot when he's home. But also I've become extremely involved with the organizations I'm part of. I'm involved in lobbying, and in coordinating efforts to send clothes and medical supplies to South America. So in my free time during the day or at night, I do phoning, mostly about fundraising or organizational paperwork, things like that. I'm pretty good at getting things organized."

Louise made it clear in the interview that her husband, although helping out with the children, also felt strongly that she should be at home during their early years. He also wanted very much to have another child, although Louise was not sure. "I feel like I'm doing a really excellent job now," she commented. "And I think you can't do as good a job if you're working outside the home. But I don't think I'd feel as fulfilled if I wasn't also involved with my organizations; I think I've really made a difference. I'm not sure I'd be able to do everything I now do if I had another child."

It was clear that Louise felt she was accomplishing a great deal in her life at the moment. She said she was glad that her family income was such that she did not have to work outside the home until her children were in school. When asked about the possibility of future employment, however, she commented that she assumed she would go back to work eventually, but that she would want to get a graduate degree first. "When the children are in school, and I'm satisfied that I really do have enough time to do it well, then I'll think about going back to school. I don't want to go to work just to have a job, just to be a salesgirl or something."

In the final follow-up questionnaire 5 years later, Louise had had a third child and was still deeply involved in organization work. She felt that their family was now complete, and that she could begin thinking about graduate school (in fact, she had begun collecting and reviewing catalogues from various institutions). She planned to return to the labor market when the youngest child entered first grade (5 years from that point). Expressing satisfaction with the lifestyle she had chosen, she reiterated that "at least for me, I've been the best parent I could be by staying home." She added, however, "to tell you the truth, I look forward to getting a little more adult time, to getting more involved in the real world, at least the real outside world. I'm going to be ready to go back to work, but I think when I do it'll be at a time when I really feel comfortable about it, that I can really commit myself to it and know I can do a good job."

Thus, Louise did not see combining work and parenting during the children's early years as a satisfying lifestyle because it would be difficult to perform both "jobs" to her best capacity, a level of performance that was obviously important to her. Given her financial security and her husband's attitudes, it made sense that she chose to focus her achievement needs on raising her children, particularly because she was also able to satisfy additional achievement-related needs through organizational work.

LOWER ACHIEVEMENT NEED SCORES: VARIABLE WORK PATTERNS

The mothers whose need-for-achievement scores were below the median for this sample were not necessarily less interested in outside employment, but they were less likely to be employed during the years immediately following their first child's birth. In their descriptions of their goals and satisfactions, they seemed less focused on personal accomplishments and more likely to describe their lives in a relational context, whether talking about home or work.

Denise: Work to Family Shift

Denise's need-for-achievement scores were below the group median at both times they were assessed. Denise was married in 1973 at age 22, moving directly from her parents' home to a home with her husband, as Sandy had done. Denise's father was an assistant foreman with the public works administration; her mother worked as a secretary from the time Denise was 10 until she died, 15 years later. Denise completed her college education at a small state college, then worked first as a secretary in a medical office and then as an airlines reservations clerk. After her marriage, she was promoted to a supervisory position, in which she oversaw two teams of reservation clerks. She enjoyed this work very much she said; she liked the responsibility, liked being in charge. "Basically, I'm a bossy person," she commented. "And I like working with other people, having them look up to me, helping them out."

Denise returned to her full-time job 2 months after the birth of her first child, Alyson, in 1977. In the first questionnaire, completed when she had been back at work for about 2 months, she said that the hardest thing for her was leaving the baby, that she really could not get used to it. Three months after that, she resigned her position as supervisor, and went back to being a reservations clerk on a part-time basis, because she wanted to spend more time with Alyson. The effect of having a child on her career, she said, was that her career was postponed. "It (my career) was really blooming before Alyson," she commented. "But I've decided to shelve it for a while." Asked about the future, she foresaw another child, and going back to work full time, although she was not sure in what area—maybe in airlines work, she thought, or maybe teaching, the field in which she held an undergraduate degree.

At the third interview, Alyson was 2, and Denise was expecting her second child. At that time she was still working at the airline, but because she was only part time, she did not qualify for a maternity leave of absence. "So when the second baby comes, that's the end of my job," she said. "Which I'm sad about." But then she went on to say, "My husband thinks I'm going to go into culture shock. He thinks I'm going to go into a complete depression. But I have more faith in myself than that. I think I'm going to miss the independence. I love the people I'm working with, I like going in there and talking with them every day. And I like the money. But to tell you the truth, after a couple of months to adjust, I'm looking forward to it. It's going to be enticing to stay home, to relax for awhile. I'll see more of my friends, and more of my kids. I know I won't stay home forever, but it'll be a question of time." It is clear from these comments that Denise's job satisfied important personal needs; the difference between her description of these needs and those of the women just described, however, is their more relational flavor. She is much less likely to describe her satisfactions in terms of individual accomplishment.

Denise did leave her job after her second child was born. During the next few years she and a group of friends became involved in making crafts and selling them at a local crafts fair. Although she said in the third interview that if she could change anything about her life it would be to be able to keep her job at the airlines, she was less committed to that perspective at the time of the final questionnaire. She indicated that she would not want to have done things differently than she had, primarily because of her discomfort with leaving children in day care—"A day-care center or day-care mother at home does not love or really care about a child's total well-being," she explained. "They are babysitters, not nurturers, ego-builders, educators—they can't give of themselves to my children the way I do. It's a job to them—it's more like a career for me."

Like the other mothers, Denise initially felt strong conflicts between working and mothering. Denise's work environment was also not particularly supportive, because her job would not provide her with maternity leave. However, she was less likely than Sandy and Nancy to describe the things she enjoyed about her work in terms of her own developing skills and achievements, and more likely to mention relational gratifications. Her comments about motherhood also have a different flavor than either Sandy's or Nancy's comments. She is less likely to talk about her child's developing accomplishments, and more likely to stress her enjoyment of the responsibilities of being a mother. Her decision to remain at home for the time being, while to some degree reflecting the realities of her workplace, also reflected her perception that work experience outside of the home, at least at that point in her life, was not as satisfying of her needs as was her career as a mother.

Janet: Lower Achievement Scores, Unplanned but Continuous Employment

Janet is included in these portraits as an example of the mothers with relatively low need-for-achievement scores who nevertheless had taken jobs outside the home by the time of the last questionnaire, and who planned to remain in the labor market. What distinguishes Janet from the employed women with higher need-for-achievement scores is not her enjoyment of or commitment to her job, but rather the particular aspects of her job that she finds satisfying.

Janet married at age 20, after completing 1 year of secretarial school. She worked full time as the assistant to the minister of a large urban church until the birth of her first child 2 years later. She enjoyed her work, she said, because she liked the people, and because she knew what needed to be done. She liked going in each day to be with people she knew and do work she was familiar with. Five months after her son was born, she said that she planned to go back to work some day, but that for the time being she had a career at home. In a later interview, she described this early period as being a very pleasurable one. "Being with my baby was so much more wonderful than I had expected," she said. "And I was nursing, which no one in my family had ever done. Everyone thought it was a wrong thing to do, and that was difficult. But I just ignored what they were saying. It was really important to me. Those first 10 months, were just so close and special. I almost hated to see him get older." Shortly after their son's first birthday, Janet and her husband bought a house and Janet returned to her old job, on a part-time basis, to "help out with the family finances." At that time Janet said that although she had not expected to go back to work, she was enjoying it because of the money and because it gave her "something extra to do." Two years later, Janet had a second child, and once again left her job, planning to return "eventually." For 6 months prior to the third interview, Janet had begun working at her old job on a very part-time basis, "just when they need me for something because I'm so familiar with everything, and because they can trust me with the confidential things like pay raises and complaints people have made, things like that."

In the last questionnaire, 4 years later, Janet indicated that her husband had been laid off shortly after the third interview. Janet had then found a part-time position as a secretary and office manager in a private health clinic near her home. "I took the job because we needed the money," she said. "But when he found a new job 3 months later, I decided I wanted to keep on working. The people are great; it's only a few miles away from our house. The hours are convenient. Also, I like a little variety in my life." Later in the questionnaire, Janet's hopes for the future included a bigger house and a better position for her husband. "And I'd like to work a little more, more than 20 hours a week, but not full time. I want to be home when the children get home from school. But having my own job is important to me too. We can use the money, but also I realize that I like working. I like being with other adults and I like having my own thing to go to."

Combining employment and parenting is not what Janet planned to do during her children's early years. Nevertheless, although it was the financial crisis of her husband's unexpected unemployment that propelled her back into the labor market, it was the need for variety, for relationships with other adults, and for some time out from mothering that kept her there. She did not pursue specific career goals with the same focused quality that some of the other women with higher need-for-achievement scores did; nevertheless it is clear that her job is an important part of her life and one that she plans on maintaining.

CONCLUSIONS

Obviously, external factors (i.e., difficulties in getting pregnant; job status and maternity leave options; husband's attitudes; financial pressures; number of children, etc.) play an important part in determining whether or not women continue to work after having a baby. These case studies, however, illustrate that individual characteristics also need to be taken into account when trying to understand women's decisions, values, and experiences regarding role combination.

Although many other dimensions of personality could have been chosen to illustrate how personal dispositions affect the way in which individual women make and experience decisions about home and work, the need for achievement has traditionally been associated with work behavior, probably because the workplace is a locus of socially sanctioned and identifiable achievements (i.e., titles, promotions, pay raises, etc.). Most of what we know about the achievement motive and work, however, comes from studies of men. In several ways, the present case studies of women validate the notion of the achievement motive as originally defined by McClelland and Atkinson (that is, as a desire for the opportunity to excel as an individual, based on a comparison of one's performance with internally or externally defined standards). They also show us, however, that this motive does not describe interest in achievement per se; women both high and low in the motive may value doing well. Nor is the expression of the achievement motive limited to a particular arena. The case studies demonstrate that the need for achievement has more to do with a concern with individual goals and feedback about individual effort, than with accomplishment within a specific sphere.

Thus, as we have seen, all of the women described in this chapter indicated that they valued being competent. However, Sandy, Nancy, and Louise, the three women with higher need for achievement scores, described their needs, satisfactions, and frustrations differently than did Janet and Denise, the women with lower need for achievement scores. For example, they seemed more likely than Janet or Denise to be frustrated with the routines and demands of early infancy. They seemed more driven to find the "right" solution to the problem of juggling roles, and they tended to view their abilities to do so (or to not do so as well as they would like) as a matter of personal accomplishment or failure. In addition, they seemed more concerned with "getting ahead" as they talked about their jobs or their future plans regarding employment, and less interested in job-related relational satisfactions. They also seemed to derive more satisfaction from achievement aspects of mothering. They were more likely to mention the importance of "doing a good job" as a mother, or to describe their pleasure in taking part in their children's "accomplishments," than did Denise and

Janet, who were more likely to mention relational aspects of mothering. In general, Janet and Denise appeared less driven by the need to "do it all" during this early period of parenthood. Although both worked outside the home some of the time, and clearly enjoyed and derived satisfaction out of their jobs, neither tended to construe role combination itself as a personal achievement.

That the women with high need-for-achievement scores seemed particularly drawn to the challenges of juggling home and work roles reminds us of the importance of considering how motives reflect prevailing social norms. More so than was the case for Veroff's national samples, the women in the present study were having their children during a time when working outside the home while being a parent was considered possible and acceptable, perhaps even desirable for the mother's sense of well being (see, e.g., Baruch, Barnett, & Rivers, 1983). Nevertheless, although combining work and parenting is still socially sanctioned, mothers who attempt to do so are faced with social and economic realities that make this a difficult choice. Although it is not uncommon these days to see images in the media of the well-dressed, successful professional woman kissing her smiling baby goodbye as she leaves for the office without a care, rather little institutional support exists for such a lifestyle. Most working mothers are not employed at a professional level, and find working their way up to such a level a difficult proposition. Furthermore, obtaining quality day care is still a problem to be worked out by the individual parent, for whom the options are often limited and/or expensive. Few workplaces are flexible with regard to such issues as maternity leave, time off for child-related emergencies, and part-time work without loss of benefits and status. It is not surprising, then, that Sandy, Nancy, and Denise experience some stress around the issue of how to best combine motherhood and outside work, given the precariousness of the institutional supports available to them.

In any case, regardless of their particular life pattern, these five women's lives demonstrate that motives are more relevant to the meaning a person gives to an event or experience, rather than to the choice of one event over another. Their need-for-achievement scores thus tell us more about how these women interpret their experiences, what kind of gratifications they get out of their jobs and their mothering roles, rather than about whether or how they choose to combine these roles. Role combination may offer to women a wider range of potentially satisfying experiences with regard to the achievement motive, but it is clear that the motive can find satisfaction in any one of a variety of roles. It is equally clear that the desire to be competent in whatever life pattern a woman chooses is not necessarily a function of her achievement motive level.

Too often researchers study the effects of individual and social variables in isolation from one another and from the unique aspects of individuals' lives. Each of the five women described here wrestled at some point during her early parenting years with the issues involved in working outside the home while parenting young children. The variation among their choices and perceptions reminds us that a person's life context shapes and is shaped by her motives, values, and attitudes, as well as by broader economic and social forces. As these case studies demonstrate, a much richer understanding of women's experience regarding combining outside work and parenting is gained by viewing the effects of both internal and external factors in terms of the individual woman's own life context.

ACKNOWLEDGMENTS

The author thanks Abigail J. Stewart for her personal and professional guidance and support throughout the 10 years the data reported here represent; and Hildreth Y. Grossman and Allan Denenfield for editorial assistance.

This research was supported in part by the Radcliffe Research Scholars Program of the Henry A. Murray Research Center of Radcliffe College, Cambridge, Massachusetts. The original data, collected by Abigail J. Stewart, and the subsequent follow-ups, collected by this author, are housed in the archives of the Henry A. Murray Research Center of Radcliffe College.

REFERENCES

Atkinson, J.W. (1958). *Motives in fantasy, action, and society.* Princeton, NJ: Van Nostrand.

Atkinson, J.W. (1981). Studying personality in the context of an advanced motivational psychology. *American Psychologist, 36,* 117–128.

Baruch, G., Barnett, R., & Rivers, C. (1983). *Lifeprints: New patterns of love and work for today's women.* New York: New American Library.

Chester, N.L. (1988). *The effect of child stage and parent motive states on the experience of parenthood.* Unpublished manuscript, Boston University, Boston, MA.

Eccles, J. (1985). Sex differences in achievement patterns. In T.B. Sonderegger (Ed.), *Nebraska symposium on motivation, 1985: Psychology and gender* (V. 32), (pp. 97–132). Lincoln: University of Nebraska Press.

Eccles, J. (1987). Gender roles and women's achievement-related decisions. *Psychology of Women Quarterly, 11,* 135–172.

Gerson, K. (1985). *Hard choices: How women decide about work, career, and motherhood.* Berkeley: University of California Press.

Jenkins, S. (1987). Need for achievement and women's career over 14 years: Evidence for occcupational structure effects. *Journal of Personality and Social Psychology, 53,* pp. 922–932.

McClelland, D. (1980). Motive dispositions: The merits of operant and respondant measures. In L. Wheeler (Ed.), *Review of personality and social psychology* (Vol. 1, pp. 10–41). Beverly Hills, CA: Sage.

McClelland, D. (1984). *Human motivation.* Glenview, IL: Scott, Foresman.

Murray, H. (1938). Explorations in personality. London: Oxford University Press.

Nieva, V., & Gutek, B. (1981). *Women and work.* New York: Praeger.

Shaw, L. (1986). *Midlife women at work: a fifteen year perspective.* Lexington: D.C. Heath.

Stewart, A. (1980). Personality and situation in the prediction of women's life patterns. *Psychology of Women Quarterly, 5,* 195–206.

Stewart, A., & Chester, N.L. (1982). Sex differences in human social motives: Achievement, affiliation, and power. In A.J. Stewart (Ed.), *Motivation and society* (pp. 172–218). San Francisco: Jossey-Bass.

U.S. Bureau of Labor Statistics (1987, August). *Press release* (No. 87-345). Washington, DC: U.S. Department of Labor.

Veroff, J. (1982). Assertive motivations: Achievement versus power. In A.J. Stewart (Ed.), *Motivation and society* (pp. 99–132). San Francisco: Jossey-Bass.

Veroff, J., & Feld, S. (1975). *Marriage and work in America.* New York: Van Nostrand Reinhold.

Winter, D.G. (in press). Measuring personality at a distance: Development of an integrated system of scoring motives in running text. In A.J. Stewart, J.M. Healy, Jr., & D.J. Ozer (Eds.), *Perspectives in personality: Approaches to understanding lives.* Greenwich, CT: JAI Press.

Winter, D., Stewart, A., & McClelland, D. (1977). Husband's motives and wife's career level. *Journal of Personality and Social Psychology, 35,* 159–166.

Chapter 6

Women's Employment Patterns and Midlife Well-Being

Jacquelyn B. James
Henry A. Murray Research Center of Radcliffe College

Until recently, part of women's socialization process included preparation for careers that could be interrupted (presumably for child-rearing purposes) and easily resumed (if desired or necessary). Young women entering the early adult phase of life were urged to prepare for marriage and motherhood; if preparation for employment was encouraged at all, it was based on the need for something "to fall back on" (e.g., teaching, secretarial work, library work) in case of disaster (see Zellman, 1976). Consequently, many women did choose careers on the basis of the facility with which they could be interrupted; others chose the traditional pattern of forging an at-home career. On the other hand, many more women than ever before have sustained paid employment since completing their education (see Corcoran & Duncan, 1979). Although some research has focused on structural factors leading to women's varied employment patterns (Elder, 1976; Gerson, 1985; Shaw, 1986; Sorenson, 1983), seldom are these patterns examined for their psychological impact at some later point in life. The purpose of this chapter is to ascertain whether one employment pattern is more facilitative of psychological well-being at midlife than any other.

MIDLIFE PSYCHOLOGICAL WELL-BEING

Although several theories (e.g., Jacques, 1965; Jung, 1916) emphasize the importance of establishing occupational commitments for the midlife transition to flow smoothly, none addresses the elements of career trajectories particular to women's midlife experience.

Although not focused directly on middle age, Erickson's (1968) theoretical model is probably the approach that deals most pointedly with employment concerns and their implications for development. In Erikson's view, the tasks of middle adulthood rest upon successful resolution of earlier adult tasks believed to revolve around identity and intimacy issues. The midlife adult who has proceeded "normatively" through these earlier stages is usually faced with the dialectic of generativity versus stagnation.

For men in Erikson's theory, the journey through the identity "crisis" is accomplished by the selection of and commitment to a career, usually at the end of adolescence. For women, however, the path is not nearly so straightforward. Even though Erikson maintains that women follow a unique approach to the course of development by taking on the tasks surrounding intimacy before identity, he never clearly specified how identity resolution for women might look. While suggesting that a woman probably resolves the dialectic of identity versus diffusion out of her disposition to care (derived from awareness of her "inner space"), he concluded that the female identity crisis "ends when she chooses a path which integrates her abilities, social responsibilities, and anatomy" (Franz & White, 1985, p. 144). What form or process that identity resolution takes is not clear.

Another troublesome aspect of Erikson's notion of identity is the way that it is typically understood in measurement terms. Marcia (1966) conceived four levels of identity status based on the amount of exploration involved in decision making (crisis) and the amount of commitment afforded the decision. A period of exploration that yielded a firm commitment was determined to be an achieved identity status, the "highest" level. Ongoing exploration, as yet unsettled, was considered to reflect an identity in moratorium. A commitment made without exploration was a foreclosure. The diffuse identity status was characterized by no exploration and no commitment, the "lowest" level.

Employment patterns, then, conceived as one aspect of identity illuminated by Marcia's criteria, could reflect different levels of development, and thus be differentially related to well-being. For example, employment that follows a straight and largely continuous pattern could be said to grow out of early resolution of identity issues or out of early foreclosures. Employment that includes some interruption followed by change to a more committed employment enterprise could be said to grow out of identity issues resolved over time. Both of these patterns could be said to facilitate growth and movement into the next stages of intimacy and generativity. Employment that is variant (changing from job to job) or nonexistent could be seen as reflecting unresolved identity issues and therefore related to stagnation.

We know, however, that women often find other resources for resolving identity issues (e.g., through volunteer work; see Gora & Nemerowicz, 1985), political causes (Schenkel & Marcia, 1972), and philosophical stands (Tesch & Whitbourne, 1982). Moreover, there has been in the past considerable cultural support for women to foreclose (not challenge traditional expectations), although women's identity formation is considered to continue well into adulthood (Helson & Wink, 1987). Taken as a whole, this line of reasoning suggests that if women do make a choice to seek employment opportunities, then some aspect of identity is probably involved. The absence, however, of employment does not necessarily imply an absence of identity formation.

In fact, after an in-depth longitudinal study of women in the aforementioned identity statuses, Josselson (1987) concluded that even when women *are* employed, their sense of self is more "anchored" in aspects of their relational life than their occupational life.

> Although they have discovered that they are capable of accomplishing productive work in a nondomestic sphere, most of these women experience their job-related selves as secondary (and often expendable) aspects of their identities. (p. 176)

Although Josselson's finding may be a result of the traditionality of her sample (most of the women were first-generation college graduates and thus had few models for resolving the identity crisis in other than the relational domain), it may well be the case that women do have a wider array of spheres within which to resolve identity issues than do men, who are more confined to the occupational domain for self definition.[1]

EMPLOYMENT PATTERNS PER SE

What elements of different employment patterns in and of themselves might be expected to contribute to well-being? Some of the psychological benefits of employment for women can be seen in the repeated findings of the positive relationship between employment and self-esteem (Barnett & Baruch, 1978; Birnbaum, 1975; Coleman & Antonucci, 1983; Verbrugge, 1982) and between employment and physical health (Nye & Hoffman, 1963; Powell, 1977). Paid employment has also been shown to be an antidote for depression (Brown, Bhrolchain, & Harris, 1975; Brown & Harris, 1978;

---

[1]Josselson reported that those women who did consider their occupational commitments to reflect identity resolution had found a mentor to guide their way, which suggests that a different model might have a profound impact on development.

Kessler & McRae, 1982). One would think, then, that continuous employment over time might predict higher levels of well-being than either interrupted employment or unresumed employment.

Recent media attention of the effects of role strain on health (see
"Feminism's identity crisis," 1986) and to the number of women in high
powered positions returning to the "hearth" (see Cardoza, 1986) have called
into question many of these beneficial aspects of women's employment and
served (on the negative side) as yet another indictment of women who work
whether for financial necessity or as a critical source of identity. There is still
some question then as to whether continuous employment (into midlife)
facilitates or is detrimental to well-being.

Would "sequencing" or allowing for a career interruption, especially
during the most intense child-rearing years, provide a buffer for some of
these concerns? The answer might be yes, except for evidence that women
who plan to interrupt their careers tend to make their career choice more on
the basis of how easily the career can be interrupted and resumed rather
than on the basis of their own talents, skills, and interests. Thus, their
choices may be based on structural aspects of the occupation (see Gerson,
1985; Shaw, 1983) rather than on the extent to which the occupation is a
reflection of one's identity resolution. These "interruptable" careers tend to
be the more "feminine" careers (teaching, secretarial work, library work,
and nursing) that require training and skill but provide low pay, few opportunities for advancement, and little autonomy within the work setting (Van
Dusen & Sheldon, 1976). Perhaps because of the disadvantages associated
with these "interruptable" careers, many women have little interest in
returning to the same occupation. Planning interruptable careers, then, may
get women into careers that do not provide the possibilities for growth and
maturation inherent in some of the more "masculine" careers (see Kohn,
1980) and makes a return to the same career untenable, both of which may
be negative predictors for midlife well-being.[2] Another potential negative
consequence for well-being of either interrupted or unresumed careers is
women's financial reality, both in middle and old age. Currently, some 60%
of older single women depend on social security as their major source of income (Long & Porter, 1984). Long and Porter, charging that lack of attention
to women's financial plight has been a matter of "genteel neglect," submit
that at midlife, the proportion of women holding well-paying jobs that provide benefits is small, whereas the chance that they may experience the loss
of a husband is large (either through divorce or death). Moreover, they point

---

[2]Just on the basis of evidence that interruptable careers may be disappointing in terms of the
rewards they provide, women might be better served by planning for involved, committed careers; several studies of men have shown (e.g., Levinson, 1977; Osherson, 1980; Sarason, 1977)
that these careers, too, can be interruptable and flexible in many unforeseen ways.

out that the poverty rate for women over age 65 is almost twice the rate for men of the same age. "Employed women, married or not, have better chances for economic survival at midlife and later than women who are unemployed. Women without their own earnings *and* without husbands fare the worst" (Long & Porter, 1984, p. 150). The midlife woman who has been continuously employed throughout adulthood is least likely, they say, to experience poverty at midlife or later. The midlife woman employed intermittently throughout adulthood and who is no longer a wife or mother fares worst under the current set of public programs. The midlife woman who has had a homemaker career has no programs available to supply financial aid should she become disabled or unable to perform her domestic occupation. This kind of vulnerability alone has the potential to be causally related to poor psychological adjustment at midlife.

There has been little research about the psychological consequences of financial vulnerability. Recent research shows that *unpaid* work is socially undervalued (Bergman, 1986) whereas *paid* work, as we have seen, is associated with enhanced self-esteem for women (Coleman & Antonucci, 1982). In addition, there is the consistent and strong relationship between family income and many different assessments of subjective mental health (see Veroff, Douvan, & Kulka, 1981). Moreover, Veroff et al. found that the middle of life (as compared to the early adult years and the retirement years) was the developmental period during which income seemed to exert its most dramatic effects. Baruch, Barnett, and Rivers (1983) have speculated that "the power to earn one's own way in the world has a profound impact on the inner landscape" (p. 152). Especially for women, committed employment and the attendant financial security may be two very important aspects of the psychological transition from young adulthood to the middle years. The question remains whether financial vulnerability (manifested in either low or no earning power, interrupted or unresumed careers) diminishes well-being at midlife.

THE RELATIONSHIP BETWEEN EMPLOYMENT PATTERNS AND MIDLIFE WELL-BEING

To address all of these questions, a year-by-year employment history (1964–1986) for a sample of women who graduated from a prestigious New England liberal arts college in 1964 was used to examine the pattern of entries and exits from the labor force, and the relationship between these patterns and various indicators of midlife well-being.

All of the women were or had been married and nearly all of the women had had at least one child (85%). Of these women, 28% had experienced divorce. Approximately 50% of the women recorded their husband's income in the highest range provided on the questionnaire—$50,000+. The women's own income ranged from none (11%) to $50,000+ (14%). The average income was $20,000–$29,999.

The women of this sample came from highly educated families and were themselves highly educated. Of the women's fathers, 43% were at the professional socioeconomic status (SES) level (Hollingshead, 1958). A full 58% of the mothers of these women had had some college education; another 16% had earned a professional degree. Although all of the women in the sample had earned BAs, 34% had earned MAs and another 19% had acquired PhDs.

Career patterns were categorized as continuous, interrupted but resumed, or unresumed. Women were considered to have worked continuously if employment had begun after education was completed and continued into the time of the data collection. Breaks or leaves of absence of 1 year or less were not counted as interruptions. If an interruption in labor force participation exceeded 1 year, and was resumed at some later date (whether same of different work), the career pattern was categorized as interrupted/resumed. Those who had terminated jobs and had not returned were considered to be unresumed.

These three employment pattern groups were then compared as to differences in psychological well-being at midlife (all the women were approximately 44 at the time of the assessment). Well-being was measured by self-esteem (a self-rating of a list of socially desirable attributes), mood disturbance (Profile of Mood States; McNair, Lorr, & Doppleman, 1971), symptomatology (The Symptoms Checklist: Veroff et al. 1981), life satisfaction (a self-rating of satisfaction with one's current situation), and ego development (based on Loevinger, 1976, taken from coding of open-ended interview material). In addition, all participants in the 1986 wave were given an Occupational Attitude Questionnaire that revealed the extent to which they valued the monetary aspects of work, the interpersonal component, or mastery.

Considering the bounty of opportunity afforded these women, it may not come as a surprise that there were no significant differences among the three groups on any of the psychological dimensions. Apparently, employment patterns, taken alone, provide little insight into psychological well-being.

There were, however economic consequences for each of the employment patterns. Of course, women with unresumed careers reported no income; women with continuous careers, however, reported significantly higher incomes than women with interrupted ($p<.05$) careers. And these distinctions were related to well-being for women who valued the monetary aspects of working. Women in unresumed careers who placed a value on the financial aspect of work found the lack of it burdensome.

Women in continuous careers who valued money showed no detrimental effects on well-being. Women in interrupted careers who valued money and had moved from earning no money to earning some money likewise showed no ill effects on the basis of the well-being indices. It appears then that some of the financial aspects of employment or lack of it do seem to have a bearing on psychological well-being.

It must be emphasized that the lack of any differences in psychological well-being among the three groups may have been very different for a sample of uneducated women. There is evidence to suggest that the college degree alone provided many resources for self-development and growth among the women studied here and ameliorated many potential negative consequences of the lack of career commitment. Betz and Fitzgerald (1987) pointed out the importance of the educational process for women's development and achievements in conveying values that remain influential throughout one's life time. They report that college education has been shown to be related to more liberal attitudes toward women's roles and "to such characteristics as autonomy and the desire for direct versus vicarious achievement" (Betz & Fitzgerald, 1987, p. 74). Ginzberg (1966) pointed out the resourcefulness with which educated women can utilize community activities for achieving "excellence, distinction, and sometimes even power" (p. 53).

It follows, then, that educated women do indeed have more choices with respect to their employment decisions than women without an education. If they feel their financial future is secure and if they have an education that is believed to create options, interests, and outlets for creative endeavors, then it appears to be possible to arrive at midlife with psychological well-being largely intact with or without paid employment.

When examined as employment pattern groups, there appear to be no global psychological effects of either working continuously, taking some time off for full-time mothering or choosing the homemaker role entirely. Where we can start to see the costs and benefits of each career pattern is when women's individual career histories are told. These stories help us ascertain women's own impressions of how career choices came about, how they felt about their choices, and what implications these patterns seemed to have for their futures.

In order to further illuminate both costs and benefits of different employment patterns one woman from each employment pattern group (continuous, interrupted, unresumed) was selected for an in-depth interview. Although no essential data about these women have been changed, they have been given fictitious names. Further, no reference is made to any identifying information, and some details have been altered slightly or changed in order to protect their privacy.

CASE STUDIES OF THREE EMPLOYMENT PATTERNS

Lydia: Continuously Employed Since College

Lydia, the director of a social services agency, reports that shortly after college graduation, she concentrated considerable effort toward finding a suitable career. She described a period of exploration and choice making with respect to various occupations and ultimately chose clinical social work.

Lydia then slowly and methodically climbed the "ladder of success" in her field. She began as psychological research assistant, followed by assisting in a social service agency during which time she obtained a master's degree in social work. She then became a clinical social worker, advanced to the position of assistant director for her agency and in recent years has become the executive director. Clearly, Lydia's occupational choice is a reflection of her own identity resolution. When asked what had been rewarding about her capacity to work continuously she replied:

> Well, I think that I chose a career that was suitable for me. So, you know I definitely see myself as a social worker and you know that's part of my identity....I wanted to be active in doing my craft....You know some people think about women's clubs and this and that but that's not part of me. Doing my work was part of who I am....I like the involvement with people on an interaction basis and the feeling that....I am effective.

The "price to be paid" for this choice, she felt, was the lack of availability to her children at times, but she felt this concern was diminished by the fact that her husband created availability for the children out of his more flexible schedule, which she felt was a plus for father, children, and mother.

Interestingly, she mentioned the monetary disappointments of women's employment experiences. Asked if social work was a good field for women, she replied that it is a traditional female field. She also said that she went into this field during the "revolutionary fervor" of the 1960s in which more men were attracted to social work.

> Interviewer: Do you think men's presence made it a better field for women somehow?
>
> Lydia: I think the result is that men tend to be better paid and the women still, you know, the front line positions still aren't paid the way they should be...my Board of Directors, they may not realize it but they presume that all these people doing the counselling are women and they have a man to support them so they don't need money and that's unfortunate.

When asked what women, in general, need to make the next decade a positive time in their lives, Lydia again referred to the financial vulnerability:

Well, I think for one thing is to have a solid educational background. If they file for divorce and if they don't have a skill, it's too late for there isn't time to get themselves in a position to support themselves....So I think that to be able to feel that you are relatively self-sufficient and prepared for unforeseen circumstances is really important.

Lydia also feels, perhaps with some prejudice, that well-being without paid employment is an impossibility.

Women need...a profession and a skill that someone in the society feels is worth paying for....it gives you a different feeling. Wandering from one volunteer activity to another just doesn't hack it. I do my share of volunteering but that is not the point.

When asked what were the major sources of growth and development for her, Lydia did not, however, mention her work directly. She described events of crisis proportions—a major flood and the suicide of her sister-in-law—both of which she said reminds one that "our control over our lives can indeed be quite ephemeral." She did mention that her sister-in-law's suicide had raised concerns about the limitations of her field in its capacity to "help," and had created no insignificant amount of personal guilt about her own inability to prevent this terrible tragedy.

Early in adulthood, Lydia had made a committed career choice. She seemed, in midlife, to be reaping the benefits—of increased status (from caseworker to administrator) and had bright prospects for moving into the next decade. The negative aspects of her career pattern seemed to reflect the negative consequences (found in the larger study) for women in high-level careers who place a value on financial gains and view their monetary compensation to be inadequate compared to men's. Her children were preparing for college and apparently doing well. Lydia reported few worries about the future. Her major concern about the future, she said, was the care of her aging parents.

Lydia's scores on measures of well-being indicated that she was "very satisfied" with her current situation. She was below the sample mean for mood disturbance and symptomatology; her ego development score was 5.61, precisely the mean ego-level score for women of this sample. She was also, however, almost one full standard deviation below the mean on self-esteem. This self-esteem score may reflect the negative impact on self-esteem found in the larger study for women in high-level careers that appeared to be due to the wage differential that exists between men and women (because this effect was found only for women who valued the monetary aspects of employment).

Dorothy: Interrupted, Resumed Career

In the years that followed college graduation, Dorothy, an economics major, was first a buyer for a large department store and then a computer program-mer for another large corporation, both occupations that she viewed as a stop-gap until the children were born. When she had her first child in 1968 she resigned her position and focused completely on homemaking, mothering, and volunteering. In 1982, Dorothy resumed work as an office manager. By her own definition, she has interrupted and resumed "work"—she has not yet pursued a career, although thoughts about that are currently being processed.

> I don't really feel that I had a career, so to speak. I worked...at two different jobs and then I stopped to have a family. I am working now again...but nothing that I would call a career, although right now I am in the process of trying to start my own business. Once that is off the ground, then I would say that's a career.

Dorothy provides a poignant description of the expectations that the women in her college class had for their future. In 1962, a sophomore in col-lege, she and 11 close friends who had shared a "hall" together for 2 years sat around envisioning themselves at age 30.

> We sat down one night and said where are we going to be 10 years from now, so that was going to be at 30, and I was the note-taker. (I still have the notes)....We took each gal and we said, "husband, home, activities." Nothing about jobs, nothing about career. I mean that's where our heads were. It didn't even occur to us that at the age of 30 we'd be anything but housewives with husbands, children, bridge club and all that kind of stuff...As it turns out, I was about the only one who actually became a housewife.

When asked what had been rewarding about this career path, Dorothy replied that it had been rewarding to be her children's primary caretaker. Connected with their care, she had forged a volunteer career for herself and felt that her volunteer career had also been very rewarding. When they were in kindergarten, she said, she had been involved with the PTA. After several years with the PTA she had been elected to the Board of Education and was the president for 3 of her 6 years in office. She reported a feeling of efficacy in these endeavors—of doing something for her children, for students in general, and for the community. She felt that she had been instrumental in changing the direction of the school board and setting their sights on high academic standards. It seems clear that Dorothy viewed her volunteer career as an extension of her "self," as a part of her identity, although, similar to Josselson's (1987) sample, she describes it as only important in the context of her significant relationships. In fact, her occupational choices up to now have seemed to her to be much less significant reflections of her personality than have her volunteer activities.

When asked what had helped her to grow and develop, Dorothy, like Lydia, described tragedies. During one 2-year period while her husband was in Vietnam, both she and her husband faced the death of a parent. It did not help, she said, that these tragedies came the year they had their first child. After some thought, however, Dorothy affirmed that indeed being on the Board of Education was a growing experience—being responsible, handling meetings, sticky issues, and so on.

> I think that has helped to develop a certain amount of confidence and ability. And it has helped me figure out where my abilities are. Organizational problem-solving—I think I'm good in these areas...those are strengths of mine. And I guess that's why when I think about this career I'm trying to start...hopefully I'm solving problems and being organized.

Thinking about this career that she was trying to get off the ground was the "down" side of the homemaker/volunteer choice for Dorothy.

> I am 46 now...a year from now I will have no youngsters at home and so much of my life has been devoted to my youngsters....But, you know, I didn't really have a job that I really wanted to go back to and certainly a down side is—here I am at 46 and I'm starting out.

This concern was also reflected in questions regarding Dorothy's future. Like Lydia, she first mentioned worries about her aging parents (her father remarried) who are in their late 70s. Then her attention turned to her own plans.

> Well, I'm eager to get this business started. If I can get it started I will be probably very satisfied. If I can't, I don't know what I'm going to do. I know I need something in my life....We're concerned about money—we've got three children in school...that has to be a concern over the next few years...I'm not exactly sure what to say to you.

Dorothy has had many successful experiences within her volunteer career. Her values and her knowledge have given shape to not only the activities with which she became involved but the direction they took. Within these volunteer settings, she has proven herself to be confident and strong. In facing the world of paid employment, although she feels a little shaky, she has taken the initiative toward starting her own business—one that, she believes, requires her special talents and skills discovered through her volunteering. She feels hopeful—if a little uncertain. Clearly, some aspects of identity (related to her volunteer career) have been resolved over time. Her occupational identity is currently being re-worked.

Although Dorothy's well-being appears to be somewhat shaky in her own mind, her scores are indicative of her success in adapting to midlife, at least in terms of psychological adjustment. Her mood disturbance score is one-half of a standard deviation below the mean; her symptomatology score is also below the mean. Moreover, she is one whole standard deviation above the mean in self-esteem. Where she seems to be showing the effects of her current moratorium with respect to occupational commitments is by reporting a higher dissatisfaction score (slightly above the mean) and a lower ego development score (which is one standard deviation below the mean for women in the larger sample).

Alice: Unresumed Career

After a few years of working in several different places as a journalistic writer for magazines, Alice left to begin a career of homemaking, mothering, and volunteering. Like Dorothy, Alice felt that a close following of the stages of her children's growth and development was critical for their development and very satisfying to her. As the children developed into adolescence, she felt her presence to be even more important, because, she said, they are moody and often uncommunicative. You have to be there, she reasoned, to be available to talk when the child does want to talk.

Also like Dorothy, Alice found herself involved in volunteering, at first in preschools and writing newsletters related to the children's activities, but later her own interests drew her into other arenas.

> I've been put in situations where I certainly am challenged to use all my re-sources...recently I was able to attend a leadership training institute with the head that once you went through the training, you would train others in your communities. We have been working on setting up a workshop, working with leaders of women's groups in this area.

Interviewer: And what would these workshops be about?

Alice: Well, how to lobby, how to testify at a public hearing, especially for women—what to do when you disagree with legislation and how to make your opinions heard.

Some of the issues Alice and her group are addressing rose to the surface as the result of a survey done by a local Women's Commission as a deliberate attempt to identify and correct problems currently being faced by the women of her county. Alice views herself as one who lobbies for women—working for equal pay for equal work and adequate child care.

Her interests expand to other political issues as well. Recently, she recounts her experience with a group lobbying to oppose a solid waste treatment plant.

> This is not just your healthful trash...my committee is trying to work on ideas to help the un-incorporated areas accept the idea of letting their trash be collected (they are not used to doing that). We are an advisory committee to the commissioners and make suggestions for their final plan. We are trying to educate them as to the concept and help it to be successful.

Like Dorothy, Alice feels that the costs of her choice of not resuming a career center around her economic vulnerability.

> If my husband were to die right now, I would have to go back into the work force. How would that be for me? Would I be adequately prepared? Would I get credit for what I've been doing and get paid? How would I convince the employer that I feel like I can do something. And also, where would I look for a job. Yes, that has certainly occurred to me, because you think that as you get older you begin to feel your mortality...but I also feel that if the challenge were presented, I'm sure I'd make my way through it.

Unlike Dorothy, Alice actually has a plan. She knows what kind of work she would seek (back to writing), she has contacts in her field and she is prepared to network to find her way. She says she has thoughts about this because she watched her mother's grievous process of entering the labor force (after the premature death of her father) with no education (beyond high school), no skill and very little self-confidence. Alice feels buffered by her education (college and graduate work), her volunteer experiences, and her knowledge that she has a marketable trade. Interestingly, Alice confides that she probably would not make the choice to completely abandon her career if she had it all to do over again.

When asked what kinds of things had helped her to grow and develop in adulthood, Alice describes the way in which her volunteer career had helped her to give of herself generously and to be able to say "no" to things that she felt would be given out of guilt or resentment. Interestingly, the woman without paid employment is the only one who mentioned her career first and foremost as a factor in her growth.

Like both of the other women, Alice's worries about the future center around aging parents (her in-laws), the health of her older sister (who has cancer), and her own vulnerability to illness and death.

What does a woman need in order to make the next decade a positive time of life?

I think she needs something worthwhile thing to do and I can see very definitely—when the children are gone and you don't have that every day contact
with them, you really need something to keep you feeling as though you have
some self-worth. Certainly that may be the time to re-enter the job market. If
you don't find that volunteer things that can satisfy you or present enough of
a consistent challenge, then I think you need to find something else to do.

For now, Alice likes the flexibility and freedom that she feels within her
volunteer career; and she feels confident that she can move beyond it if or
when it is no longer fulfilling or she needs to be self-supporting.

Alice appears to be riding a wave of success in her midlife development
as confirmed by her ego-level score, which was one full standard deviation
above the mean. She reports that her choices have facilitated her development, and indeed her score indicated that this is so. She is also slightly above
the mean on self-esteem and below the mean on symptomatology. Like
Dorothy, however, she is above the mean on dissatisfaction. Perhaps she
would be more satisfied with her volunteer career if she were properly
remunerated for her efforts. Perhaps her dissatisfaction score is simply a
reflection of her regret—that she had not pursued her writing career. In any
case, it seems clear that Alice has not neglected aspects of identity development by eschewing paid employment.

All three of these women exemplify the ways in which educated women
find outlets for their talents and abilities regardless of their employment
pattern or career choice. All three report worries and disappointments
about their economic vulnerability even though two of them are currently
employed and one of the two is earning enough money to be self-supporting. Women have been shown to be disappointed in the degree of financial
security they are able to attain (Adams, 1984). Interestingly, none of the
women mentioned menopause as a central concern or even any apprehen-
sion about their own aging process. The biggest worry for all three of these
women was the care of their own or their husband's aging parents—which
is similar to recent findings of McKinlay and McKinlay (see Dietz, 1988),
authors of the Massachusetts Women's Health Study, who reported that
midlife women are most concerned about aging parents, husbands with ill
health, and adolescent children, in that order.

In some ways Alice's career as homemaker and volunteer lobbyist has
been the most facilitative of psychological development. She has made it
happen herself and it has evolved out of her own inclinations and priorities.
She also has had to stand up against subtle and not-so-subtle cultural messages that suggested that her choice was not valid. She does, however, appear to be less satisfied with her current situation than Lydia, who
continued her career.

Of the three, Lydia seems to be the most satisfied with her life in general.

She does, however, have considerably lower self-esteem scores than either of the two other women. Although this finding goes against the grain of other research that provides considerable evidence for a positive link between employment and self-esteem, there is reason to believe that some of today's women are expressing disillusionment relative to their employment situations due to disappointing factors within the workplace (see Hardesty & Jacobs, 1986; McIntosh, 1985; Stiver, 1983). Lydia herself pointed out the discrepancy between her own status and that of men in comparable positions. Moreover, even as she quite skillfully climbed the ladder of success she complained about the lack of proportionate increases in wages. To the extent that money represents value in our society, the lack of monetary reward alone could be enough to put a damper on one's self-esteem (see Sanford & Donovan, 1987).

Dorothy, on the other hand, had high self-esteem and low affective distress scores, but reported the lowest satisfaction with her life and showed the lowest ego development score. Dorothy seems truly exemplary of the women who got caught in the middle, between the old norms of "husband, kids, volunteer" and the newer norm of combining work and family. Interestingly, only Dorothy's career path seemed to exemplify Josselson's (1987) conclusion that women's concern with identity could only be seen in the context of relationships. Both Lydia (employed) and Alice (unemployed) considered their work lives to reflect important aspects of the self.

All of these women reflect the influence of the cultural pendulum swing. Dorothy had no plans for a career, didn't really make any during the "winds of change," and now is struggling to launch a career at midlife. Alice seems to have profited from her volunteer career and seems set up to move into paid employment if she needs to, but confesses that she would not choose this career path if given a second chance. Lydia has somewhat blindly adopted the new message that work is the only pathway to identity resolution.

Marcia (1966) has suggested that the most complete form of identity resolution comes about as a result of exploring options. examining (maybe rejecting) the "shoulds" embedded in social mores, making conscious choices and then committing to one's chosen path. In this view, women who adopt the cultural prescription of the day, whether Betty Friedan's sample of the 1960s or some fast track "super moms" of today, would be considered to be foreclosing on identity issues, thus suffering some developmental consequences.

Clearly there were consequences for each of the employment patterns considered here, yet the generally high well-being scores suggest each had found her own path to identity resolution. These portraits suggest, too, that identity concerns are not resolved once and for all, but are often re-worked throughout the life cycle. In some ways, all of these women appeared to be in the process of re-working some identity issues in midlife. With the wisdom of their age and experience they could all be seen as approaching new choices with self-examination and reflection.

By such a process, (examining one's inclinations and priorities), long-term as well as short-term goals are more likely to be considered. In addition, options become more evident and structural forces less influential. It may well be the case that women at midlife have the potential for much richer identity resolutions than they do during earlier phases of life. It follows too, that we should think of well-being at midlife as determined not so much by what patterns have been followed of choices made, as by the extent to which one's endeavors are reflections of identity resolution.

ACKNOWLEDGMENTS

This research used the *Longitudinal Study of the Life Patterns of College-Educated Women, 1960–1986* data set (raw and machine-readable data files). These data were collected by Abigail Stewart and donated to the archive of the Henry A. Murray Research Center of Radcliffe College, Cambridge, Massachusetts (Producer and Distributor).

This research was supported, in part, by the Jeanne Humphrey Block Dissertation Award Program of the Henry A. Murray Research Center of Radcliffe College.

REFERENCES

Adams, D.M. (1984). The psychosocial development of professional black women's lives and the consequences of career for their personal happiness. *Dissertation Abstracts International, 44*(12), 3920.

Barnett, R., & Baruch, G. (1978). Women in the middle years: A critique of research and theory. *Psychology of Women Quarterly, 3*(2), 187–197.

Baruch, G., Barnett, R., & Rivers, C. (1983). *Lifeprints: New patterns of love and work for today's women.* New York: Signet.

Bergman, B. (1986). *The economic emergency of women.* New York: Basic Books.

Betz, N.E., & Fitzgerald, L.F. (1987). *The career psychology of women.* Boston: Academic Press.

Birnbaum, J. (1975) Life patterns and self esteem in gifted and career committed women. In M. Mednick, S. Tangri, & L. Hoffman (Eds.) *Women and achievement: Social and motivational analysis* (pp. 396–419). New York: Wiley.

Brown, G.W., Bhrolchain, M.N., & Harris, T. (1975). Social class and psychiatric disturbance among women in an urban population. *Sociology, 9*, 225–254.

Brown, G.W., & Harris, T. (1978). *Social origins of depression: A study of psychiatric disorder in women.* New York: The Free Press.

Cardoza, A. (1986). *Sequencing.* New York: Atheneum.

Coleman, L.M., & Antonucci, T.C. (1982, Winter). *Women's well being at midlife.* Ann Arbor, MI: ISR Newsletter, Institute for Social Research, University of Michigan.

Corcoran, M., & Duncan, G. (1979). Work history, labor force attachment, and earnings differences between races and sexes. *Journal of Human Resources, 14,* 3–20.

Dietz, J. (1988, May 30). What *really* bothers women in midlife? *The Boston Globe,* pp. 33–34.

Elder, G.H., & Rockwell, R.C. (1976). Marital timing in women's life patterns. *Journal of Family History, 1,* 34–53.

Erikson, E. (1968). *Childhood and society.* New York: Norton.

Feminism's identity crisis. (1986, March 31). *Newsweek,* pp. 58–59.

Franz, C., & White, K. (1985). Individuation and attachment in personality development. In A.J. Stewart & B. Lykes (Eds.), *Gender and personality,* (pp. 136–168). Durham, NC: Duke University Press.

Gerson, K. (1985). *Hard choices: How women decide about work, career and motherhood.* Berkeley: University of California Press.

Ginzberg, E. (1966). *Educated America women: Life styles and self-portraits.* New York: Columbia University Press.

Gora, J.G., & Nemerowicz, G.M. (1985). *Emergency squad volunteers: Professionalism in unpaid work.* New York: Praeger.

Hardesty, S., & Jacobs, N. (1986). *Success and betrayal: The crisis of women in corporate America.* New York: Watts.

Helson, R., & Wink, P. (1987). Two conceptions of maturity examined in the findings of a longitudinal study. *Journal of Personality and Social Psychology, 53,* 531–541.

Hollingshead, A.B. (1958). *Social class and mental illness: A community study.* New York: Wiley.

Jacques, E. (1965). Death and the midlife crisis. *International Journal of Psychoanalysis, 46(4),* 502–513.

Jung, C. G. (1916). *Analytical psychology.* New York: Moffat, Yard.

Josselson, R. (1987). *Finding herself: Pathways to identity development in women.* San Francisco: Jossey-Bass.

Kessler, R.C., & McRae, J.A., Jr. (1982). The effect of wives employment on the mental health of married men and women. *American Sociological Review, 47,* 216–227.

Kohn, M. (1980). Job complexity and adult personality. In N. Smelser & E. Erikson (Eds.) *Themes of work and love in adulthood* (pp. 193–212). Cambridge, MA: Harvard University Press.

Levinson, D. (1977). *The seasons of a man's life.* New York: Knopf.

Loevinger, J. (1976). *Ego development.* San Francisco: Jossey-Bass.

Long, J., & Porter, K. (1984). Multiple roles of midlife women: A case for new directions in theory, research and policy. In G. Baruch & J. Brooks-Gunn (Eds.), *Women in midlife* (pp. 109–160). New York: Plenum Press.

McIntosh, P. (1985). *Feeling like a fraud* (Work in Progress, No. 18). Wellesley, MA: Stone Center for Developmental Services and Studies, Wellesley College.

Marcia, J. (1966). Development and validation of ego identity status. *Journal of Personality and Social Psychology, 3,* 551–558.

McNair, D.M., Lorr, M., & Doppleman, L.F. (1971). *Profile of mood states.* San Diego: Educational and Industrial Testing Service.

Nye, F.I., & Hoffman, L.W. (1963). *The employed mother in America.* Chicago: Rand Mc-Nally.

Osherson, S. (1980). *Holding on or letting go: Career change at midlife.* New York: The Free Press.

Powell, B. (1977). The empty nest, employment and psychiatric symptoms in college educated women. *Psychology of Women Quarterly, 2*(1), 35–43.

Sanford, L.T., & Donovan, M.E. (1987). *Women and self esteem: Understanding and improving the way we feel about ourselves.* Harrisonburg, VA: R.R. Donnelley.

Sarason, S. (1977). *Work, aging and social change: Professionals and the one life-one career imperative.* New York: The Free Press.

Schenkel, S., & Marcia, J.E. (1972). Attitudes toward premarital intercourse in determining ego identity status in college women. *Journal of Personality, 3,* 472–482.

Shaw, L. (1983). *Unplanned careers: The working lives of middle-aged women.* Lexington, MA: Lexington Books.

Shaw, L. (1986). *Midlife women at work: A fifteen-year perspective.* Lexington, MA: D.C. Heath.

Sorenson, A. (1983). Women's employment patterns after marriage. *Journal of Marriage and the Family, 45,* 2, 311–321.

Stiver, I.P. (1983). *Work inhibitions in women* (Work in Progress, No. 82-03). Wellesley, MA: Stone Center for Developmental Services and Studies, Wellesley College.

Tesch, S., & Whitbourne, S. (1982). Intimacy and identity status in young adults. *Journal of Personality and Social Psychology, 43*(5), 1041–1051.

Van Dusen, R., & Sheldon, E. (1976, February). The changing status of American woman: A life cycle perspective. *American Psychologist,* 106–116.

Verbrugge, L. (1982). Women's social roles and health. In P. Berman & Estelle Ramey (Eds.), *Women: A developmental perspective* (pp. 49–78). Washington, DC: National Institute of Health.

Veroff, J., Douvan, E., & Kulka, R. (1981). *The inner American: A self portrait from 1957 to 1976.* New York: Basic Books.

Zellman, G. (1976). The role of structural factors in limiting women's institutional participation. *Journal of Social Issues, 32,* 33–46.

Chapter 7

Divorce and Work Life Among Women Managers

Faye J. Crosby
Smith College

Freud and others are credited with having observed that life's two major tasks are to love and to work. Accepting the basic wisdom of the observation, one may wonder what happens to love when work goes poorly and what happens to work when love sours. These are deep questions and do not admit of simple, universal answers. But although we cannot hope to find noncontingent global answers, we can approach empirically a small section of the larger question of the relationship between work and love.

One of many possible starting points is to limit the scope of inquiry by examining love that has taken the institutionalized form of marriage and work that has been formalized as paid employment. We can then look at how life in the employing organization affects life in the home and vice versa. As Repetti (1987) has noted, most investigators have been preoccupied with seeing how work affects home life and virtually no one has thought to examine empirically and systematically how domestic life manifests itself in the workplace. I prefer to turn the question around and see how domestic life impinges on work life.

This chapter looks at the connection between work life and divorce among professional women. Informing the observations here are three studies conducted over a period of 5 years: (a) a study of 18 women and 22 men working from a corporation who had experienced divorce and talked to us about their experiences; (b) a study of 20 additional individuals, including some in the process of divorce, who worked for a same organization and who completed questionnaires over 1 year; and (c) a continuation study of approximately 25 individuals in a number of different work settings. Although I have relied on all three studies to formulate my thoughts, the data that I report here come almost exclusively from the 18 female managers in the first study who spoke retrospectively of their divorces.

Two questions drive the present analysis and form the core of the chapter. First, how does professional life figure in the ways that a woman copes with divorce? Second, in what ways does a woman's divorce manifest itself in her professional life? Before turning to these questions, I describe the data that form the basis of my answers. The chapter ends with a few general observations.

STUDYING DIVORCED PEOPLE AT SNET

In 1983 I gained entry into a forward-looking company noted for its willingness to conduct socially relevant research. The company was the Southern New England Telephone Company (SNET), a Bell System Company that provided telephone service to Connecticut. At the time I conducted my studies, the company was in a state of transition—although not of upheaval—because of two legal decisions. First, as a member of the bell system, it had been required to develop a vigorous affirmative action program following the 1973 AT&T consent decree on affirmative action. Second, it was moving from being the sole provider of telephone equipment in an area to being one among several providers. These factors affected the climate of work at the company.

SNET employed over 3,700 managers in 10 divisions of the company. The organizational chart showed a broad-based pyramid: most of the managers in the company were at Level 1; Level 5 included a handful of vice-presidents and Level 6 included the president of the company. There were few women in management beyond Level 2, and a tiny band of women at Levels 4 and 5 were clearly quite visible. Participants in the study often mentioned the upper level females by name even when the participants worked in different towns and in different divisions from the women they discussed.

Prior to our study, the company had no way of knowing how many of its managers were divorced. Official records on marital status were not kept, as "interference" into family life was against the company's ethic and also against the law. Although no official documentation existed, however, the common impression among the executives with whom I spoke was that a sizable proportion of both men and women in management were, or had at some point, been divorced. Indeed, according to an unofficial count by a high-ranking executive, every manager at one of the offices had gone through a divorce.

The Sample

Good sampling was critical to the divorce study. How could I trust the information people gave us about their experiences with work life and divorce unless I felt that the people who elected to be our informants were truly representative of the managerial force of SNET? But how, in the absence of official records, could I feel certain that the people in the study constituted a representative sample?

With the generous help of in-house consultants, I created a packet of recruiting materials that went to every manager in the company. The materials contained a letter from me explaining the study and a letter from one of the assistant vice-presidents urging people to read the packet. The recruiting materials also contained a questionnaire that we requested all managers—whether or not they were eligible for our study—to complete and to return to us in a stamped enveloped. The questionnaire asked for the standard demographic and organizational information (e.g., age and level in the company, respectively) and asked the person if he or she had had a marriage that ended in divorce sometime in the last 5 years. If the person had gone through a divorce and was willing to consider participation in the study, he or she was asked to provide name, address, and phone number. Potential respondents were assured that the company would receive a report of the major findings of the study but that total anonymity was guaranteed. All correspondence and all interviewing were to (and did in fact) take place away from SNET offices.

Our sampling efforts yielded excellent results. Two thirds of the 3,703 managers returned the reply questionnaire to us. Among the replies were 161 people who were potentially eligible for our study on all the relevant criteria. Of the people who were eligible (i.e., met all the eligibility requirements), 75% did elect to join the study. Detailed comparisons showed that the 125 eligible people who elected to be in our study matched the population of managers in the company in terms of gender, race, religion, parental status, and level in the organization. In all regards save one, they also matched the people who had indicated on our questionnaire that they declined to join the study. Joiners were less likely than nonjoiners to have remarried.

Because of the overwhelming reply and finite (albeit ample) resources, we were able to include only a portion of the eligible respondents in the study. We decided that our resources allowed us to interview 40 people in depth. We decided to include roughly equal numbers of men and women in order to be able to gauge gender differences. We restricted the sample to people who had children and who were between the ages of 30 and 49. In this way, we had people who were old enough to have had some experience in the company and young enough not to be thinking about retirement. To balance for age, we decided to divide the study into roughly equal numbers of people aged 30–39 (the younger group) and aged 40–49 (the older group).

Our sample, thus, included four categories: divorced male managers between 30 and 39; divorced male managers between 40 and 49; divorced female managers between 30 and 39; and divorced female managers between 40 and 49. The last category contained only 8 people. (It appeared from the recruiting questionnaire that most of the women who had been professionally successful in the company prior to the AT&T sex discrimination case—and who, hence, were over 40 years of age—had remained single. It seems probable that the company employed only 8 or 9 divorced female managers over 40 and that all of them elected to talk to us.)

The final sample included 11 men in each age group; 10 women between the ages of 30 and 39; and the 8 women over 40. All of the people selected for the study had children from the union that had ended in divorce; all had been employed at SNET at the time of the divorce. All of the divorces had occurred between 5 years and 1 year prior to the start of the interviews.

The Data

Nonrepresentative findings could emerge even with a totally representative sample. The respondents in the study could be misrepresenting information in their accounts—either intentionally or unintentionally—and we, as interpreters of the accounts, could be misconstruing the information ourselves. Qualitative research contains its own set of perils.

The SNET study employed several techniques to safeguard against bias. The first and most basic was to use multiple sessions with each respondent. Following the techniques developed by Levinson (1978), we interviewed each of the 40 people (22 men and 18 women) in the study four times. The first interview asked the person about his or her family background and career path. The second interview focused on the marriage. In the third and fourth interviews we looked at the parallels and the interconnections between work life and home life. Each interview lasted between 45 minutes and 3 hours. For some respondents, we had 12 hours of taped interviews. The second interview typically elicited strong emotional and sometimes tearful reactions.

Repeated interviews helped built trust. Virtually all participants in the survey commented about how much they had generally benefited from and enjoyed being in the study and also about how much they had found themselves revealing to the interviewer. Many times a participant would preface his or her comments with the observation "I've never told this to anyone before" or "I've never thought about this in quite this way before." Most participants felt that they experienced a marked increase in trust after the first interview.

Two additional types of evidence attested to the validity and openness of the accounts we obtained in our in-depth interviews. First, at the end of the third interview, we informed the respondents that we would like to interview a sample of their co-workers and supervisors. We gave the respondents the list of questions that would be asked of the supervisors and co-workers. Three quarters of the respondents nominated their supervisor and some of their co-workers for further interviewing. Only one fourth showed some hesitation about having us interview others in the company. We did conduct short interviews with 30 supervisors and co-workers and, by and large, their accounts corroborated the accounts of the participants in our study. (In order to avoid the danger of information leakage, the supervisors and co-workers were interviewed by a new interviewer—unfamiliar with any of the 18 women or 22 men who had been interviewed.)

I also felt reassured about the truth of people's accounts by personally listening to how the respondents talked about their lives. Most people, including managers at SNET, speak ungrammatically and unevenly. The tempo of speech changes as people speak about materials that are more or less emotionally arousing or as they speak about events that they remember more or less clearly. The great majority of the interviews had enough grammatical errors, enough hesitancies, and enough unclarities to sound unrehearsed.

An honest self-representation does not, of course, assure valid conclusions. Not only must one deal with the phenomenology of the respondent in qualitative research. One also has to contend with the phenomenology of the researchers. The generosity of SNET permitted me to include methodological precautions against researcher bias. One very important feature of the study was the use of several different interviewers. I had developed the interview schedule during pretesting and I trained the interviewers, but I personally conducted only three of the sets of interviews. This meant that I had no way of directly influencing the respondents to reflect back my own preconceptions. The use of several different interviewers—with different personal styles and different backgrounds—helped assure us that whatever patterns emerged from the data were not simply patterns that any one person had imposed on them. Two final means were used during the interviews themselves to minimize the chance of interpretive distortion. During all four interviews, and especially during the first two, we asked the respondents for exact and specific dates to trace the chronology of their careers and of their marriages. In many instances, the participants consulted their records between interview sessions. We, for our part, lined up the chronologies of careers (obtained in the first interview) with the chronologies of marriages (obtained in the second) and worked with the participants to correct any inconsistencies. We also reflected back to the respondents what we had heard and inferred. Each interviewer reviewed with each respondent what had been heard during the four ses-

sions so that the participants could corroborate the interviewer's conclusions and check any inferences.

The final precautions against research bias occurred when I was preparing the report for SNET. As I reviewed the hours and hours of tape-recorded
interviews, I noted themes that seemed to emerge. I then created a grid in
which I cross-listed themes and individual respondents. I checked to make
sure that at least 10 people had mentioned each theme. Next I presented my
tentative conclusions to the team of interviewers and deleted or modified
any conclusions that seemed to any interviewer not in accord with the sense
of what he or she had felt to be the case during his or her particular set of interviews. In writing the report for the company, I made sure to quote every
respondent (anonymously, of course) at least two times and no more than
five times. I then shared with each respondent those sections that pertained
to him or her, and the respondents corrected any misunderstandings. There
were a few corrections at each stage, enough to reassure me that people
were honestly responding to the task of detecting misunderstandings, and
yet not so many that I worried about the validity of the findings.

THE PAIN OF DIVORCE

Given our methods, what did we find about the 18 women in the SNET
study? How did work life and divorce connect? To understand the connections between work life and divorce, we had first to recognize one basic fact:
People experience extraordinary pain when they go through a divorce. All
but one of the women characterized divorce as a terrible process. Typical of
the responses was this:

> When I was going through the divorce, it was a nightmare, really bad. It was
> like nothing I've ever experienced. I would hope to never go through that
> again.

Asked how divorce compared with other major life stresses, one women
spoke for many: "Nothing," said she, "comes close." Another woman
responded to the question of comparisons by first enumerating other major
stresses in her life, including the death of her mother; a car accident in which
her sister had died after 6 months in a coma; and the family situation when
her husband lost his job. The respondent did conclude, however, by saying
that the divorce "was definitely the most stressful thing I have been
through." This woman, and many others in the study, acknowledged the
positive aspects of ending their marriages even as they described the pain
they felt. One participant spoke of how she could only develop into a ma-
ture human being once she had parted from her husband; nevertheless, her

characterization of the divorce as eventually growthful did not blind the woman to the fact that, as she was going through the process, divorce was "a baptism by fire."

The women's accounts of their work and family lives made clear that their divorces had taken a toll. Many of the respondents had become ill during or following their divorces. Several developed drinking problems. Several experienced mild depressions. Our sample did not seem unique in this regard. As Riessman and Gerstel (1985) have shown, women tend to suffer health disturbances when they go through a divorce.

We had expected that women who initiated their divorces would feel less pain than those who did not initiate their divorces. Our expectation grew from Weiss' (1975) description of divorce and separation in his book, *Marital Separation* and from Vaughan's (1986) study. For our respondents, however, it was extremely difficult to separate women into instigators and noninstigators. Typically the deterioration of the marriage occurred over several years. Most story lines were complex. When the husband filed for a divorce after the wife flaunted an affair in his face, who was the instigator? When the wife filed for a divorce after the husband asked her to, who initiated the divorce? When two people woke up one morning and realized that they had grown apart, who was the instigator?

Perhaps the major reason why we could not distinguish between the instigator and noninstigator was that all of our respondents had, at some moment, felt ambivalence about the divorce. As one participant put it: "Between morning and night, you feel a thousand different emotions."

Our sample may have included more ambivalent people than did Weiss' or Vaughan's samples because we restricted ours to divorced parents. Children enormously complicate the picture. Virtually every women in our study worried about how her children would be affected by the divorce. The existence of children also precluded, in almost every instance, the possibility of a clean break with the former spouse. One woman said that "The thing that is ironic about divorce is you never get away from what you went to so much trouble to get away from if there are children."

Another respondent contrasted her divorce with the recent death of her father. Her father's death brought her acute pain, but the painful feelings of the divorce lasted longer. Death, she said was "once and for all, but when children are involved, divorce never ends."

Another reason why nearly all of the women experienced deep upset about the divorce was that they viewed it as a personal failure. One of the managers, who described her girlhood as strictly Catholic, admitted during the interview—3 years after her divorce was finalized—"I still feel I've failed." Another woman described the long deterioration of her marriage and then puzzled out loud about why she had remained in the marriage so long. She presented and dismissed several possible explanations, settling finally on the idea of failure. "It's hard," observed the woman, "to admit failure. And that is what divorce is—failure." In a later interview, the same woman said: "I didn't want to tell my mother." She did not want to have her mother see how she had failed. For women in the SNET study, born between 1934 and 1953, marriage was a prized accomplishment. None of the women had entered marriage thinking they might leave it through divorce, and to do so seemed a terrible failure.

PAID EMPLOYMENT AS A COPING DEVICE

Work, for the 18 women managers in the SNET study, provided great relief from the misery of divorce. One woman captured the sentiment of virtually all respondents in the study. She said: "Work saved me."

Other respondents were less laconic. One respondent said:

> Work absorbs my energies and my interest. I have a friend who is retired [and divorcing]...and I can see her going in a thousand directions. She tries yoga; she tries a little tennis; she tries a play. She does this; she goes there. And yet, I really feel she's missing something that ties everything together and gives a purpose to everything. And, uhm, while another person definitely contributes to that feeling of satisfaction, a job can do almost as much, if not more. So, yes, I have sought refuge in the job. A bad weekend or an upset feeling and I say, 'welp. goin' to work on Monday!'

In the words of another: "I can remember days, weekends, when I couldn't wait for Monday to come." This woman was anticipating the relief of work especially because at work she "could get [her] mind off the problems [she] had no control to solve."

Only one woman felt, on balance, that immediately after her divorce going to work proved more difficult than helpful. This woman had been in an abusive marriage for years; and, as is usually true in such cases, her spirit as well as her body was badly bruised. To leave the marriage required enormous courage. In this instance going to the office made the task more difficult. The woman's co-workers, to whom she had confided nothing, believed that the woman was sinful to "break up the home" and daily berated the respondent for the damage she was causing her son. Even the unfortunate woman who worked with "the three harpies" (her characterization), however, recognized that in the long run, she would have found it harder to cope with divorce had she not had paid employment.

Reasons for the Value of Work

What made paid employment so helpful to the divorcing women? Four interrelated aspects of work account for much of its healing power. First, for managers in a large corporation, at least, work gives structure to the day. Second, the absorbing activities of work give people "time out" from their domestic troubles. Third, being a good worker allows a person to repair her damaged self-esteem. Fourth, having a job helps a woman decrease the extraordinary financial worries that arise during divorce.

Structure. When a couple divorces, routines change. For 16 of the 18 women in the SNET study, the end of the marriage involved major changes in daily living arrangements. (Each of the other two women had lived apart from her husband for years before bothering to obtain the divorce.) Many of the women moved. Those who remained in the same community, even those who remained in the same house, found their social life vastly altered when they reverted to being single. Child-care arrangements shifted, sometimes quite dramatically, for the women.

Lives need structure. Daily routine, even when it causes minor irritations, often gives life a sense of security. Changes in one's daily routine at home might make it all the more urgent that paid employment lend structure to the day. The point was openly acknowledged by many of the respondents. Typical of the women's statements are these:

[Work helped me simply because] I had to get up. I had to get dressed.

My job totally occupied my mind.

I used my job to keep the feelings [about divorce] within bounds.

It seemed like the more pressure I got at home, the harder I worked....I figured that if I would keep busy...I wouldn't have to think about [the chaos at home].

The importance of structure, recognized by the participants in the SNET study, made me wonder if jobs that lacked a daily structure would provide the same tonic effect for divorcing people as the managerial positions did. The answer, derived from my subsequent studies with additional people inside and outside SNET is that a structured work day helps heal the wounds of divorce much more rapidly than does an unstructured day. People like writers, artists, and self-employed real-estate agents have all found their recovery from divorce hampered by the flexible schedules that they so highly value in times of health and happiness.

Time Out. Jobs provided more than a daily structure for the participants in the SNET study. They also helped respondents forget their domestic miseries because a day at work was a day filled with activities, most of which require the expenditure of some energy and thought. Many of the managers in the SNET study reported that they spent extra hours at work around the time of the divorce. If they were not in charge of the children—if the children were with their fathers or off at school—the women found themselves arriving early at work and staying late.

Ms. X, who experienced an extraordinary surge of energy around the time of her divorce, anchored one end of the continuum. Ms. X was unable to sustain her efforts at any one task and did not concentrate well at the time; but she filled the long work days with flurries of different tasks. By coincidence, Ms. X was assigned temporarily to a new work location soon after she and her husband separated. The children were at summer camp. Ms. X found herself working as late as 10 or 11 p.m. and then arriving at work the next day as early as 6:30 a.m.!

Most other participants had more moderate histories, but almost all claimed that the demands of a managerial job helped them cope with the stress of divorce by providing an outlet for energy and a focus for thought. Work, opined one respondent, "absorbed my energies and my interests." Said another: "Things [at work] were so busy that I *had* to forget my personal life."

Even when the office tasks do not fully engage a person, the business of interacting with other people allows a way out from the pain that a woman feels as her marriage comes apart. Virtually all of the women in the SNET study kept their work life and their home life rather distinct. Many of the women told us about close friends who helped them through the divorce, but for the particular sample of management people in a large corporation, at least, most of the closest friendships existed outside the office. At work, people had what Rubin (1985) has called "friends of the road" rather than "friends of the heart." Most office interactions were pleasant and rather impersonal.

Social scientists have sometimes assumed that the only "true" friendships are those in which people can bare their innermost secrets to each other (Cancian, 1986) or can "bond" with each other in some primordial fashion (Tiger, 1984). The accounts of the women and men at SNET indicate the limitations of the traditional social scientific view. For the respondents in our study, the familiar and repetitive office interactions acted as a salve in the healing process. One woman in the study illustrated the point. She claimed that work was the factor that helped her more than anything else in her life recover from divorce and that work helped her primarily "because I had people around me who had other things to talk about than my divorce."

Self-Esteem. Although superficial conversations can help people take their minds off their family troubles, they can also aid people in repairing the torn fabric of their self-esteem. For many women in the study, failure in marriage threatened their view of themselves as individuals with the capacity for pleasant social interactions. Positive interactions at work provided the women with a necessary contrast to hateful exchanges with spouses. The simple knowledge that her colleagues enjoyed interacting with her did much to help the typical respondent maintain a positive self-image.

The maintenance of self-esteem was described by one participant in exquisite detail. She said:

> So we're fighting openly. And I'm saying, "I want a divorce. I don't love you anymore. I am beat." At work I was another person. I was becoming a schizoid. At work I was—certainly no one would know. I never talked about home life problems to anybody. I was always just bubbly and cheerful, because I was happy at work. I loved my work. I was somebody at work. People liked me. I liked them. I truly enjoyed my work life....[At home] my son was smoking pot. His grades started going down. He started hanging around with a bad bunch. That devastated me....I left home for a week. I felt that everything was my fault and that if I just left, he would straighten out and his father would take care of everything.

Work life builds self-esteem in many ways. For a person who is suffering through a divorce, it can be especially gratifying to complete tasks competently. One women in the study expressed rather succinctly the sentiment of most people. She said that "The fact that you can do a good job means that you can't be all bad."

Another woman, somewhat older than the first, amplified the same theme. The older woman spoke at length about the importance of paid employment for a woman whose self-image is threatened:

> I think my feeling was that in divorce, by the time you've been through that horrible period, you're so beaten down that you begin to feel awful, I mean, because you have somebody telling you "you can't do this, you can't do that." You get to the point where you say, "How could anybody survive and be as stupid as I am?" My feeling is that you have to start building yourself back up again so that you have some respectable self-image. And I think that's where the job comes in....I don't think you can feel good about yourself just because you can clean the house well.

Another respondent said:

> Even though my job right now is not very rewarding, I get a great deal of satisfaction out of knowing that I can support myself and my daughter.

Financial Resources. The last observation brings us to the final reason why a career helps a woman cope with the trauma of divorce. The reason is simple and obvious; the reason is money. A job provides income; a career provides the expectation of continued, and perhaps even enhanced, income. Divorce causes severe financial strain (Weiss, 1975, 1979). As Weitzman (1987) has shown, furthermore, the financial ax of divorce cuts mainly at the woman. In California and presumably most other states, some of the very laws that were meant to protect women, particularly displaced homemaking women, have come to be used against them.

Many of the women in the SNET study spoke of the financial difficulties of divorce. They told us of pinching pennies and of worrying. They told us of the struggles over money and over the other forms of property held in the marriage. Many of the women also noted that they felt well off, personally, compared to their more traditional sisters and friends who had faced divorce without any career capabilities.

The Downside

To acknowledge the therapeutic value of work is not to claim that work life never interferes with coping. Even women who waxed eloquent about the ways in which their jobs had helped them muddle through and recover from their divorces also spoke of the ways in which work life could exacerbate their pain. The two problems that seemed especially noticeable concerned criticism and proximity to the former spouse.

When a woman is being constantly criticized at home, she may have a special susceptibility to criticism at work. One woman, referred to previously, found it very difficult to go to work because her closest colleagues disapproved vociferously of her divorce. The woman was unable or unwilling to tell people at work about the physical and psychological abuse that she suffered at the hands of her husband. Throughout most of the worst period, however, the woman's immediate supervisor seemed quite supportive. Then an incident occurred in which the supervisor also turned away from the woman. In the respondent's own words:

> I had been promoted to management. And actually two things happened. The first was that I was supposed to be sent to————[another city] for a week for training. And he [the husband] told me that I could not go. He said that he forbade it; I could not go; that he knew that it was just a big shack-up place; that he knew what people did when they got together; nobody could fool him. He knew what went on, and I could not go. [He said] that if I went, he would kill me. And I had no doubt in my mind that—while he probably would not kill me—I would probably end up with some more mangled bones or something, you know. And he meant it. And I tried to talk with my supervisor, and I didn't want to tell her at that point that I was getting clobbered. [exhale with a laugh] And I tried to tell her just how strong his feelings were. I did not intend this. And she said, "well, Mary, it is an honor that you be selected to go" She said: "don't you understand that I think that, out of all the managers, you are the

best qualified to go?" She said, "I want you to." She said: "It's part of your job....this should not come as a surprise." And I just could not make her understand simply because I couldn't tell her. So being torn like that was....[voice trails away]

Few other women experienced the dilemma faced by this woman. But several participants did note how "touchy" they had become during points in the divorce. Remarks that would not have affected them at other times seemed to provoke emotional reactions, sometimes surprisingly large ones. Many of the respondents, recognizing at the time how sensitive they were, avoided situations that might call forth an emotional response. When asked if the divorce meant any compromises on her work performance, one woman replied:

I was more emotional at that time. Because most of my conversations with him [the husband] were unfortunately during working hours,...I was a little more emotional. So maybe I wasn't as supportive of my subordinates as I could have been, *should* have been because I avoided confrontation....Anything where I might have been upset or was a situation where I had to remain in control, I guess I avoided these at all costs. In such situations I thought I might cry.

The one other aspect of employment that can retard recovery from divorce is proximity to the former spouse. As Weiss (1975, 1979) noted, when there are children in a marriage, divorce usually does not *end* but rather only changes the relationship between the woman and the man. Weiss also noted how upsetting it is for women and men to be reminded of their failed hopes and dreams and how contact with the former spouse tends to have an upsetting effect. Certainly among the women and men in the SNET study, people fared best if they had minimal (and highly structured) contact with the former spouse for at least 1 or 2 years following their separations. For one woman and one man in the study, the former spouse worked in a company that conducted business with SNET. Both the woman and the man had to have professional contact with the former spouse. For both, the necessity of contact kept alive some of the hurt and anger of the divorce. Speaking of her professional interactions with her estranged husband another woman said: "It was just painful every time I talked to him."

DIVORCE AS AN INFLUENCE
ON PROFESSIONAL LIFE

Given that work proves very beneficial to people going through a divorce, how does divorce influence life at work? For the vast majority of respondents in the SNET study, divorce interfered with professional life—usually quite severely but usually also for a delimited period of time. In the long run, the divorce experience contained some benefits from the organization's point of view. Most of the respondents deepened their attachment to SNET during and after the divorce, in large part because they felt well treated by the company. The men also seemed to gain a measure of compassion. For the women, becoming a single parent meant that they began to label themselves as breadwinners and no longer felt that work commitments conflicted with home commitments as they had done previously.

Problems

On the basis of the literature on divorce (Bloom, Asher, & White, 1978; Gerstel, Reissman, & Rosenfield, 1985; Vaughan, 1986; Wallerstein & Kelly, 1980), I had expected that the process would prove emotionally painful to people, and—as discussed earlier—the pain of divorce was amply evident among our sample. What I was unprepared for, however, was the extent to which divorce penetrated people's work lives. We asked our participants to compare the stress of divorce with other major life stresses. Many of the participants noted that divorce interfered with effectiveness at work far more than other stresses they had experienced, including the death of a spouse or of a parent.

When asked point blank if the divorce had compromised their work performance, only 1 of the 18 women said no. She maintained that, if anything, the divorce improved her performance at work. The other 17 women replied in the affirmative, usually with some vigor. Typical were statements such as: "I know my work suffered" or "My battles with my husband affected my attitude and my performance."

Ironically, for many managers the recognition of how much their work had suffered seemed to have dawned at the moment of improvement. One women spoke of how, after months of defective labor, she began to come to terms with the divorce and to improve her performance at work. "I *then* realized that I was running on anger and pure adrenalin." Another manager, working in sales, declared: "I spent a lot of time during the divorce saying 'I'm fine. Everything is fine.' But later, I saw it differently."

Professional work suffered for three reasons among the female managers at SNET. First, the divorce process disrupted work hours. Second, motivational deficits appeared. Finally, ruminations about marriage and divorce disrupted people's concentration.

Lost Time. Divorces take a great deal of one's time, especially when property needs settling and custody needs arranging. Many managers in the study lost hours due to court appearances. Other people had to take time away from the office to consult with lawyers and financial advisors.

Several women told us about how they spent some time at work acquiring information relevant to the divorce or in other ways sleuthing. Near the extreme on this dimension was one woman who said:

> When I went into work each day, that was when I got everything done as far as my personal life. Really, I took a lot of time off. I went into work. But I was doing things there that were nonwork related. You know, I would get in and first thing I would do was call my friend Sally. After I spoke with Sally, I called my brother. After I spoke with my brother, I called my attorney. I'd be calling this one and that one. I was so obsessed with the divorce, that I spent hours at the office checking my phone bills back over the last eighteen months to see how long things had been going on between my husband and his girlfriend. All this happened during work hours.

Diminished Motivation. Marital conflict can also undermine a manager's motivation. Many of the participants in our study reported that they had suffered depressions before, during, and after their separation and divorce. Quite a few of the women noted that they felt less depressed at work, where the structured day and absorbing activities pushed troubles out of consciousness, than outside work. A few respondents commented on their separate selves—the home self, where all seemed hopeless and worthless; and the work self, where they felt at least somewhat more alive and competent. Even among women who extolled the tonic effects of work life, however, a certain decrease in energy occurred at various points throughout the divorce. Virtually everyone acknowledged how difficult it could be to muster the usual enthusiasm for the usual tasks of professional life during a divorce. For some, motivational deficits lasted only a few hours and occurred sporadically. For others, episodes of diminished motivation occurred more often.

Impaired Concentration. Although there was quite a bit of variety among the respondents in terms of how much depression interfered with functioning at work, there was much more agreement on another problem: impaired concentration. One women said:

> While I was going through my divorce,...I went through this whole period of time when I didn't care about my job. I just spent hours I think just gazing out, doing nothing. And, of course I was supervising people. When they would come and ask me questions, I would say, "ehrr, I don't know." I was in the...I was not at all helpful. I am really surprised the company kept me on.

It is not always helpful to distinguish between emotions and cognitions (Lazarus, 1982, 1984; Zajonc, 1980, 1984), but it is nevertheless interesting to note that the impaired concentration of the people in the SNET study did not seem to be merely a symptom of their depressions. A clue that the impaired concentration was more than an epi-phenomenon of depression came from considering the timing of the two sets of events. During the course of our first two interviews, we constructed chronologies of people's work lives and family lives. For each individual, it seemed possible to identify, in retrospect, a time when she finally decided that the marriage would end. (How the timing of this decision related to marital separation and divorce varied from person to person.) Sadness and a lack of energy often followed the time of the decision. Impaired concentration, in contrast, usually preceded the decision.

Why should concentration at work be most impaired prior to the decision to end the marriage? The reason is that the managers were devoting all of their cognitive attention to their domestic situations. The divorce process demands attention. One searches for good solutions when, in fact, there are only solutions that are bad and solutions that are worse. The managers at SNET had been trained to be excellent problem solvers; presented with a problem that essentially admitted of no solution, they functioned like a computer stuck in a feedback loop. It is also possible that the participants experienced difficulty concentrating at work because one common way of coping with divorce is to work and rework the situation mentally.

Positive Consequences

Energy. In contrast to the sharp and severe but rather time-delimited problematic ways in which the stress of divorce manifested itself at work, there were some benefits for the organization resulting from the managers' domestic distress. Some women found that they experienced an increase in "nervous energy" during the divorce. Often the energy alternated with bouts of depression and lethargy. Sometimes, the women experienced an upsurge in activity. When asked, "how did you cope with the stress of divorce?" for example, one woman reported: "I stopped eating, and I cleaned house." After she had scrubbed and scrubbed her house from top to bottom, this woman focused her vigor on the job. Other women, such as the one already mentioned who arrived at work at 6:30 a.m., channeled all of their excess energy into their paid employment.

The heightened energy level of the women at SNET was not necessarily as valuable an asset as one might think. What muted the value of the energy was the women's lack of ability to concentrate. Several respondents characterized their movements at the time of the divorce as rather frenetic and unthinking. The flight into work was not an uncommon response to stress.

Gratitude. Of much more substantial value were the long-term benefits that resulted from the divorce process. Almost all of the participants in our study expressed gratitude for the way that they had been treated during the times of their distress and especially during the times when they were not performing up to par at the office. For most of the participants the gratitude was directed most specifically at their immediate supervisor. Typical of the sentiment expressed by the managers were these:

> There were times when I said "I can't talk." I was filled [with emotion] up to here. And he [my supervisor] knew it and was wonderful.

> I was fortunate at the time to be working for a supervisor who was very understanding.

> I was lucky I was working for [my boss]. I don't know if somebody else would have put up with my craziness.

The gratitude of the managers took expression in deed as well as word. Many of the women we interviewed described how they had "made up for" their impoverished performance at work by working harder after the divorce was over. Several respondents had engaged in extra un-remunerated work in order to compensate for the latitude that the company had shown them. Indeed, for some of the women, participation in our study, painful as it was to them personally, seemed to constitute a way of paying back the debt of gratitude that they felt to a supportive organization. Many people correctly construed participation in the survey as a way to help other people in their company decrease some of the pain of marital dissolution, and they wanted to help others in the organization in part because they felt they themselves had been helped.

GENDER AND COPING

Did the women in the SNET study differ from their male counterparts in how they experienced divorce or in the relationship between work life and domestic distress? By and large gender differences were less impressive than gender similarities. Some differences did emerge, however, that seem worthy of note.

The Stress of Divorce

Concerning the way in which the divorce unfolded, more men than women seemed to have been surprised to learn that their spouse was disaffected, angry, or hurt. One high-ranking man came to see, in hindsight, that for years he was "happy but dumb" while his wife was "furious but silent." A

few other men also characterized themselves as having been blissfully ig-
norant of wifely disaffection; only one woman seemed to have been taken
completely by surprise when her spouse declared himself unhappy in the
marriage.

Virtually no other important themes emerged to distinguish the men's
accounts of their divorces from the women's accounts. The men were as
upset and as troubled as the women about the disintegration of their marriages. The men felt themselves to be personal failures in much the same
way as did the women. The men worried about the children and about the
former spouse in much the same way as did the women.

Work As a Coping Mechanism

If women and men were basically similar to each other in the stress they felt,
they were also basically similar in their coping. For the men as well as for the
women, work was the primary coping mechanism during and immediately
following the stress of divorce. The men in the study recognized this stark
truth as fully as did the women. The reasons that work helped women cope
were, furthermore, the very same reasons that work helped men cope with
the stress of divorce.

Against the backdrop of similarity, there were, nonetheless, some nu-
ances of differences. More specifically, it seems to me that the salutary
aspects of work existed in different proportions for women and for men. I
would speculate that the men benefited even more than women from the
ways in which work structured the day. Some of the men in the study had
limited access to and day-to-day responsibility for their children; some had
joint custody; only a couple of men had full custody. Most of the women in
the study had full custody; all had at least shared custody of the children.
The presence of children does much to structure identifiable portions of the
day; without children, divorced and divorcing adults are in greater need of
organized activities to give shape to their waking life.

Another difference concerned self-esteem. Certainly the men, as well as
the women, experienced a drop in their feelings of self-worth as they went
through the pain of marital breakdown. And of course for the men, as for the
women, competencies at work bolstered their self-esteem. It did seem, nonetheless, that the women in the study were more conscious than the men
about how events at work helped mend damaged self-esteem: They explicitly and spontaneously recognized the importance of work in repairing damaged self-esteem more frequently and articulately than did the men.

Doing well at work may have been more of a source of pride to the
women in the study than to the men—perhaps because a professional
career was still more unusual for women than for men in the cohort of our
sample. Perhaps, too, women's greater involvement in the day-to-day run-

ning of the household gave them a perspective on working that sensitized them to the importance of a job for the creation and maintenance of self-esteem. One of the women said:

> I think because I was in that situation of being home, working, being home, working that I was able to see even more [clearly] how important a job is when you are going through a divorce.

Manifestations of Divorce at Work

Concerning the ways in which divorce influenced people's behavior at work, once again women and men appeared more similar than different. Two changes that appeared (both to us researchers and to the participants themselves) to be related to the process of divorce seemed to unfold differently for the women and the men. First, some respondents found themselves becoming more tolerant of others at work as a result of the "deepening" that stress can bring. As one woman reflected, "I try to be nicer to people now because I've been hurt...[and I] appreciated that people were nice to me when I was down and out."

Although the numbers are slight, I have the impression that more men in the study than women experienced a growth in compassion as a result of their divorces. In any event, more men than women remarked on their own increased tolerance. The reason for the gender asymmetry may be that most female managers had already developed a compassionate or person-oriented style prior to the stress of divorce, whereas most male managers had not. For several of the men an awareness of how family life can place legitimate demands on a professional person came only when they had to manage their children on a day-to-day basis.

Mr. H illustrated how the exigencies of divorce can make a man a more tolerant manager. Mr. H was in charge of a number of mostly female clerical workers. Prior to the breakdown of his marriage, he had always felt impatient and disappointed with staff who requested time away from work for family matters. Absenteeism was his nemesis. During his divorce, Mr. H had times when he had to function as a single parent. Through his personal experience he came to the realization of how the women working for him had, in fact, shown extreme dedication to the organization. Instead of chiding workers who sought personal time, Mr. H formulated a policy of mutual trust and respect. When a clerical worker needed time to accompany her child to the dentist, for instance, the reformed Mr. H would automatically allow her the time and ask her to make up the hours later. "I don't know how single mothers make it," commented Mr. H during one of his interviews.

The second gender-related change in professional life that accompanied divorce concerned career commitment. Whereas men gained enhanced compassion, women gained enhanced career commitment. For the majority of women in the study, the divorce was associated with taking their careers quite seriously.

Sometimes the new attitude preceded the divorce. One woman, for example, first thought to divorce her husband when she realized that she could not count on him for stable financial support and that she had come to see herself as a career woman. Sometimes the redefinition occurred concurrently with the divorce. When she was first promoted, the same year she divorced her husband, Ms. W discovered that her "job became a career." Rather than think in terms of an isolated position, Ms. W now thought in terms of a succession of positions requiring increasing skills and containing increasing responsibility.

Most often the change in career commitment followed the divorce. When asked if anything positive had come from the divorce, one of the participants replied: "Yeah! It made me take my career seriously." Until her divorce, this woman had seen her husband's salary as the primary one in the family. Another respondent portrayed her early family life as one in which both she and her husband worked long hours and then she also took care of the child. Her husband, she commented, did not spend time with the youngster because he had a job. "Of course, I had a job too," the woman recognized, "But my job didn't matter. It was 'extra' money." After the divorce, all this changed.

Women's increased commitment to a career after they became single parents stands in sharp contrast to men's reactions. Whereas divorcing women tended to redefine their careers in one way, divorcing men seemed to rethink their careers in another. Not one man in the study reported that he took his career more seriously as a result of the divorce. On the contrary, several men said that the divorce posed a major challenge to their assumption that work constitutes a central life value. Thus, divorce coincided with a revision toward greater career ambitions of women, while among men, it coincided with a revision of the assumption that the best way to be "a good family man" (or, indeed, a good man) is to climb the corporate ladder.

Other Studies

Other researchers (e.g., Reissman, in press) have found rather pronounced differences in the ways that males and females experience divorce. At SNET gender differences existed as a matter of emphasis but, overall, the women and men generally resembled each other in how they experienced divorce and in how their divorces related to their professional lives. How can we reconcile our findings with those of other researchers?

The answer lies, no doubt, in the populations studied. In American society, gender and social roles remain largely confounded, even today. Many woman, for example, are housewives; but few men are househusbands. Typically mothers, but not fathers, retain responsibility for maintenance of the house and the daily minding of children. Any study that examines a cross section of the population is likely to find gender differences that relate, in part, to role differentiation. In our unusual sample, where the women and men did not differ in terms of occupational involvement, differences that were actually role determined, rather than gender determined, were brushed away.

SUMMARY

What happens at work to a professional woman when she goes through a divorce? Typically, the divorce interferes with effective performance at work, in very noticeable ways but only for a discrete and short period of time. In the long run, a divorce often fosters a deepened career commitment among professional women. The person who had suffered through a divorce in a tolerant organization also tends to develop a richly deserved gratitude toward her employer.

Professional life proves enormously helpful to the typical woman as she goes through a divorce. Managerial—and presumably many other types of jobs in and out of corporations—help structure the day and provide engrossing activities. The job also allows people to rebuild their self-esteem through the successful completion of tasks at work and through pleasant social interactions. Not all aspects of work life help heal the wound of divorce. On-the-job contact with the former spouse may prove especially difficult. But, the evidence of our small sample of women, corroborated by data from other data in our program of research, shows clearly that for professional women, the tonic effects of paid employment far outweigh the dystonic ones.

ACKNOWLEDGMENTS

I express my thanks to Maureen Skrilow and Jean Handley for their initial support; to Alan Dann, Thomas Gavaghan, Joyce Redinger, and Robert Tucker for their wise counsel and good support; to Herbert Atherton, Michael Barrios, Edith Hanf Flagg, Kathryn Cowgill Harding, Gregory Herek, Sara Ohly, Lisa Silberstein, and Carol Weiss for their integrity and skill as interviewers in the SNET studies; to Virginia Farmer and Sandra Vanden for their dedicated work in follow-up studies. I would also like to thank the Southern New England Telephone Company for supporting the research financially as well as otherwise and to thank very warmly the managers at SNET who shared their lives with me and my colleagues. Thanks too to the PEW Foundation and to Smith College for financial support of the work.

REFERENCES

Bloom, B.L., Asher, S.J., & White, S.W. (1978). Marital disruption as a stressor: A review and analysis. *Psychological Bulletin, 85,* 867–894.

Cancian, F.M. (1986). The feminization of love. *Signs, 11,* 692–709.

Gerstel, N., Riessman, C.K., & Rosenfield, S. (1985). Explaining the symptomatology of separated and divorced women and men: The role of material conditions and social networks. *Social Forces, 86,* 84–101.

Lazarus, R.D. (1982). Thoughts on the relations between emotion and cognition. *American Psychologist, 37,* 1019–1024.

Lazarus, R.D. (1984). On the primacy of cognition. *American Psychologist, 39,* 124–129.

Levinson, D. (1978). *Season's of a man's life.* New York: Knopf.

Repetti, R. (1987). Linkages between work and family roles. *Applied social psychology annual, 7,* 98–127.

Riessman, C.K. (in press). *Making sense: Women and men talk about divorce.* New Brunswick, NJ: Rutgers University Press.

Riessman, C.K., & Gerstel, N. (1985). Marital dissolution and health: Do males or females have greater risk? *Social Science and Medicine, 20* 627–635.

Rubin, L. (1985). *Just friends. The role of friendship in our lives.* New York: Harper & Row.

Tiger, L. (1984). *Men in groups* (2nd ed.). New York: Marion Boyars.

Vaughan, D. (1986). *Uncoupling. How relationships come apart.* New York: Oxford University Press.

Wallerstein, J., & Kelly, J.B. (1980). *Surviving the breakup. How children and parents cope with divorce.* New York: Basic Books.

Weiss, R.S. (1975). *Marital separation.* New York: Basic Books.

Weiss, R.S. (1979). *Going it alone.* New York: Basic Books.

Weitzman, L.J. (1987). *The divorce revolution. The unexpected social and economic consequences for women and children in America.* New York: The Free Press.

Zajonc, R.B. (1980). Feeling and thinking. Preferences need no inferences. *American Psychologist, 35,* 151–175.

Zajonc, R.B. (1984). On the primacy of affect. *American Psychologist, 39,* 117–123.

Chapter 8

Crossing Boundaries Between Professional and Private Life

Judith Richter
Tel Aviv University

CROSSING THE BOUNDARIES

The purpose of this chapter is to explore the relationship between professional and private life by examining the ways individuals cope with the daily transitions between these two arenas and to examine whether women and men experience these passages differently.

In the transition between the work and home worlds, two kinds of boundaries are crossed—the sociophysical ones, which demarcate the territorial boundary of each system; and the psychological ones, which relate to the shift in self derived from the change in task activities.

A simplified schematic pattern would suggest that the transition starts when the person physically leaves one domain and ends when he or she physically enters the other. In reality, however, the process of transition is more subtle and thus more complicated.

The dynamics of the shifts between two life worlds involve forces that may act on the doing (physical) level and on the cognitive (psychological) level (Lewin, 1951). Thus, it it suggested that along with the physical transfer between the domains of work and home, a corresponding move across the individual's psychological region occurs, too. Moreover, one may experience a transition even though one is still physically situated in one or the other domain. For example, one's thoughts may turn to home before one has actually left work; or, upon arriving home, one's mind may still be at work, meaning that one has yet to effect the psychological transition.

At this point, an elaboration of the action of transition between the domains of work and home is required. Considering the occurrence, time, and location of the psychological shift, any definition of transition patterns should take into account the possible discrepancy in timing between the physical and the psychological shifts. Operationally, this could be examined by a person's acknowledgment that his or her concerns have switched before actual departure from a given domain. Simultaneous concerns with the work world and personal/family world may lead to role conflict, which in turn may reduce effectiveness in a given role, and produce stress (Katz & Kahn, 1978).

Gilligan (1982) observed that women tend to base their definition of self on their simultaneous functions in different role sets, whereas men's definition of self tends to be less relativistic. Thus, men and woman may experience boundaries and transitions differently. Supporting this suggestion is the argument of Evans & Bartoleme (1979) that even in more liberal and advanced cultures, the married woman who chooses to pursue a career is still expected to be responsible for the quality of the couple's life. Consequently she is under more pressure to manage skillfully the boundaries between professional and private life. A similar observation was made by Kanter (1977a), who noted that in the corporate world she was exploring, women were often criticized for carrying their private life issues into the workplace.

The process by which one effects home/work transitions, and how men and woman differ in handling these transitions, are the major questions examined in this chapter. Toward these ends, I differentiate between two kinds of transitions: (a) *planned transitions*, which occur regularly in the morning and evening; and (b) *interposed transitions*, which occur when a person, physically engaged in one domain deals with issues from the other. Interposed transitions may be *imposed* by others or may be *initiated* by the individual him or herself.

PLANNED TRANSITIONS

Transition Style

I use the term *transition style* to describe the pattern of planned transitions between work and home. Three basic styles (anticipatory, discrete, and continuous) represent the different possible combinations of time and location in which the daily cognitive–psychological or behavioral–physical shift can occur. Each style reflects a defined sequence of psychological and physical shifts. I illustrate these styles using the morning, home-to-work transitions.

Anticipatory. The psychological transition precedes the physical transition. It starts before leaving home and ends upon arriving at the workplace. The person is concerned with work while still at home and the psychological transition is complete by the time the territorial boundaries of the workplace are encountered. For example, the individual might be rehearsing a speech to be delivered to a committee in the afternoon while she or he is still in bed in the morning.

Discrete. The psychological transition begins upon leaving home and ends upon arriving at work. The psychological and physical transitions occur simultaneously and all boundaries are crossed at the same time. This transition style might typify a person who is fully involved mentally and actively in home chores until leaving the home and starts to be concerned with work duties only upon arriving at the office.

Continuous. The psychological transition starts when one leaves home, but is still in process when one enters the physical boundaries of work. Because the individual is not yet involved with work, he or she may need what we call some "transitional warm-up time." In this case, the individual, although he or she starts to be concerned about work upon closing the door to his or her home, is still concerned to a certain degree with his or her home-life chores upon arriving at the office, and gets fully involved in the office life only after a certain period of time.

Strategies for Coping With Planned Transitions

A person coping with transition-generated role differences needs to engage in cognitive and emotional maneuvers, in addition to the overt activities in which he or she is involved.

Different strategies for coping with situations of role conflict were defined by Levinson (1959) and applied later to the realm of the married woman (Hall, 1976; Hall & Hall, 1979). These strategies may be proactive, in which case they are based either on (a) changing others' expectations by redefinition of role demands, or (b) by changing one's own expectations and attitudes by a process of reorientation. They may, alternatively, be reactive, in which case they are based on accepting and meeting all demands.

The use of proactive strategies presumes that people act according to schemes that they devise. Embodied in this presumption is the notion that the situation is already so familiar that one can employ a "transition ritual." For example, one of the persons participating in our research told us that morning home chores in her family are well defined in advance and each member of her family has a clear share in taking care of the breakfast, feeding the dog, warming up the car, and shoveling the snow in front of the garage in the winter. Such a ritual may be developed for acts of departure and entry by the individual or by the system through which one transits. Families may develop a joint routine to help a partner cope with the transitions, and an organization may develop a ritual to ease the process of crossing its territorial boundaries or to symbolize this process. In one organization, for example, communal coffee drinking was a common habit to symbolize the ending of the work day.

The reactive style is based on a different image of the individual, which holds that behavior can be better explained by the individual's consideration of others. Reactive style calls for greater awareness and flexibility. That is, self-awareness should accompany the demand for diagnostic sensitivity to the situation itself and should be followed by flexibility in behavior. For example, the individual's plans to work at home are deferred because a family problem requires his or her involvement.

Beyond individual, personal transition style and coping strategy, family members are faced also with the need to decide to what extent each of them will be involved in the management of the other's transition. However, it may be necessary for the family members to rely on some established mode of rejoining and departing. This routine has to include a set of task activities and responsibilities, as well as some patterned transactions and relationships in order to support a sense of security.

INTERPOSED TRANSITION

Maintenance of Boundaries

More complicated than the daily transitions made at the beginning and end of the work day are the interposed transitions, which entail dealing with issues from one domain while physically located in the other; that is, dealing with home issues that arise while one is at work, or work-related problems that present themselves while at home.

Interposed transition is a state whereby boundaries are crossed either as a result of external factors imposing the shift on the individual or by factors within the individual initiating a shift by him or herself. In these cases of transition, the *maintenance* of boundaries is indicated by the extent of their permeability. Thus, the more focused the person is with issues relevant to the world in which he or she is presently located, and the fewer the issues from the other world penetrate into it, the less permeable these space boundaries will be. Thus, a person engaged to a high degree with home issues at work would demonstrate high permeability of work boundaries, whereas carrying out work chores at home would reflect high permeability of home boundaries. Interposed transitions raise the question of congruence between the person's experience of self and the social and physical space in which he or she is acting.

Establishing boundaries between life worlds plays a central role in the individual's adjustment to this transition process. The dynamics of the boundaries between work and home then are tested when conflict situations arise: when a person considers violating the established boundaries or when the employer or the family place a specific demand on the person. In interposed transition, boundaries are challenged each time they are crossed, either as a result of external factors imposed on the individual, or at the individual's initiation, and issues of changing the boundaries become salient.

Maintenance of boundaries may vary according to what filters through them, and how. As boundaries demarcate role discontinuities, what might penetrate them are role behaviors and concerns originating in one domain and penetrating into the other. Moreover, boundaries might be less permeable to penetration from one direction and more permeable from the other direction. For example, issues of home life, such as a child's birthday party, might not be reported at the office, whereas a party to celebrate a colleague's raise in rank would be talked about at home. These examples show higher penetration from the work domain into the home domain than vice versa.

Setting of Boundaries

Being involved in the two life worlds, a person has to deal successfully with the existence of structural and/or attitudinal boundaries set up to differentiate between the two. From a dynamic point of view, the individual will have to cope with the *setting* of the sociophysical boundaries that may be characterized by the degree of their rigidity or flexibility. Rigidly set boundaries define a context in which work must be carried out between, say, 9 a.m. and 5 p.m. in a specific location, while setting flexible boundaries means that the working individual can choose his or her own time limits and work locations. Finally, the setting of sociophysical boundaries could be challenged, in fact, by the individual, the organization, or the family.

Strategies for Coping With Interposed Transitions

On the individual level, issues of self-image become prominent in coping with interposed transition. Gofman's (1959) view pointed to the importance of the relation between the structure of the self and the sort of performance one gives in interactions with others. He drew attention to the relationship between the "performed self" and the "phenomenological self" (the self one experiences). Thus, when boundaries are intruded upon, the performed self is challenged and a state of tension might arise. It is the management of an image that becomes an issue to be dealt with. In the interposed transition, and especially in those cases where it is imposed, there could be a need to cope with the potential threat to the present role image, if disequilibrium is experienced.

As a way of coping with interposed transitions, individuals use differently constructed barriers to defend themselves against disturbances. The barrier's function is to help the person protect the self-image he or she wants to keep and to follow the norms of the work world or the personal world. For example, construction of a *topic* barrier that places limitations on the private life issues to be exposed at the office might help maintain a certain image at work. Another barrier involves selectively limiting the particular audience present when home life issues are being discussed with home members who call during a meeting with people at work. These and other measures can be seen as setting boundaries that limit the intrusion of one world into the other.

THE RESEARCH QUESTIONS
AND THE SCOPE OF THE STUDY

The nature of the physical and psychological shifts experienced when home/work boundaries are crossed provided the context of this study. The focus of the research was on gender differences in the way home/work boundaries and transitions are experienced. The first research question thus addresses potential differences between women and men in the way they handle the planned transitions between home and work. Toward this end, I examined differences in transition style employed by men and women in their daily morning shift from home to work and in the evening from work to home. In addition, I explored whether differences exist between women and men in the way they cope with interposed transitions. For this purpose, I looked into variations in the operation of home/work boundaries in terms of both their setting and their maintenance.

Participants

The selection criteria for individuals participating in the study were: (a) a management position in a corporation; (b) between 35 and 45 years old; (c) members of a dual-career family and having at least one child of preschool or grade-school age.

Participants for the research were recruited from among the alumni and their referrals of a graduate school of management. Each candidate was contacted by phone, predominantly while at work. Approaching the candidate, the researcher presented the research idea and suggested the candidate be interviewed at a time and place convenient for him or her. Most people were enthusiastic about participating and remarked how important the topic of the relationship between professional and private life seemed to them. Of the 48 people contacted, 42 were willing to participate. I interviewed all 42, but included only 30 of them in the data presented here. The rest were excluded because they did not fit one or more of the criteria (i.e., they had only older children, or the wife had stopped working).

The choice of these criteria was based on the four-factor model suggested by Evans and Bartoleme (1979) in which it was suggested that the overall relationship between work and family is influenced by the personality, the work environment, the life stage, and the spouse. Recruiting of participants focused on the last three factors in the following terms.

Work Environment

Participants held management positions and had at least four people reporting directly to them.

Resemblance Between the Environments. The influence of the work domain on family life may be greater when an individual's role in the two domains is similar (Aldous, 1969). The occupational context of managers is characterized by frequent interaction with other individuals, resembling the interactive context of family life. This contextual analogy was elaborated by Kanter (1977b) who found that individuals in management positions, especially those whose work involves intensive interpersonal encounters during the day, can develop for what she called "interactive fatigue" and withdraw from personal contacts at home, from their burn-out at the office.

Salience of the Relationship Between Work and Family. Studying the career paths and life concerns of people in different business-related occupations, Schein (1978) found that, compared to academics and engineers who tended to be highly involved in only one domain, managers show high involvement with both their work and their families.

Job Design. Management positions often follow a "protean" design (Hall, 1976), allowing the individual greater flexibility in job definition (e.g., scheduling). Thus personal preferences, as defined by one's own concept of the boundaries between private and professional life may influence the transition process to a greater extent than in other occupations. Nonetheless, the findings of the present study could still be applied to benefit those worker populations for which this "freedom of structuring" is more limited.

Life Stage

The overall relationship between professional and private life is most strongly affected by the way managers experience their lifestyle (Evans & Bartoleme, 1986). Male managers in their mid- to late-30s and early 40s were found to have the highest preoccupation with the overall relationship between their private and professional life. The decade between 30 and 40 has been characterized by Gould (1976) as a stage of questioning for men. There is a tendency for introspection: Individuals begin to question their commitments, relationships with others, and the roles they assume. The focus of women in this life stage is argued by Lopata (1966) to be influenced by their children's ages. Having a child in the preschool or grade-school range calls for greater home-presence obligations and thus makes the tradeoff between time at home or at work more salient.

Spouse

Dual-Career Family. It has been suggested that the effect on the interplay between the domains of work and home should be considered within the joint structure of the family and the demands for commitment and involvement that this structure presents (Richter, 1985; Sekeran & Hall, in press). Participants in the study were members of dual-career families in which both partners pursue independent careers outside of the home, and for whom work involvement is a source of self-identification and satisfaction rather than merely a source of economic gain (Sekeran, 1986). When both spouses spend most of their day at work, issues of home management are more likely to intrude upon the work setting and crossing of boundaries becomes a more serious issue. This suggests that the problem of maintaining boundary reliability (especially of the workplace) as well as coping with the transitions is particularly complicated for dual-career families.

The Interview

The interview lasted approximately 2 hours and included three general parts. The initial part aimed at gathering background information concerning (a) personal characteristics—age, education, position; (b) family characteristics—number of children, ages, spouse's working position; and (c) work characteristics—position, scheduled hours, personal working schedule, career stage, and employer.

The second part of the interview was aimed at generating information of psychological region shifts, the two dimensions of activity and concern were simultaneously explored. Participants were asked to concentrate on specific segments of their transition and to report their concerns and activities in a diarylike manner. I chose a chronological order in conducting the interviews as it seemed most convenient for the participants to report their daily experiences sequentially. They also were encouraged to bring up any relevant issue even if it did not follow the daily order. The morning and evening transitions were studied through the use of parallel questions. Reinvolvement within the family was further explored, however, by looking at the other family member's experience as well.

The third part of the interview focused on the boundaries between work and home. First, the individual's concept of the relationship between professional and private life was examined. Next, the setting and maintenance of boundaries were explored. Finally, the ways individuals, families, and organizations cope with boundary violations were investigated.

Data Analysis

The primary aim of this study was phenomenological exploration of the daily transition. What was required for the findings of the study was to document that a psychological shift accompanies the transition, and that transition-related occurrences can be traced along the transition process, which in turn define different ways of handling the shift. Much of the data collected and analyzed, therefore, were descriptive in nature.

Quantitative analysis provided indications of the degree of transition differences between the sexes and between transition directions. These analyses included cross-classification of handling of the transition and boundary setting and maintenance, by gender and by direction. Analyses appropriate to the level of the scales of the data were used in each of the instances just mentioned.

SEX-RELATED DIFFERENCES IN EFFECTING TRANSITIONS AND SETTING AND MAINTAINING BOUNDARIES

Transition Styles

The first question explored whether there is a sex-related difference regarding style of transition. Two "transition periods" were identified: the morning transition—going from home to work; and the evening transition—going from work to home. Each transition period was composed of three subperiods: the time at the domain of departure, the commute, and the time upon arrival at the domain of destination.

Analysis of participants' descriptions of their morning home engagements, both in cognitive terms and in actual activities, indicated the preferred transition style in the transition from home to work. I looked into the role of the work-life interaction in people's mornings at home by exploring the frequency with which they were engaged in their work role while still at home and by the timing employed in disengaging themselves from home life along their commute or upon starting their day at the office. Further indications of the transition style were supplied from the description of activities in the office during the subperiod of starting the working day and time needed for warming up.

I studied the evening transition styles in a parallel way by exploring the ways people concluded their working day, commuted, and got reinvolved in their home life. Along with the actual transition activities, I also traced the ways people would "unwind" from their office life, and become involved in their home life. For this purpose, I also included in the inquiry the type of engagements people would get into during the period of time after dinner.

From Home to Work

In the morning, more women were engaged with home chores than men: More men in this sample reported being engaged only with taking care of themselves. However, in contrast to common stereotypes, husbands were considered by half of the women to have a fair share of home chores in the morning. At this time of day, most men showed a higher level of concern with work, suggesting a preference for the anticipatory style in the transition from home to work. The men who did not take an active part in the home activities were those who routinely left home earlier. Where children were older, they were frequently expected to free their parents from any engagements with home-related activities.

Although women reported lower concern with work while being at home in the morning, they were found to undergo a dramatic increase in work concern during the commute. This suggests that, because women almost never shift their concerns to work while still at home, they compensate for this delay by a very quick shift, starting once they leave home. The rapid shift enables women to be fully concerned with work once they arrive at the workplace. In fact, the preoccupation questionnaire results showed that women's starting level of work concern is somewhat greater than that of men. All this indicates that women's shift of roles, although delayed in comparison to men's, is typified by an *abrupt* transition from one domain to the other. This quick shifting was further demonstrated in their dealing with their entry to work in the morning. On the average, women were quicker in their entry into work and reported a need for a shorter warm-up time to help them get involved in work.

Overall, women and men were engaged in similar activities once they started their work. However, women more frequently used the first 15 minutes of their day for review of the previous day's work, whereas men tended to use this time more often for solving specific problems. This difference may reflect a difference in working style, whereby women prefer to first establish contextual continuity, while men more frequently cope with work by isolating events. Women may also experience a greater segmentation between their professional and private lives and therefore a greater need to first bridge over the two separated working days.

From Work to Home

No gender differences were found in the extent of cognitive involvement with work concerns before leaving work. Differences between women and men, however, were apparent in the different functions served by the concluding hour at work. For women, the last hour at work was frequently experienced as the most hectic time of the day. This could be related to women's need to keep their working hours within rigid boundaries. Attempting to accomplish more work before leaving for home typifies their coping with the potential for impending role conflict.

For men, the last hour was experienced as a loosening up time, some men even reporting a higher engagement with home-life activities before leaving work.

Further exploration of these gender differences revealed that women would very often rush to end the working day. Men very often would enjoy a more relaxed departure, which would allow them to conclude preparations for the next working day still in the office and free them from work concerns while driving. It was found that men often call home just to let their wives know when to expect them for dinner. This pattern was frequently followed when the boundaries of work were extended by staying later than usual. On the other hand, men were rarely at home earlier than their wives, so there was no point in women calling home (especially because men rarely considered it their responsibility to prepare dinner).

For most of the way home, women were concerned with work. In comparison, men were concerned with leisure activities, and considered the commute to be leisure time rather than work time. Thus, women often reported that while driving home they would make a mental list of things to be continued in the office the next day, whereas men often reported listening to their favorite radio program while driving or planning their weekend program. Thus, men detached themselves more easily from work. Although for many men, the commute serves the function of helping them unwind, they still reported taking additional time to unwind from work once they got home, so that overall their shift is very gradual.

The stage of reentry into home is more of a routine for women, as they are tuned in to responding to family needs. Men have more freedom in their manner of getting reinvolved at home, and experience this reentry as less routine. Men more often encounter their spouse first when arriving home, whereas women more often than not encounter their children. An interesting typology was suggested by one of the male participants. He described two phases in the evening transition: getting into one's "personal" home and getting into one's "social" home. Men's reentry is characterized by first entering their personal home and then their social one, whereas women must first enter the social home and only some later time do they get to their personal one. One woman described the routine of reentry into home life in the evening as follows:

> I walk in the door and say, "hello kids how was school?" and we talk about that for a few minutes and then I start, and they've had dinner and sometimes they've had a bath and Lloyd has generally done most of his homework so we can start in on the practicing and whatever else they have to do. They're tired and they really don't like to do it anyway, a lot of what I described is a very unpleasant—he [husband] just disappears and I don't know what he does, he reads or rests or goes outside and works in the garden, but I'm the one who comes in and feels the obligation, he doesn't see why we do all this music anyway, to him. He doesn't become really interrelated with them very much until bedtime and then he will pick up again. If I ask him, he will go over Lloyd's spelling or something like that. I initiate, he probably doesn't. I don't unwind. I do after the children are in bed, or after he's taken over getting them to bed.

In summary, men's transition from home to work is characterized by an anticipatory style, whereas women's transition style is more discrete, and women tend to start shifting only after leaving home. Both tend to follow a routine in their departure from home and to adopt proactive coping strategies in their entry into work. In the evening, the transition style of both sexes is what I named in this research as "discrete," meaning that no work concerns are carried over to the home domain and both work and personal worlds are clearly separated. However, men tend to delay their shift until after they have arrived home, whereas women are fully shifted immediately after entering the home. Women follow a routine in their reentry to home, indicating a proactive coping strategy, while men's reentry to home life is less routine, indicating a reactive style. Overall, men showed a tendency for *gradual shifting*, whereas women were characterized by an *abrupt style* of transferring from one role to the other.

This gender difference in the evening transition into home life was illustrated by two of my study's interviewees. One man described his getting into home life as follows:

> I am not fully involved. I don't want to answer a lot of questions, I do like 15 minutes to get reinvolved...I may walk in, put the brief case down, look at the mail, then talk to my daughter. Usually she'll come in and chit chat quietly. You prefer some quiet time when you get home. For the first 15 minutes, I don't talk to my wife, just my daughter about the events of her day and her trials and tribulations.

The same period of the day was described by a woman as following:

> A lot of people, and my husband is one of them, go home and they just have to rest, they have to have some time, and I don't. I just go right home and keep on going. I'm compulsive. I get more vocal at home, and I think I get more tense at home when the children won't do what I expect them to do in a relatively short period of time, and that's unreasonable of me I know. They're tired, I'm tired. A lot has to be done in a short period of time and it's not a good situation. Which is why I like to come home earlier.

This rapid shifting between roles for women exemplifies the lack of a *buffer zone* between their professional and private lives and typifies the role strain many of them experience. It can be argued that this stems from women's tendency to deal simultaneously with their different roles (Gilligan, 1982; Pleck, 1977), but, at the same time, it almost certainly reflects the reality that working full time does not free them from most of their home responsibilities.

Operation of the Boundaries

The second research question explored was whether there are gender-related differences regarding the operation of home/work *boundaries*, in terms of both their setting and their maintenance.

The Setting of Boundaries

The setting of boundaries was measured by (a) the *extending* of the time one stays in a particular domain beyond the regular hours, and (b) by the *erosion* of the time one is supposed to spend in that domain. These indices were considered to reflect the degree of rigidity–flexibility of the boundaries. Rigidity was indicated by infrequent changing of the time setting of boundaries, and flexibility was determined by frequent changing of the time setting or interposing of time demands.

The issue of the timing of the daily transition epitomized another difference between men and women. This was reflected in how the boundaries were set between professional and private life. Women reported staying late at work less often than men. This suggests that the home boundaries of women are more rigid in terms of time than those of men. For all women, the major concern in deciding to stay late was their children. Men's decision to continue working was more commonly affected by their own desire to stay, and only then by concern with their children or spouse (and often it was a matter of approval rather than home responsibilities that was the consideration).

Coping with extended boundaries of work was different for men and women. Finding out that they have to stay later in the office, most men would inform their wives, and that was that. While for women the extension of working would cause more complications, if their spouses were not available, as they would have to call in a back-up system such as a friend, neighbor, or pre-arranged babysitter to substitute for them in their absence from home. One might conclude from this that it is the wife's responsibility to deal with the repercussions of work on family life, whereas the husband is relatively free of this concern.

All this suggests that women's work boundaries are more rigid because less support is offered from their families, and, at the same time, they are expected to fully support their husbands and enable them to have greater boundary flexibility. This pattern of setting the boundaries between work and home reflects the traditional socialization of women, whereby they make a priority of family obligations over professional performance and take exclusive responsibility for home chores.

Pleck and Staines (1985) supported this position when they speculated that, compared to husbands, wives more often experience conflict between their work schedule and their job within the family. They suggested that this possibly higher level of "job-to-job" conflict may be part of a more general pattern of women's greater acceptance of responsibility for accommodating to other family members' schedules. Furthermore, unique to dual-earner families is that although the individual's own job schedule has presumably the stronger effect on his or her work–family conflict, the spouse's schedule also has an influence on the wife (especially in situations where nonstandard work schedules are expected).

The present research supports these assumptions. As I have already shown, when the women had to expand their work boundaries they assumed responsibility for the effects on other family members, by arranging for a substitute for themselves. In contrast when husbands stayed late, they merely called their wives, who again assumed responsibility for the home life.

The setting of the work/home boundaries by the dual-career family is the arena where gender-related differences were most salient in the present research. Very often, the participants voiced support for an equal sharing of responsibilities for work and home between spouses. At the same time, many of the men were aware that in reality the responsibility for work and family is unequally distributed, with the woman having primary responsibility for the family and simultaneously for her own work. Moreover, negotiations would most often taken into consideration the man's need to establish his career first. The preferred mode of the accommodation between work and family life is the "independent" mode (Bailyn, 1978); that is, one in which decisions concerning allocation of responsibility are based on individual negotiation. In reality, however, many families follow to a greater extent the traditional pattern, whereby responsibility is determined by traditional expectations of gender roles.

The Maintenance of Boundaries

Maintenance of the *home* boundaries was indicated by their permeability or impermeability to penetration by work life into the home domain. This was measured by the frequency of bringing work home to be done during the evening or over the weekend, and by the frequency with which subjects called up the office or colleagues from their own residence after work hours or during vacations. These are examples of boundary permeability under *initiated* penetration of work into home life. However, such penetration could be *imposed* by work colleagues who choose to intervene in one's home-life engagements.

Maintenance of *work* boundaries was indicated by their permeability to penetration by home-related issues into the work domain. This was measured by the frequency of calling home or calling spouses at their workplace, which indicated the level of initiated interposed transitions, and by the frequency with which family members intruded upon work—indicating the level of imposed interposed transitions.

Consistent with the differences found between women and men in setting boundaries between work and home were the differences in maintaining boundaries between work and home. Men assumed that their working at home was approved or at least accepted by their wives, whereas women felt that they were not able to work at home without their husbands' approval. One woman described her husband's attitude as follows:

He resents it more than I do, because it doesn't really happen to him and it invariably happens to me. Just the other night, we were just sitting down to dinner, a weekend dinner, when we all try to eat together; the phone rang and he answered it. I usually make him answer the phone, because he can usually postpone the call. I mean there are some people who call and I just say tell them I'm not there, I don't want to talk to them. Anyway, it was this woman and she said she really needed to speak to me, and he said well she's just sitting down to dinner could she call you in 20 minutes. No. Right then and there she had to talk to me, and as it turned out it didn't take just a few minutes and it was a question that really need to be answered.

Women would often discourage their husbands from working at night out of concern for their well-being. At the same time, a wife would tend to view her husband's objection to her working at night as resulting from a desire for her to be available for joint home life.

Women also experienced their working at home at night as a source of family conflict to a greater extent than men. As another woman commented, "He doesn't like it when my clients call on the phone. He feels that it interferes with my life and is very mean to me, too, when they call. That's alright."

Men were able to detach from work in the evening, but were more concerned with it in the morning. Women, however, indicated being concerned with work issues at home in the evening to a greater extent than men. At the same time, although women's levels of work concerns at work do not differ from men's, women admit to being concerned with home issues at work to a greater extent than men; that is, while at work they will think about home issues. As one of them put it, "There is always a low hum to cope with," especially in the late afternoon hours when the children may already be home from school. Women's concern with home issues is often further increased by the children's tendency to call their mothers at work much more often than they call their fathers.

Thus, it appears that women who work outside the home and have families have psychological boundaries that are more permeable in both directions. Comparing the actual timing of the evening transition for men and women, it was found that men's evening transitions often occur later than those of women. At the same time, women's physical boundaries were more inflexible in the sense that they were less willing to stay longer at work. In this sense, the higher tendency of women to return to work issues at home may be seen as a compensatory act derived from trying to balance two jobs at once. Obviously, this leads to higher workload and potential conflict and is indicative of women's tendency to be concerned simultaneously with different segments of the life space (Gilligan, 1982). One should keep in mind that although women may put in fewer hours at work because of family demands, they may compensate by being more efficient than their colleagues who spend more hours in the workplace.

Many of the women who participated in this study were pioneers in their professional careers and felt that they were "test cases." Their high work involvement may have stemmed from excessive motivation to establish their position. A typical remark follows:

It [work] is very much with me all the time. Even on the weekend, dealing with friends. Particularly because many of the men, my friends, think it is probably a bigger deal than it is because it is still relatively unusual for a woman to be a big deal in a big company. It does affect everything you do.

Career and Life Stage

Several differences were apparent between men and women in the way they coped with transitions and boundaries during the different stages of their lifetime.

Generally, male participants admitted that career stage was the predominant factor in the setting and maintenance of their work/home boundaries. Age of children, which may be taken as an indication of life stage, had less of an effect on them than on female participants. Mothers of young children noted very clearly that the setting of their boundaries was much more rigid and less flexible than that of their spouses. Day-care timing was the major factor governing their boundaries. Freeing themselves from the time constraints of a babysitting system was looked upon as the means to achieving greater boundary flexibility. Women professed that, during these early life stages, instead of staying late at the office they would bring work home, thereby trading boundary permeability for boundary flexibility. The relationship between career stage and home boundaries permeability was well illustrated by another woman who said the following:

Sometimes a client may be upset, but I'm used to it, because I've been doing this for so long, I'm better able to cope with it and go home and forget about it. I'm much better than I used to be. If I were more ambitious I would probably let it bother me and I would work longer and do more at home. I try real hard, for my own sake as well as the children, to separate work and home. I didn't use to do that. As the children have gotten older I've become better.

However, having growing children still affected the way some women handled the boundaries between work and home. At this life stage, the maintenance of the boundaries, as indicated by their level of permeability, was affected in two ways. Home concerns tended to penetrate into the mother's work life, because the growing children tended to call their mother rather than their father at the workplace, thus imposing on her an interposed transition. At the same time, some mothers admitted to being concerned about the activities of their growing children. A number of women expressed their desire to be in touch with their children, particularly at that time of the day when they were due home from school. Thus, these women demonstrated a tendency to initiate interposed transitions, indicating the permeability of their work boundaries.

Burnout

These findings also lead us to the problem of burnout amongst women. Different research findings (Etzion & Pines, 1986; Freudenberger & North, 1985) suggest that women are more prone to experience burnout than men. They experience less control over their work environment, tend to deny their personal needs, and use less-effective strategies for coping with stress. In research that compared men and women (Pines & Aronson, 1981; Pines & Kafry, 1981) it was found that women perceive their jobs less positively than men, attribute more negative characteristics to their jobs, feel they are being underpaid, and attribute higher significance to their personal life than to their professional life. This point gains greater importance among women who work out of necessity rather than because of intrinsic motivations.

Some studies contend, however, that a woman's age is the major factor in strain between her work world and her personal world. Etzion (1987) for example, found among women engineers in the United States that, as they get older, they tend to perceive themselves as being more successful and less burned out, and enjoy their work more. As women get older and their children become more independent, the strain of performing the duties of a mother and managing a job decreases. With age, the level of self-confidence of women increases while with men it decreases. These findings support other research on professional women (Pines & Kafry, 1981), who in mid-career were characterized as having more positive attitudes toward life, perceiving their career to be more rewarding, and enjoying a more varied and satisfying lifestyle. Thus, it seems that work/home conflict, which is so prominent in the first stages of a woman's career and is such a dominant factor in her burnout (Bailyn, 1973, 1978), tends to decrease in later career stages, allowing her to rebuild and rebase her career.

However, it may be that the major factor determining the level of the professional woman's burnout is not necessarily her age or her career stage but rather the stage of the family life cycle. The findings of the present study support this argument, as strategies for coping with boundary flexibility and permeability have been shown to be related to the age of the woman's children.

CONCLUSIONS

In conclusion, I would like to suggest some practical applications of the findings for helping women cope with balancing home and work life. Three levels should be considered: the organizational, the family, and the individual.

On the organizational level, I would like to suggest that scheduling meetings during the work day should take into consideration the stressful impact of meetings scheduled at both ends of the day. In light of this, organizations should be advised to adopt any flexitime work procedures to allow individuals' needs to be met. The effect of a late meeting is reduced when it is predictable so that reasonable substitute procedures for the working mother could be arranged in advance.

Boundaries between work and home are sometimes violated by work intrusions into the home after work hours. This phenomenon has unfavorable effects on the individual and the family and should be discouraged. Thus, although it is the individual's responsibility to take care of his or her own personal life at home, it is the organization's moral role to make sure that proper conditions are allowed for doing so.

On the family level, the most demanding and troublesome time in the daily life of the family turns out to be the final part of the transition from work to home—the phase of entering the home and the start of private life. Only rarely was it an egalitarian situation where both partners took equal responsibility for the home chores. The predominant experience was one of stress. As one woman said:

> It's all the same, I simply continue to work, but now under greater stress. Everybody wants me and there's no time for myself. I have so many things to do, that sometimes I don't even have time to change my clothes.

Many men acknowledged the inequality of home-chore responsibility, the gap between their values and their behavior, and the need to change the status quo.

The issue of boundaries between work and home causes much stress, especially during early career stages. To help cope with this, couples might discuss a contract between them regarding the violation of home time, either by staying late at work or by working at home.

On the individual level, one way for women to cope with the accelerated transition into home life and the stress of role overload caused by it would be simply to acknowledge its existence and to structure a transition period into the home life. This could be done by structuring an individual "unwinding period," such as one woman did by forming the habit of taking a shower before any actual encounter with her family. Another technique would be to perform the different roles of parenting and home maintenance sequentially.

As a constructive way to deal with the daily setting of work and home boundaries, one might schedule one's transition to home to be at a fixed time on certain days and fully flexible on others. This approach might benefit individuals and organizations equally because the employer's request for longer hours on these days would be fully legitimized. For the family, this predictability would make scheduling easier. Spouses might alternate times so that the career aspirations of both might be satisfied.

In these days of accelerated technological change, work conditions are characterized by increasing variability and responsibility. Family patterns are vastly different, as are individual values regarding the relationship between private and professional life. Addressing the question of how people manage their transitions is essential since this interface affects workers' efficiency, satisfaction, involvement, stress (in the short term) and burnout (in the long term).

REFERENCES

Aldous, J. (1969). Occupational characteristics and males' role performance in the family. *Journal of Marriage and the Family, 31*, 707–712.

Bailyn, L. (1973). Family constraints on women's work. *Annals of the New York Academy of Sciences, 208*, 82–90.

Bailyn, L. (1978). Accommodation of work to family life. In R. Rapaport & R. Rapaport (Eds.), *Working couples,* (pp. 159–174) New York: Harper & Row.

Etzion, D. (1987). *Career success, life patterns, and burnout in male and female engineers: A matched-pairs comparison.* Paper presented at the Third International Interdisciplinary Congress on Women, Trinity College, Dublin, Ireland.

Etzion, D., & Pines, A. (1986). Sex and culture as factors explaining coping and burnout among human service professionals: A social psychological perspective. *Journal of Cross-Cultural Psychology, 17*(2), 191–209.

Evans, P.A.L., & Bartolome, F. (1979). Professional lives versus private lives—Shifting patterns of managerial commitment. *Organizational Dynamics, 7*, 2–29.

Evans, P.A.L., & Bartolome, F. (1986). The dynamics of work–family relationship in managerial lives. *International Review of Applied Psychology, 35*(3), 371–398.

Freudenberger, H.J, & North, G. (1985). *Women's burnout.* New York: Doubleday.

Gilligan, C. (1982). *In a different voice.* Cambridge, MA: Harvard University Press.

Gofman, E. (1959). *The presentation of self in everyday life.* New York: Doubleday.

Gould, R.C. (1976). *Transformation, growth and change in adult life.* New York: Simon & Schuster.

Hall, D.T. (1976). *Career in organizations.* Santa Monica, CA: Goodyear.

Hall, D.T., & Hall, F.S. (1979) *The two-career couple.* Reading, MA: Addison-Wesley.

Kanter, R. (1977a). *Men and women of the corporation.* New York: Basic Books.

Kanter, R.M. (1977b). *Working and family in the United States: A critical review and agenda for research and policy.* New York: Russell Sage.

Katz, D., & Kahan, R.L. (1978). *The social psychology of organization.* New York: Wiley.

Levinson, D.S. (1959). Role, personality and social structure in the organizational setting. *Journal of Abnormal and Social Psychology, 58*, 170–180.

Lewin, K. (1951). *Field theory in social science.* New York: Harper & Row.

Lopata, H.A. (1966). The life cycle of the social fate of the house-wife. *Sociology and Social Research*, 51(5), 2.

Pines, A., & Aronson, E. (1981). *Burnout: From tedium to personal growth*. New York: The Free Press.

Pines, A., & Kafry, D. (1981). Tedium in the life and work of professional women as compared with men. *Sex Roles*, 7(10), 963–977.

Pleck, J. (1977). The work-family role system. *Social Problems*, 24, 417–427.

Pleck, J., & Staines, G. (1985). Work schedules and family life in two earner couples. *Journal of Family Issues*, 6, 61–84.

Richter, J. (1985). *Switching gears between the office and the living room*. Paper presented at the 56th annual convention of the American Academy of Management, San Diego, CA.

Schein, E.H. (1978). *Career dynamics*. Reading, MA: Addison-Wesley.

Sekeran, U. (1986). *Dual-career families: Contemporary organizational and counseling issues*. San Francisco: Jossey-Bass.

Sekeran, U., & Hall, D.T. (in press). Dual career and family linkages: Implications for career development theory and practice. In M. B. Arthur, D.T. Hall, & B. S. Lawrence (Eds.), *Handbook of career theory*, Cambridge, England: Cambridge University Press.

Chapter 9

"Liberated to Work Like Dogs!": Labeling Black Women and Their Work

Cheryl Townsend Gilkes
Colby College

The moral value of people and groups in society is expressed through their placement in a hierarchy of social statuses. The devaluation of some people and groups in society diminishes the degree of humanity and respect they receive and lowers their position in this hierarchy of social statuses. We call this devaluation, *labeling*. This devaluation and labeling is a power contest in the form of a stigma contest (Schur, 1980) and a conflict over rules, the power to make and enforce rules that define the situations in which people exist (Becker, 1973). It is a sociopolitical contest in which losers are forced to survive in society with diminished moral claims on goods, services, political efficacy, social honor, and respect. This chapter focuses on the labeling of Black women and their work and the consequences of that labeling for Black women's definition of their situation in relation to self, work, the women's movement, and activities for social change.

LABELING AND BLACK WOMEN

In a pluralistic society such as the United States, diverse groups find themselves faced with a variety of survival problems in the hostile interaction contexts that labeling produces (Rubington & Weinberg, 1987). Many groups, for example the mentally ill, the physically disfigured, and gay women and men, have experienced the impact of this labeling process.

Labeled groups can be stripped of their legal personhood through the misuse of medical ideology and the manipulation of cultural images and stereotypes (Scheff, 1966), socially discredited and pushed out of occupational settings (Goffman, 1963), or victimized by extralegal violence and various forms of discrimination (Becker, 1973, pp. 35–36).

Women and racial-ethnic groups are distinctive victims of labeling. Gender and race-ethnicity, along with class, are major sources of social inequality that have deep moral meaning. These moral meanings have serious consequences. In a culture of affluence, the poor are victimized by stereotypes labeling them lazy and profligate. In a culture of white-skin dominance and privilege, dark skin is associated with danger and degradation. And in the patriarchal culture of the United States, women are imaged as fragile, ineffective, and intellectually inferior to men. All groups who fall outside the norms of affluence, whiteness, and maleness encounter demeaning and sometimes hostile stereotypes that assign them to specific cultural roles with limited and limiting expectations. The labeling of such groups is intensified when, as Murray (1973) pointed out with reference to Black people, social scientists codify idealized and unrealistic models of White norms and institutions by which they measure the conformity or nonconformity of Black people.

The moral relationship of women and minorities to the labor force is probably the most dramatic indication of their powerlessness and their moral devaluation. Indeed much of the rhetoric concerning affirmative action implies a normative hierarchy of access to jobs based on the assumption that all White[1] males should be employed before White women and before Black women and men. Such problems of access are further complicated by the cultural assumption that good clean people should have good clean jobs and that bad, dangerous, and dirty people should have bad, dirty, and dangerous jobs, if any jobs at all. A good job is a high paying job and, historically, when traditionally dirty jobs were redefined as "good," Black people were often excluded.

In an analysis of White women's place in contemporary society, Schur (1984) argued that "under the gender system as presently constituted women are subject to an enormous array of increasingly questioned, but still dominant norms" (p. 51). This complex of "gender norms" governs women's presentations of self, marriage and motherhood, sexuality, criminality, and occupational choice. A "normal" woman is a warm, attractive,

---

[1]Although I use the term *White* I am aware that the dominant racial category is socially constructed and does not exclude all men of color with equal hostility. The focus of this chapter is on the problems of Black women within a racial-ethnic community of Black people located in a racist society, and therefore, share with Black men many of the hostilities and stereotypes reserved exclusively for people of African descent native to the United States.

fragile, White wife, and willing mother with a decorous sexual image who refrains from permanent participation in the labor force. Any woman who falls outside of this narrow definition suffers from the general devaluation of things female and from the punishment meted out to those who stray beyond these demeaning boundaries of normal womanhood.

For "Black women in White America" (Lerner, 1972), there is a peculiar interaction of norms and expectations governing society's historical evaluation of their work role. White institutions with their power to define have pointed to Black women's work roles as evidence of their deviance. As Dill (1979) pointed out, the image of Black women laborers as "beasts of burden" contradicts a dominant cultural image of White women that emerges as "fragile, white, and not too bright." As laborers, Black women must contend with stereotypes and images that have labeled them inferior and defective females. As victims of the labeling process, Black women must collectively resist these negative definitions and a negative social identity while engaged in their so-called improper conduct in order to survive. Black women, slave and free, were exempted from the usual complex of gender norms (Davis, 1981), punished for that exemption, and, as laborers, assigned to bad, dirty, and dangerous work. This additional burden of labeling shapes an extremely stressful situation for Black women—perhaps the most stressful in America's racial-ethnic order.

These cultural and historical distinctions foster contrasting and often conflicting definitions of social reality among Black women. Such conflicting perspectives have fostered an ambivalence on the part of Black women toward "women's liberation." Attempts to explain this ambivalence have focused on hostility rooted in inequality (King, 1973; LaRue, 1971; Noble, 1978; Reid, 1972), on Black women's lack of consciousness (Wallace, 1978), on their overall disadvantage compared to White women (Jackson, 1971, 1973, 1978; King, 1973; Lewis, 1977; Mitchell & Bell, 1978), and on Black women's concern with the problems of the total Black community (Cade, 1970; Davis, 1971, 1981). Andolsen (1986) identified explicit conflicts between White and Black feminists over the issues of rape, work, beauty, and male–female solidarity. These Black feminist perspectives reflect Black women's overall discomfort with the prevailing ideologies of American feminism (Williams, 1986).

Black women's participation in the labor force and their involvement in the public affairs of community and society, historically, are important contrasts to the experiences of White women and, in addition to their experiences as family members, primary sources of their "definition of the situation." Black women's responses to the feminist movement include hostility, ambivalence, cautious acceptance, and complex theoretical criticism. Many Black women attach such great importance to the distinctiveness of their experience, they embrace Walker's (1983) term *womanist* to describe their Black-woman-centered definitions of self, critiques of culture, and praxis. Their responses are rooted in a sense of self that is historically grounded in their consciousness concerning their labor experience and in their experience of isolation, conflict, and devaluation stemming from the negative labeling of their selves and their work.

THE RESEARCH

In order to explore Black women's "definition of the situation" with reference to work and to the women's movement, data are utilized which were gathered on 25 Black women community workers in a northern city. These women were recognized by the local Black community as its full-time activists and advocates. These women also worked as appointed and elected politicians and human service professionals. Each participant was recommended by members of the community as women who had "worked hard for a long time for change in the Black community." They had also been similarly recognized by the Black press at least 8 years prior to the commencement of the study. Each woman provided a taped open-ended interview averaging 2 hours in length but ranging from 45 minutes to 6 hours. The interviews explored childhood, educational, occupational, and cultural experiences with special reference to their careers in community activities and their daily work lives—work lives that were thoroughly integrated with their work for social change and community survival (Gilkes, 1982, 1983).

Although the study did not focus primarily on the women's attitudes and feelings toward the feminist movement, the women voluntarily expressed their feelings when asked about their perception of the problems that contemporary Black women face and about their experiences working with White people. Additionally, women provided perspectives on their work and labor histories during the narrative section of the interview in response to the question, "Tell me about yourself."

Although the sample is small, these women's perspectives are significant. They are the most admired women in the local Black community, and, in spite of their visibility and public honor, they represent the spectrum of the Black experience, in their class, ethnic, regional, and status origins. In spite of their current white-collar, managerial, middle-class occupations and their great prestige, their social networks involve the entire Black community. Two of the women were in their 80s and retired from full-time paid work. The 23 younger women, ages 30 to 60, were employed full time in a variety of human service agencies where they integrated fully their roles as professionals, advocates, and activists in order to advance the economic, political, and social interests of the Black community. Their definition of "the Black community" included not only the diverse, segregated, disproportionately poor urban community in Hamptonville (a pseudonym) but also "wherever Black people can be found" and "people of African descent." All of these women were married at some point in their lives and had worked full time during the child-rearing and childbearing years. Although two women were childless, they defined the importance of their work with reference to the community's children in precisely the same terms as those women who were mothers.

THE DEFINITION OF THE SITUATION

Perspectives on self, work, and the women's movement were expressed with reference to the social and labor histories of Black women. A typical statement usually pointed to both history and contemporary reality: "I guess I have to think about what I am and what I am is a Black women, living in America,...and all that means historically and realistically." Realistically and historically, the meaning of being a "Black woman living in America" is tied to the social history of Black women in the world of work and political conflict. These women's assessments of their situation demand an examination of the historical problems of Black women and their work outside the home for explanations of their attitudes toward the women's movement. Although much of the concern of the feminist movement has been with work, the movement has not spoken loudly to the conditions created for Black women through the interaction of their color, gender, and labor history, and the society's labeling of Black women and their assertive management of their difficulties.

Black women have had a higher labor force participation rate at consistently lower wage and status levels than White women. This work has been a response largely to the demands for survival. The society's response to this work has been to generate negative images and stereotypes that focus largely on the Black woman laborer. Concrete expressions of this deviantizing or labeling are found in such labels as "Mammy," "Sapphire," and "matriarch" by which Black women are depicted as bad women and dangerous mothers. Such labeling structurally and ideologically isolates Black women from the experiences and problems of other women. The nature of Black women's work, particularly domestic work (Dill, 1980, 1988; Rollins, 1985), is such that non-Black women are often implicated in the deviantizing process. The moral isolation of labeling represents a victimization distinct from that experienced by White women. Although isolated from White women, the same process prompts Black women to integrate themselves into the public affairs and social problems of the Black community and fosters a tradition of political activism and autonomous Black women's movements. As Becker (1973) pointed out:

Members of organized deviant groups of course have one thing in common: their deviance. It gives them a sense of common fate, of being in the same boat. From a sense of common fate, from having to face the same problems, grows a deviant subculture: a set of perspectives and understandings about what the world is like and how to deal with it, and a set of routine activities based on those perspectives. Membership in such a group solidifies a deviant identity. (p. 38)

Keeping in mind that the "deviance" of Black women is conferred on them by the larger society, the realities of their work and community lives demand that they develop and communicate "a set of perspectives and understandings about what the world is like and how to deal with it."

Black women do have a distinct set of perspectives and understandings about the world concerning their social image, their work, and contemporary feminism. The perspectives of these community workers are important because they shape and are shaped by the attitudes and concerns of the larger community. They sit on boards, attend meetings, and work in organizations and agencies that are highly visible. They are vitally connected to all segments of the Black community and are crucial links to the realization of both community survival needs and aspirations for social change. As visible participants in all movements affecting black community life, these women are occupational, political, and social role models to other Black women and men at all socioeconomic levels of the Black community. The honor and prestige accorded these women within the Black community (and occasionally outside of it) places them in the position of trendsetters and contributors to the ideological perspectives and practical strategies extant within the Black community at any given time.

Community workers volunteered perspectives on their relationship to the feminist movement in response to my question, "What are some of the most important problems which Black women face today?" The women consistently referred to their powerlessness in the face of the racism that dictated the terms of employment of the Black community in general and Black women in particular. They emphasized the degraded and coerced circumstances of some of their past jobs, the problems of Black family life, and the negative definitions attached to Black women's working. They spoke plainly of the isolation that encouraged Black women to develop an interdependent approach to their problems. Observing that adjustment to the problems of labor force was a focal concern of White women, community workers insisted Black women had already adjusted. They were more concerned with Black women's structural isolation at the bottom of the labor market and the emotional and social isolation that stemmed from the negative labels attached to Black women's economic roles.

One elected official summarized the overall theme of community workers perspectives on liberation and work. She stated flatly, "We've had the opportunity as black women to be forever liberated—to go out and work like dogs!" During her interview, she described her own work history. Her sense of working "like a dog" came from her early jobs in factories. She described her first job where she refused to be treated "like an animal." She said:

> Well, I remember that when I first went to work...right after the Second World War,...I was working in a meat packing factory and started smoking quite young. They would give us breaks, but I would get tired. I'd do my work but I'd go to the Ladies Room and have a cigarette. And the floor lady came telling me to stop doing it. Well I knew she was doing the same thing, so she'd say "stop" to me and I said to her, "You stop, and I'll stop." And I had no business saying that...but I just felt that if she had those kind of privileges, why couldn't I. And I didn't have to sit there like an animal! But I had a right to get up and rest myself if I was producing what I was supposed to produce.

After marriage and her first child in the early 1950s, she left the meat packing factory and sought a job in the garment industry. She encountered difficulties because "jobs were scarce":

> I went looking from place to place, for a job and everybody kept telling me that I didn't have any experience. I went into this one particular place and the man told me you don't have any experience. And I turned around and looked him dead in the eye and said, "How can I ever get any if nobody hires me!" and was walking out the door. So as I started out, he said, "Hey, com'ere! You want a job?" I said, "Why do you think I came in here?" [He said,] "OK, I'll hire you."

She described her general feistiness in the labor force as the foundation for her public involvement. Her basic philosophy asked, "Why can't I do it?" when faced with a new opportunity. She said, "And I never hesitate to apply." Always involved in community activities as a volunteer, by the 1960s she said, "I was ready to come out of the factory." Another woman with similar experiences, described how she fought and threatened legal action in order to gain admission to a clerical training program. After criticizing clerical work as demeaning, she explained her struggle to end her long career in factories by stating, "I was sick and tired of getting my hands dirty."

Regardless of their class origins, the women all complained about dirty work such as domestic service, sweat shops, and factories that they or their close friends had endured. Some complained openly about White female supervisors and employers and vividly recounted instances of direct conflict with them in early jobs. One elderly woman instituted a program in her women's club to teach fellow domestic workers how to be assertive about receiving the agreed-upon wages for their day's work. They all saw the problem of Black women as the "overall level of work." One professional with middle-class origins said:

> The level of work is something that is a problem to Black women. We are still found to be in the domestic jobs....The other is if it is not domestic work that one is involved in, it is work that is considerably low paying.

Not only did community workers cite their disadvantaged structural position, but they described the injury caused by the labels attached to their work and their economic contributions to the family. The image of the matriarch was particularly burdensome isolating them from the larger society and from many Black men who saw them as rivals and embarrassments to "the Race." A child welfare worker related her perception of Black women's problems, saying:

> A really big problem for most of the Black women I know is trying to find out where we fit in the social system,...particularly when the matriarchal system has been so stereotyped—trying to get out of the stereotypes. And getting help, being so isolated....We've had to lean on each other a lot and that has made it more difficult for us to relate to any black males....It's a vicious a cycle.

Many other women also observed this conflict with Black men and that it stemmed both from the misidentification of Black women as matriarchs and from the specialized pressure racism placed on Black men. They also complained that there seemed to be fewer Black men, especially fewer who were sympathetic to the problems of Black working women.

The social and emotional isolation from Black men was seen as a recent problem. The two elder community workers, both widows, were concerned and puzzled by their observations of increasing conflict between Black men and women and of a change for the worse in the situation of the Black working women and their families. These elders had successfully combined paid work, long marriages, and child rearing. One had been a household domestic and the founder of numerous clubs and programs, some of which addressed the problems of household domestics directly. The other had been a successful businesswoman—at one time the owner of the largest Black business in the Hamptonville metropolitan area. Both had been distinguished executives in the local NAACP. One said:

> I think a good many of the young [Black] women of today have a hard time finding men who have the same ideas that they have and seem to want to cooperate with them enough....I've noticed that and that's why a lot of them have broken marriages so much; most of the time I've found that it's been the

women that are most progressive and, it seems, want to do more in making a home and preparing for the future.

The community workers' perspectives were linked to their present reality, their personal work histories, and their understandings concerning Black women's history. Although two thought incorrectly that Black women were doing better than Black men, they all expressed a sense of victimization stemming from inequity, isolation, and the status degradation fostered by negative images and stereotypes. One woman shared the outline of a lecture that she had presented to Black professional women. One prominent topic heading was entitled, "Labels—aggressive, domineering, hardnosed." Another topic, referring especially to those Black women "wearing two hats" as breadwinners and parents, described Black women's victimization through labeling in similar terms. Describing their situation as "very difficult" she described the effects of labeling as follows:

> You're footing two bills—being known as too aggressive and being professional and not being warm enough and womanly enough....Black women perceived by the total community at large are the victims of a lot of superficial values of the society—more than White women, more than White men, more than Black men or other minorities—because at this point [White and other minority] cultures dictate that [White and other minority] women take the position they have taken.

She insisted that the negative perception of Black women as different came from Black men as well as the dominant culture. Addressing labeling as "that syndrome," she concluded, "I just think that Black women who [must] break out of that syndrome are beset with problems from 'Jumpstreet'."

The most prominent community worker openly criticized the ideology of the matriarchy in her discussion of problems confronting the Black community. She said:

> When I first started to work in the NAACP, for example,....there was a certain kind of togetherness that we don't feel now....We have allowed ourselves to become divided by White people's philosophies such as the matriarchal society—you know, Black women have all the power [over] Black men....We've allowed all these divisions it seems to me to interfere in a way it didn't seem to me they interfered [before].

She perceived the problem of labeling in Black women's lives and also recognized it as a problem in the Black community's internal organization. She felt that the labeling of Black women as matriarchs had increased the amount of disrespect in the political community and had undermined Black women's ability to contribute to the efforts of the entire community. She was particularly conscious of the extra pressure of the labels. She said:

> Well I see a real need for Black women to do some kind of united [action]. I think Black women have severe problems that have been put on us....There's this put-down constantly of Black women. I think of the little girls because...you look at the TV and I said, "What can little girls think of when they look at TV with this long flowing hair?" The image that's been put out there is not going to be happening for Black women....I think that Black women have a problem in the kind of image that's been portrayed about them...that we've been cut off and set aside and kind of isolated. That there are certain myths about how Black women can proceed.

She concluded with an insistence that Black women of all age and occupational and professional statuses shared a common problem that required a collective response. She said, "I just think that it would be good if Black women had some way of getting together across age lines, across professional lines and see that they have a common problem dealing with the kinds of put-downs...."

The inequities in the labor force and the difficulties Black women were facing in their communities were part of the consciousness with which Black women viewed the concerns of the women's movement. One woman, who viewed the movement as important but problematic, argued that the movement seemed to be pre-occupied with "some of the fluff." They were particularly unsympathetic to the problems of affluent White women who were seeking opportunities to enter the labor force. One woman, an elected official said, "I'd like to be able to stay at home and just get bored and want to go look for a job." There was, however, an overall rejection of simply aspiring towards the luxury of staying home. One woman actually quoted LaRue (1971) when she warned of the "trap of 'Miss Ann's warmed over throne.'" There was little sympathy, however, for those women who were actually denigrating the homemaker role.

Another professional, who was very much involved in several national Black women's organizations provided some extended criticism of Black women's relationship to the feminist movement. She said:

> I hate to keep using the same words but we've got to straighten out in our own minds who we are and what we're about. Some of us I think have gotten a little off track in being with quote unquote "women's liberation" in the narrowest sense—I'm talking about the middle-class White world's interpretation of women's liberation. We need indeed to be about the business of the equal rights for all women. I really don't want to low-rate that part of it at all but some of that other esoteric intellectualization! I'd hate for us to get too far off in that ball game because we've got too much work to do within our own Black

communities, within our own families, within our own relationships with each other and if we've got extra energy we've got to invest it in our own communities. Now, for example, that business of reading skills: I think we'd better be about that then worrying too much about whether we're M-S or M-R-S or M-I-S-S.

Community workers recognized White America's moral evaluation of them as morally dangerous women and deviant mothers and of their work as dirty, degrading, and deviant. They perceived this labeling as divisive for the whole community. This recognition when tied to their consciousness of Black women's social history fueled their criticism of the dominant society and its White feminist movement. For Black women, the labeling of their persons and their work was the crowning blow in a history of economic exploitation, political victimization, and cultural assault.

"EVEN IN SLAVERY TIMES": HISTORY AND CONSCIOUSNESS

The problems these women identify are historical in scope and they are conscious of that history. They refer to it and their sense of history is part of the definition of the situation. Work has been the defining element in Black women's experience and the stereotypes with which these women feel battered are tied to their work history.

That work history includes slavery and rural southern peonage, experiences that institutionalized the "mammy" and "the bad Black woman" (Lerner, 1972). "Mammy" and "the loose Black woman" were stock characters of the antebellum South (Christian, 1980) and the "loose Black woman" emerged as "Jezebel" (White, 1985). These stereotypes were much larger than reality (Genovese, 1974; Parkhurst, 1938). Northern migration, urbanization, the civil rights movement, and Black demands for empowerment modified these images but did not erase them. The newer images became the "castrating force of Sapphire" (Bond & Peery, 1970) and "the matriarchy" (Rainwater & Lancey, 1967; Ryan, 1971; Staples, 1971, 1973). Christian (1980) identified "the sapphire and the matriarch" as "two variations on the mammy image..." (p. 77). However, these images, both direct assaults on the Black working woman, became publicly institutionalized during the 1950s and the poverty policy debates of the late 1960s. These debates became the vehicle through which the deviant image of Black women was widely publicized and communicated through the culture, making the stereotypical images of Black women more intractable and culturally pervasive than that of men (Andolsen, 1986). The life and times of these stereotypes are tied to the role of Black women laborers at specific times in the history of the United States.

As slaves, Black women participated fully in rural and urban work forces, beginning their history with 100% labor force participation. Because of their sex, they were burdened with additional tasks as mothers and wives. Women who refrained from bearing children were often punished or sold, so the role of working mother was inescapable. The plantation system, with its preponderance of men, actually encouraged slave women's fertility resulting in one of the highest fertility rates at that time (White, 1985, pp. 65–70). Slave women feigned sickness and weakness in order to prolong periods of lying-in. As working wives and mothers, they confronted limited choices of survival strategies. Less than 20% of the runaways were women and the more famous female fugitives ran with their families or, as in the case of Harriet Tubman, had no children (Genovese, 1974; White, 1985).

One community worker pointed to these precise historical realities in describing the contemporary problems of Black women. She said:

> Even in slavery times, the man could leave but the woman had to stay. Not only stay but take care of the children and the work. Very few Black women would leave their children to that situation. And the same thing is true now; we still can't leave; we still have to stay in the struggle but I think we've been about the struggle at the most basic level and our realism and our pragmatism reflect that; and we still have ideals and we still have *lofty* ideals which we carry on in the form of culture bearers.

Her perspective was reflected in Angela Davis' (1971) analysis of Black women's roles in the slave community—a role that involved the integration of "toiling under the lash from sun-up to sun-down" with the care of family yet "annulled as woman" so that she could "function as slave."

This life stood in stark contrast to that of White women, who were deemed to be the quintessential definition of womanhood. The stereotypes that stripped black women of their feminine humanity became ideologies by which slave masters justified their sexual exploitation of slave women and further intensifying the "Jezebel," "bad," or "loose" image. Ironically, this immoral woman also raised the master's children. As the large sexless mammy, Black women's nurturant and biological capacities were exploited by the planter class, not only for the sake of their children's material welfare but also for the ideological defense of slavery. Although the actual number of "mammies" was small, they were the ideological and material base for the pedestal on which the planter class placed upper class southern White womanhood. The *ideal* of White womanhood became *reality* where "mammy" existed.

Sociologically, "mammies" were imaged as the highest ranking slaves on plantations sharing the closest and most sentimental relationships with the master and mistress. They were invested with a false image of power. As deviant mother—a corollary of the "myth of the bad Black woman," the White children's needs took precedence over the needs of these slave women's own. Masters used this reality to demonstrate the good will and love present within the "peculiar institution," and to negate the Black woman's humanity and to emphasize the slave's lack of commitment to the family. This powerful image, what DuBois (1972) called "a perversion of motherhood" (p. 41) in response to southerners' attempts to erect a bronze statue to "mammy" in Washington DC, loomed large in popular culture. This physically large woman remains the only role for which a Black woman has received an academy award (Noble, 1978).

The "mammy" with her illusion of power performed all of the drudgery of the female world. The tasks of housekeeping and child care became "mammy's." Her White mistress was projected as dependent on mammy's loyalty, devotion, and skills. The image of "mammy's" competence and her mistress's dependence was based on another dimension of deviant womanhood, strength—physical, emotional, and spiritual strength. Emotional stability and physical strength were required for capable management of mansions and planter class children. Emotional instability, vapors, and fragility were "privileges" reserved for upper class women. By doing all of the dirty work of womanhood, mammy's labor supported and enhanced the ideal woman.

According to Hughes (1971), the moral enhancement of a profession and its exercise of power often depend on its ability to pass on its dirty, routinized, boring, and least rewarding tasks to workers under their control. These repugnant tasks are supposed to elevate the status of those lower in the hierarchy. Mammy contributed to the elevation of White women in a similar way. The dirty work of elite home and child care were passed along to Black women, creating a cultural milieu in which it was unseemly for White women to do it. Christian (1980) pointed to the implications of this arrangement:

> When the Black woman first began to experience and understand the contradictions about motherhood among the southern planters, she must have been truly appalled....[T]hat the planters could relegate the duties of motherhood, a revered and honored state, to a being supposedly lower than human, reveals their own confusion about the value of motherhood. That they could separate spiritual aspects of motherhood, which they acknowledged in their religion, from the physical aspects and give the duties of childrearing to a "subhuman" gives us some indication about the value they placed on women's work. (p. 11)

The enhancement of the status of White women depended on the mistress's passing her dirty work on to Black women. By raising "mammy" above the rest of the slaves and conferring upon her the ambiguous privilege of White women's dirty work, the White woman's status was protected, purified, and dignified. The Black woman's status became the dialectical opposite of the White woman's (Dill, 1979). Ultimately, the ideological stability of slavery rested on the perception of Black women as deviants—bad and dangerous women and mothers who became the ideological centerpieces in cultural institution of American racism.

An irony of slavery was the relative social equality between Black women and men. This social arrangement elicited another set of stereotypes assaulting both women and men. After slavery, Black women continued to work in large numbers, by the turn of the century at two and one half times the rate of White women and this work was targeted as further evidence of racial inferiority (Cox, 1940; DuBois, 1969; Frazier, 1939; Miller, 1905/1968).

As the labor force demanded more female labor (Oppenheimer, 1970, 1973), White women increased their labor force participation and Black women continued their participation at higher rates with more continuity and at lower economic and prestige levels. Every upward shift in the demand for female labor placed White women into job levels higher than those held by Black women. This occupational pattern reflected social patterns of the women's world established during slavery. Black women, as deviant women, were denied access to many of the "female" occupations, especially those such as secretary and department store clerk where feminine image was involved. One community worker described her early job as the "first" department store clerk in downtown Hamptonville as evidence of the problem. Anecdotes, such as that told by labor executive Addie Wyatt, indicate that Black women, because of their "unfeminine" image, were occasionally sent to better paying male jobs. Addie Wyatt had applied for a job as a secretary and was sent to work in meat packing, a higher paying men's job that led to her achieving the rank of vice president of the international union. Such incidents point to the importance of employers' moral evaluations of Black women. The rigidity of White over Black in the women's labor market is so evident that equality between Black and White women "is likely to take at least several generations to attain" and "one might well predict continuing discontent with American society among Black women" (Feagin, 1970, pp. 31, 33). Although the negative stereotypes persist, Black women do not retreat from the labor force. Within this context of economic inequality and moral denigration, organized Black women, as is evident in the present sample, maintain a high level of race pride, political activism, and community uplift.

"LIFTING AS WE CLIMB": A RESPONSE
TO LABELING AND INSTITUTIONAL RACISM

Black women's response to their labeling, historically, has been organized, public, and national, "the first national articulation of Black prophetic practices...[p]redating the National Urban League and the National Association for the Advancement of Colored People..." (West, 1988, p. 45). Black women organized the National Federation of Afro-American women partly in response to insults published in the White press calling Black women prostitutes and liars as an attempt to undercut Ida B. Wells's antilynching efforts. The Federation merged with the Colored Women's League, to form the National Association of Colored Women after the two groups had held their 1896 national meetings in Washington, DC (Barnett, 1970; Davis, 1933; Fields, 1948; Giddings, 1984; Holt, 1964; Lerner, 1972; Terrell, 1940b).[1] These organizations provided the foundation for Black women's energetic organizing on a variety of political, economic, and cultural issues and levels. Later when northern migration and urban politics had placed civil rights on the federal agenda, Black women, under the leadership of Mary McLeod Bethune in 1935, brought these organizations together with many others under the umbrella of the National Council of Negro women.

These efforts consistently stressed the problems of "the Race" and the special problems of Black women at work and at home. Although this was an era of White feminism, the color line and the negative moral evaluations that White women themselves placed on Black woman fanned racial antagonism. White suffragists exacerbated these antagonisms with their accommodation to lynch law, particularly, and racism generally (Andolsen, 1986; Barnett, 1970; Giddings, 1984; Terborg-Penn, 1977; Walker, 1973).

Prompted by these assaultive labels, organized Black women concerned themselves with lynching, peonage labor, prisons, unionization, professional and industrial education, and many other problems affecting both men and women. They initiated surveys of Black working women, sent organizers into areas with no clubs, organized economic cooperatives and mutual aid associations, and developed social services for poor Black women and youth. In response to degrading moral attributions and

---

[1]The Colored Women's League, organized by Mary Church Terrell in 1893, represented the interests of members of the black elite who were allies of W. E. B. DuBois and his arguments regarding the "talented tenth." The National Federation of Afro-American Women, organized by Josephine St. Pierre Ruffin and Margaret Murray Washington (Mrs. Booker T.), was composed of elite and mass Black women. Both groups held their national conventions in Washington, DC, in the summer of 1896. Each organization formed a committee of seven which was responsible for hammering out the details of the merger of the two groups. Mrs. Terrell, a founder of the League, was on the Federation's Committee; Mrs. Fannie Jackson Coppin, a founder of the Federation, was on the League's committee.

stereotypes, the women worked to erase the situations among Black women that fed these stereotypes. This meant organizing across economic and status boundaries. Educated Black women did what feminist Audre Lorde (1988, p. 130) identified as the most liberating thing one can do with one's privilege—acknowledge it in order to make it available for wider use. They organized many clubs to *include* "women in industry"—factory workers, laundresses, and household domestics, and not just educated white-collar workers and professionals.

Such inclusion resulted in the leadership training for women of all social classes. One elderly community worker was a former household domestic whose newspaper column during the 1940s focused on the club activities of Black women in Hamptonville and its surrounding communities. At the time of her interview, she was the president of a club affiliated with the National Association of Colored Women whose projects and programs focused on Black working women. She described the importance of her first "community service club":

> Well I learned a lot about leadership and all that and how to lead a club and how to deal with people and I was president two or three different times; and helped to write the by-laws, those kinds of things. And you learn what different people are like too—different women....We had some women who were very very deprived and some of us who weren't quite as deprived were able to help them a great deal by example and how to really have the proper decorum and everything that some of them didn't have. And some of their habits changed, particularly those who would drink a little too much and use profane language a little too much. They learned that that just wasn't the thing to do and they'd curb themselves and they became a little bit better oriented. All those things were done, and it wasn't done for any sort of lessons or anything that anybody would put a person through. But they learned from association, from other kinds of women; they could see the difference and some of them became wonderful [leaders] and some of them couldn't understand any kind of parliamentary procedure and they started to learn things and after a while they became leaders....So we had a wonderful club.

Examples like this illustrate DuBois's observation that the distinguishing feature of the Black women's club movement was its creation of networks and connections throughout the Black community (DuBois, 1970). Black women understood the implications of their organizing for the entire community. They asserted that by working together for the material and ideological uplift of Black women who were on the bottom, then it would follow that the whole race would rise. The National Association of Colored Women's motto, "Lifting as We Climb," reflected this belief. The activities of Black women in the organizations of the National Council as well as their activities in the Young Women's Christian Association (Lerner, 1972) continued the basic philosophy of the National Association of Colored Women with a more professionalized political strategy that included lobbying and Congressional testimony. Several community workers held volunteer and paid positions with the YWCA and underscored this historical importance. During the Depression and on through World War II, organized Black women continued their concerns for southern rural women, urban women workers, domestic workers, professional women, the economic and social problems of the Black family, birth control, juvenile delinquency, women and children under colonialism, and apartheid.

One can argue that organized Black women are ahead of White women in their concerns, perhaps one of the reasons many Black women prefer Walker's (1983) term *womanist*. These movements recognize that Black women's special problems are tied to the economic, social, and political problems of an entire community. Black women recognize clearly that the negative stereotypes of them are tied to ideological assaults on Black men. In spite of these labels, and perhaps partly because of them, Black women work aggressively in the public affairs of the Black community, using their autonomous organizations as a springboard to community wide leadership. The formation and growth of these movements demonstrate that Black women are not antagonistic to the ideals of contemporary feminism. Instead one must point to the labeling of Black women and their work as that which isolated their potential contributions. This was indeed the case for many community workers in Hamptonville.

"FIRST AND FOREMOST, POWERLESSNESS": DEBUNKING THE MATRIARCHY

Community workers felt most abused by the label "matriarch." As part of an inept analysis of the historical role of Black women, the "matriarch" legitimated the Sapphire stereotype in an unprecedented way. According to a report issued by the Johnson administration, Black women violated the norms in "a society that presumes male leadership in public and private affairs. The arrangements of society facilitate such leadership and reward it" (Rainwater & Yancey, 1967, p. 45). In the process of addressing the problems of Black poverty, family structure, and male unemployment, Black women and their work became part of the Black problem. It was implied that Black male employment problems were exacerbated by the labor force participation of Black women and that efforts to "insure equal employment opportunity for Negroes...have redounded mostly to the benefit of Negro women, and may even have accentuated the comparative disadvantage of Negro men." Many analyses, especially Jackson's (1971, 1973, 1978), demonstrate that the disadvantage of Black men is purely relative to White men and that there is *no* Black male disadvantage in the labor force *relative to Black women.*

The "matriarch" label undermined Black women within their own communities. Murray (1970) described the consequences of the matriarch label at a more general level. She noted that *Ebony*, in a special issue on Black women in 1966:

> felt it necessary to include a full-page editorial to counter the possible effect of articles by women contributors. After paying tribute to the Negro woman's contributions in the past, the editorial reminded *Ebony*'s readers that "the past is behind us," that "the immediate goal of the Negro woman today should be the establishment of a strong family unit in which the father is the dominant person," and that the Negro woman would do well to follow the example of the Jewish mother "who pushed her husband to success, educated her male children first, and engineered good marriages for her daughters." The editors also declared that the career woman "should be willing to postpone her aspirations until her children, too, are old enough to be on their own." (pp. 354–355)

Some community workers in Hamptonville, heads of their own agencies, were asked, as one administrator told it, "to step aside and let a man take over. It looks bad for 'the Race.'"

Black women responded to this label, "matriarch," and its implications, by producing a spate of literature criticizing erroneous assumptions concerning Black women's advantage in the labor market. They also explored the Black female experience with reference to Black men in order to correct distortions, battle myths, and to provide self-affirmation in spite of the labeling (Cade, 1970; Carson, 1969; Exum, 1974; Lewis, 1978). Reid (1972), in a national sampling of ideologies at the grass roots level, identified a deep discontent among Black women with the matriarch label. Many felt that the label presented Black women to Black men in White middle-class terms and they repeatedly underscored Black women's lack of access to Black men. Writers and community workers alike emphasized the importance of Black women's defending themselves. As the White feminist movement was beginning, Black women were forced to prove their femininity, to examine seriously their culpability in Black male "emasculation," and yet at the same time to maintain their position in the civil rights/Black power movements and in their communities. As Cade (1970) described the situation:

> Unfortunately, quite a few of the ladies have been so browbeaten in the past with the Black Matriarch stick that they tend to run, leap, fly to the pots and pans, the back row, the shadows, eager to justify themselves in terms of ass, breasts, collard greens just to prove that they are not the evil, ugly, monsters of tradition. (p. 163)

One community worker saw the matriarchy label as an extension of the southern myth of free White men and free Black women. She challenged this label, insisting:

> The Black woman is never a threat to a White man no matter what position she holds, and no matter how many of us come together in a group....We can't define Black womanhood...it's been defined for us [referring to the "matriarchy."] Black womanhood means first and foremost powerlessness. I think that that myth that the White male and the Black female are the only ones who are free is manifestly absurd because you can't be free if you're powerless and there's no question that we're the most powerless group in the culture, in the society today. We can't even protect our own children and that is the ultimate test of powerlessness as far as I'm concerned. We can't even protect our own children.

Ultimately, the designation of an activity in society as deviant is a political act. The status of a deviant group, or the effectiveness of a society's label, is determined through political conflict. Some viewed the matriarchy thesis as a purely political device that blamed the victims and weakened the national Black community's political organizing by creating hostility toward Black women (King, 1973; Patton, 1970). In light of the history of Black women's political movements, particularly their visibility as lobbyists and advocates in Washington, DC through the Women's Bureau in the Labor Department, it is not unreasonable to assert a political motive identifying Black women as the matriarchs who crippled the economic and political aspirations of Black men. Labeling Black women and their work a matriarchy intensified the moral devaluation they faced historically. At the height of change and transition within Black communities, Black women faced the need for a time consuming and politically deflective response to this intensified labeling.

CONFRONTING THE POLITICS OF ISOLATION

Labeling also separates and isolates "bad" people from "good" people. For Black women this isolation is heightened at the beginning of a new women's movement. Labeling adds to existing political and economic gaps, and undermines much of the potential for a racially unified women's movement. The labeling of Black women and their work also isolates them, as Black men viewed them through the prism of White definitions. Such isolation and conflict diverts Black women's critical energies away from the hierarchies of injustice in the overall society. One community worker, an educator critical of the matriarch label and involved with White women's groups described the problems. She said:

There *are* white people in the world who understand the limitations of the dominant culture as it has manifested itself....Women in women's groups or women's movements who want to do serious studies about Black women, and how black women are at the bottom, and [these White women] associate the socioeconomic structure and all of that, [White women] who want Black women to join the fight against sexism and see that there's no natural coalition unless you see those same [White] people fighting racism over here. They [White women] can't leave that [the fight against racism] to us and capitalize on the benefits and privileges of being White while still hoping that some of those [Black] women will come in and help them fight their battles with their men which essentially a lot of that comes down to for some women.

That conflict with "their men" makes Black women cautious about applying the White feminist critique to Black men. One community worker cautioned:

Many of our men labor under anti-African definitions of themselves and they can be as sexist as anybody and some of our internal structures reflect that including our families....I think it's true that while Black men suffer from racism and classism, that we [Black women] suffer from racism, classism, and sexism, even within the group and that's a problem. [But], I don't think Black men are the first people we need to direct our attention to.

In spite of their separation and critique of feminism, some middle-class Black professional women did form Black women's feminist organizations (Lewis, 1977). While disagreeing with White definitions of feminist issues, community workers maintained close working relationships with diverse White women's organizations. Aware of the isolating effects of labeling, they also pointed to the practical importance of their involvement. One elected official argued, "We cannot permit the White woman to control the women's movement and to set the agenda. [Black women] have got to be in it in order to help direct that agenda."

The position of Black women in society and their relationship to White feminism cannot be understood without reference to the moral isolation of labeling. Pointing to the structural isolation of Black women in the job market, Lewis (1977) was optimistic about the feminist potential of Black women, particularly as they face more and more sex discrimination. However, community workers and the organizational history of which they are a part demonstrate that Black women espouse feminist or womanist ideologies within their organizations and movements and combine this with a collective historical self-consciousness in response to labeling. It is not only the structural isolation in the economic system that blunts Black women's participation, but it is also the moral isolation of labeling.

As part of their response to labeling, Black women examine every White organization critically. Their community and church experiences teach them to cherish their autonomy. My own data on Black women community workers show that these women participate in a wide range of organizations simultaneously: labor, public educational groups, health organizations, traditional civil rights organizations, religious groups, churches, professional associations, party politics, and radical political organizations. These multiple affiliations are pragmatic and address acute survival problems all Black people face. Community workers as women experienced in the work of the Civil Rights movement, local community organizations, and autonomous Black women's organizations, are realistically critical of white feminist organizations. Until Black women are freed from the deviant labels that are ideologies of domination and racism, they will continue to keep a cautious distance from many aspects of contemporary feminism.

Isolated by their conflicts with labels, Black women are still forced to expend additional energy convincing the Black community that their "deviant" contributions of time, money, energy, talent, and leadership are not a threat to the credibility and advancement of "the Race." These intragroup strains and stresses exacerbate the pre-existent economic and political antagonisms. The labeling of Black women is a function of a society that is both racist and sexist in not only its institutional arrangements but also its moral hierarchy, placing additional burdens on Black women. The labeling of Black women and their work represents an additional barrier to be removed before a truly united and integrated movement for total human liberation can be achieved.

ACKNOWLEDGMENTS

Earlier versions of this chapter were presented to the American Sociological Association, 1979 Annual Meeting, and distributed as Working Paper No. 66 of the Wellesley College Center for Research on Women. Support for research and various stages of writing were provided by the National Fellowships Fund and the Minority Fellowship Program of the American Sociological Association. Blanche Geer, Joan Arches, Carol Owen, and Murray Melbin provided valuable comments on this paper.

REFERENCES

Andolsen, B.H. (1986). *Daughters of Jefferson, daughters of bootblacks: Racism and American feminism.* Macon, GA: Mercer University Press.

Barnett, I.B.W. (1970). *Crusade for justice: The autobiography of Ida B. Wells*. Chicago: University of Chicago Press.

Becher, H. S. (1973). *Outsiders: Studies in the sociology of deviance*. New York: The Free Press.

Bond, J.C., & Peery, P. (1970). Is the black male castrated? In T. Cade (Ed.), *The black woman: An anthology (pp. 113–118). New York: New American Library*.

Cade, T. (Ed.). (1970). *The black woman: An anthology*. New York: New American Library.

Carson, J. (1969). *Silent voices: The southern negro woman today*. New York: Dell.

Christian, B. (1980). *Black women novelists: The development of a tradition, 1892–1976*. Westport, CT: Greenwood Press.

Cox, O.C. (1940). Sex ratio and marital status among negroes. *American Sociological Review, 5*, 937–947.

Davis, A. (1971). The black woman's role in the community of slaves. *The Black Scholar 3*(4), 2–15.

Davis, A. (1981). *Women, race, and class*. New York: Random House.

Davis, E.L. (1933). *Lifting as they climb: A history of the National Association of Colored Women*. Washington, DC: Moorland-Spingarn Research Center, Howard University.

Dill, B.T. (1979). The dialectics of black womanhood: Towards a new model of American femininity. *Signs: Journal of Women in Culture and Society, 4*(3), 543–555.

Dill, B.T. (1980). The means to put my children through. In L.R. Rose (Ed.). *The black woman* (pp. 107–123). Beverly Hills, CA: Sage.

Dill, B.T. (1988). Making your job good yourself: Domestic service and the construction of personal dignity. In A. Bookman & S. Morgen (Eds), *Women and the politics of empowerment* (pp. 33–52). Philadelphia: Temple University Press.

DuBois, W.E.B. (1969). The damnation of women. In *Darkwater: Voices from within the veil* (pp. 163–192). New York: Schocken Books.

DuBois, W.E.B. (1970). *The gift of black folk: The negroes in the making of America*. New York: Washington Square Press.

DuBois, W.E.B. (1972). The black mother. In D. Walden (Ed.), *The crisis writings* (pp. 340–342). Greenwich, CT: Fawcett. (Originally published 1912)

Exum, P.C. (1974). *Keeping the faith: Writings by contemporary black women*. Greenwich, CT: Fawcett.

Feagin, J.R. (1970). Black women in the American work force. In C.V. Willie (Ed.), *The family life of black people* (pp. 23–35). Columbus, OH: Charles E. Merrill.

Fields, E.L. (1948). *The women's club movement in the United States, 1877–1900*. Unpublished master's thesis, Washington, DC, Moorland Spingarn Research Center, Howard University.

Frazier, E.F. (1939). *The negro family in the United States*. Chicago: University of Chicago Press.

Genovese, E. (1974). *Roll Jordan roll: The world the slaves made*. New York: Random House.

Giddings, P. (1984). *When and where I enter...: The impact of black women on race and sex in America*. New York: William Morrow.

Gilkes, C.T. (1982). Successful rebellious professionals: The black woman's professional identity and community commitment. *Psychology of Women Quarterly, 6*(3), 289–311.

Gilkes, C.T. (1983). Going up for the oppressed: The career mobility of black women community workers. *Journal of Social Issues 39*(3), 115–139.

Goffman, E. (1963). Stigma: Notes on the management of spoiled identity. Englewood Cliffs, NJ: Prentice-Hall.

Holt, R. (1964). *Mary McLeod Bethune: A biography.* Garden City, NY: Doubleday.

Hughes, E.C. (1971). The sociological eye. Chicago: Aldine.

Jackson, J.J. (1971). But where are the men? *The Black Scholar 3*(4), 30–41.

Jackson, J.J. (1973). Black women in a racist society. In C.V. Willie, B. Kramer, & B. Brown (Eds.), *Racism and Mental Health* (pp. 185–258. Pittsburgh, PA: University of Pittsburgh Press.

Jackson, J.J. (1978). The mythological black woman, she ain't nowhere to be found. In D.J. Mitchell & J. H. Bell (Eds.), *The black woman: Myths and realities (pp. 10–23). Cambridge, MA: Radcliffe College.*

King, M.C. (1973). The politics of sexual stereotypes. *The Black Scholar, 4*(6–7), 12–23.

LaRue, L.J.M. (1971). Black liberation and women's lib. In I.L. Horowitz & C. Nanry (Eds.), *Sociological realities II: A guide to the study of society* (pp. 282–287). New York: Harper & Row.

Lerner, G. (1972). *Black women in white America: A documentary history.* New York: Random House.

Lewis, D.K. (1977). A response to inequality: Black women, racism, and sexism. *Signs: A Journal of Women in Culture and Society 3*(2), 339–361.

Lewis, T.L. (1978). The imbalance of black males and black females: Implications for black family structure. In D.J. Mitchell & J.H. Bell (Eds.), *The black woman: Myths and realities* (pp. 61–64). Cambridge, MA: Radcliffe College.

Lorde, A. (1988). *A burst of light.* Ithaca, NY: Firebrand Books.

Miller, K. (1968). *Surplus negro women. Radicals and conservatives and other essays on the negro in America.* New York: Schocken Books. (Originally published 1905)

Mitchell, D.J., & Bell, J.F. (Eds.). (1978). *The black woman: Myths and realities.* Cambridge, MA: Radcliffe College.

Murray, A. (1973). White norms, black deviation. In J.A. Ladner (Ed.), *The death of white sociology* (pp. 104–105). New York: Random House.

Murray, P. (1970). The liberation of black women. In M.L. Thompson (Ed.), *Voices of the new feminism.* Boston: Beacon Press.

Murray P. (1972). Jim Crow and Jane Crow. In G. Lerner (Ed.), *Black women in white America.* (pp. 592–599). New York: Random House.

Noble, J. (1978). *Beautiful, also, are the souls of my black sisters: A history of the black woman in America.* Englewood Cliffs, NJ: Prentice-Hall.

Oppenheimer, V. (1970). *The female labor force in the United States: Demographic and economic factors governing its growth and changing composition.* Westport, CT: Greenwood Press.

Oppenheimer, V. (1973). Demographic influence on female employment and the status of women. In J. Huber (Ed.), *Changing women in a changing society* (pp. 184–199). Chicago: University of Chicago Press.

Parkhurst, J. (1938). The role of the black mammy in the plantation household. *Journal of Negro History, 23,* 349–369.

Patton, G.C. (1970). Black people and the victorian ethos. In T. Cade (Ed.), *The black woman: An anthology* (pp. 143–148). New York: New American Library.

Rainwater, L., & Yancey, W.L. (1967). *The Moynihan report and the politics of controversy.* Cambridge, MA: MIT Press.

Reid, I.S. (1972). *"Together" black women.* New York: Emerson Hall.

Rollins, J. (1985). *Between women: Domestics and their employers.* Philadelphia: Temple University Press.

Rubington, E., & Weinberg, M.S. (1987). *Deviance: The interactionist perspective* (5th ed.) New York: MacMillan.

Ryan, W. (1971). *Blaming the victim.* New York: Random House.

Scheff, T.J. (1966). *Being mentally ill: A sociological theory.* Hawthorne, NY: Aldine.

Schur, E.M. (1980). *The politics of deviance: Stigma contests and the uses of power.* Englewood Cliffs, NJ: Prentice-Hall.

Schur, E.M. (1984). *Labeling women deviant: Gender, stigma, and social control.* New York: Random House.

Staples, R. (1971). The myth of the black matriarchy. In *The black family: Essays and studies.* Belmont, CA: Wadsworth.

Staples, R. (1973). *The black woman in America.* Chicago: Nelson Hall.

Terborg-Penn, R. (1977). *Afro-Americans in the struggle for woman suffrage.* Unpublished doctoral dissertation, Howard University, Washington, DC.

Terrell, M.C. (1940a). *A colored woman in a white world.* Washington, DC: Ransdell.

Terrell, M.C. (1940b). The history of the club women's movement. *The Aframerican Woman's Journal, 1*(2–3), 34–38.

Walker, A. (1983). *In search of our mothers' gardens: Womanist prose.* San Diego: Harcourt Brace Jovanovich.

Walker, S. (1973). Frederick Douglass and woman suffrage. *The Black Scholar, 4*(6–7), 24–31.

Wallace, M. (1978). *Black macho and the myth of the superwoman.* New York: Dial Press.

West, C. (1988). The prophetic tradition in Afro-America. In *Prophetic fragments* (pp. 38–49). Grand Rapids, MI and Trenton, NJ: William B. Eerdmans and Africa World Press.

White, D.G. (1985). *Ar'n't I a woman: Female slaves in the antebellum south.* New York: W. W. Norton.

Williams, D. (1986). The color of feminism. *Journal of Religious Thought, 43*(1), 42–58.

Chapter 10

Work, Relationships, and Balance in the Lives of Gifted Women

Diane Tickton Schuster
California State University, Fullerton

Gifted women. The label conjures up diverse images: an assortment of accomplished scientists, politicians, and feminist activists on the one hand, and a range of undiscovered artists, reclusive academics, underemployed reentry women, and ambivalent teenage math students on the other. Our images sometimes are supported by the stories of celebrated women, women whose autobiographies or poems or essays have given us glimpses into the struggles and achievements that have accompanied personal or professional growth. More often, however, we read that most gifted women are underachievers struggling to find genuine outlets for their interests and abilities, impeded by personal and societal barriers to success. Recently, Noble (1987) speculated that: "By adulthood it is likely that the majority of gifted women...settle for far less than their full potential" (p. 368).

Social pressures, cultural expectations, and negative self-concepts all appear to work against gifted women's confidence, achievement, and visibility in the work force (Noble, 1987). Psychological interpersonal vulnerabilities have been identified as significant inhibitors to the full development of gifted women's competence (Hollinger & Fleming, 1984; Kerr, 1985; Reis, 1987; Schwartz, 1980). Despite the conventional expectations that intellectually talented girls will have an "edge" on coping with the demands of the academic world and that gifted college graduates will have a head start on career pursuits, there is little empirical evidence that giftedness is the critical variable in the success or well-being of educated women (Reis, 1987).

Curiously, in recent efforts to document and explain the accomplishments and concerns of gifted women, only rarely have these women been asked to describe their life experiences, their work, their relationships, or the significance of "giftedness" in their personal or professional development. We have not determined whether the lives of gifted women are notably different from those of their nongifted midlife peers, or whether during adulthood gifted women have felt affirmed or burdened by their intellectual strengths. Moreover, much of our conceptualization of the gifted has been framed by studies of earlier cohorts, such as the Terman group (Terman, 1925; Terman & Oden, 1947, 1959) that was born around 1910 or the Ginzberg (1966) and Birnbaum (1975) groups that were born during the Depression years. As Bardwick (1980) pointed out, when we seek to evaluate the adult experience of women, we cannot ignore the sociohistorical context of their personal and career growth. To date, little research has been conducted on gifted women who were raised with "traditional" values and whose education predated the women's movement; relatively little is known about that cohort that entered adulthood concurrent with the resurgence of feminism in the 1960s, and arrived at midlife when professional opportunities for bright women had become more widely available. During the past decade, the experience of talented women in a variety of careers has been documented (Abramson & Franklin, 1986; Gallese, 1985; Morantz, Pomerlau, & Fenichel, 1982; O'Connell & Russo, 1983; Sternburg, 1980) but cross-sections of midlife gifted women have received limited attention.

In order to address the lack of information about the personal and phenomenological experience of gifted women, I recently conducted a longitudinal follow-up study of gifted women who had first been studied in the late 1950s. This study provided an opportunity for a close, detailed examination of the adult development of a group of gifted women now at midlife. Quantitative and qualitative data from 35 women were used to assess how women identified as gifted in the 1950s have experienced giftedness and competence in the personal and interpersonal domains of their lives. In addition, analyses of extensive interview data provided new insight to "the experience and meaning of work" for gifted women.

PREVIOUS RESEARCH ON GIFTED WOMEN

This investigation was informed by earlier studies of gifted women. As previously stated, the seminal research on gifted women was conducted at a time when educated women typically did not seek to enter fully or compete in the work force. Of the 671 gifted girls studied by Terman, only 253 were working full time at midlife; among the married women in his study, fewer than one third worked full time (Terman & Oden, 1959). In 1968, Terman's associate, Melita Oden, compared the gifted women to their male counterparts and concluded that, "On the whole, the gifted women have not shown marked interest in, or ambition for, a high degree of vocational achievement outside the home" (Oden, 1968, p. 25).

Later studies of gifted women (Birnbaum, 1975; Faunce, 1967; Ginzberg, 1966; Helson, 1967; Yohalem, 1979) revealed that, during the post-World War II years, gifted women tended to be persistent in their efforts to utilize their intellectual or creative talents, despite inequitable pay in the labor market and inhospitable social milieux that discouraged career-plus-family lifestyles. Birnbaum (1975) reported that the most satisfied gifted women were married professionals who viewed themselves as both "unconventional" and "dependent." Birnbaum concluded that, for gifted women of the 1940s and 1950s, career and personal gratification rested heavily on the willingness of the individual to "buck the tide" and be an independent thinker; at the same time, life satisfaction was correlated with the availability of a supportive spouse on whom the gifted professional woman could rely for emotional reinforcement.

During the past decade, Birnbaum's findings about gifted women have been echoed in studies of gifted girls who have been compared to their female nongifted peers; typically gifted girls have been described as follows:

> From an early age gifted girls appear to be more achievement-oriented, more interested in non-traditional professions, more rebellious against sex-role stereotyping, and more rejecting of outside influences that hinder their development. (Noble, 1987, p. 371)

Despite this general profile of gifted girls and despite the increased education of women and the broader involvement of talented women in the work force, recent reports (Kerr, 1985; Reis, 1987) have documented that gifted women still hesitate to seek careers in traditionally male-dominated fields, do not advance in most career fields as rapidly as male counterparts, and do not feel particularly adequate in their pursuit of multiple roles in adult life. In this sense, Reis (1987) has suggested that although, as children, gifted girls may look academically and socially dissimilar to their nongifted peers, their giftedness likely will be gauged by career-related standards in later life and they ultimately may not seem so different from other women of their age cohort.

The issues of *social awkwardness* and *problems with social efficacy* have begun to emerge as major concerns of gifted females. Kerr (1985) and Reis (1987) identified diverse emotional constraints such as conflicts about femininity, ambivalence about success, perfectionism, "imposter" concerns, and unrealistic planning, that may have long-term consequences for gifted women. Hollinger and Fleming (1984) reported a high incidence of low social competence among gifted female adolescents. Rodenstein, Pfleger, and Colangelo (1977) and Noble (1987) articulated the mixed societal messages that likely confound gifted women in their pursuit of the "multipotentialed" life. Noble (1987) concluded that during adulthood gifted women may be especially vulnerable to feelings of inadequacy and conflict. Burdened with their own high standards and the expectations of the society around them, these women may feel inordinately pressured to be superwomen, to put their intellectual competencies at the center of their lives, and to neglect the need for "balance" that has been identified as a central issue in the adult well-being of women (Baruch, Barnett, & Rivers, 1983). For women generally, the achievement of balance requires an ongoing calibration—a fine-tuning of how energies are distributed, how relationships are sustained, and how choices are made. The existing literature on gifted women suggests that for this group—women who may bear the scars of long-term social vulnerability as well as the burdens of high self-demands—the achievement of balance in adult life may remain distressingly "out of reach."

THE GIFTED FOLLOW-UP STUDY

In 1957, 41 women who entered the University of California, Los Angeles, as freshmen were selected for participation in a new program for students who had been identified as "gifted." These students ranked in the top 10% on a battery of national scholastic aptitude examinations and constituted approximately the top 5% of UCLA's incoming class. When tested as freshmen, they demonstrated significantly higher ego strength, greater appreciation for theoretical and aesthetic issues, and greater interest in nontraditional occupations than their nongifted peers. While attending UCLA, the gifted women were offered special counseling designed to encourage the full expression of their interests and abilities. Their undergraduate experience was reported by Langland (1961), and data about these students' academic performance, aptitudes, and values were stored for later analysis.

In 1984–1985, I located 38 of the 1957 group of UCLA gifted women (Schuster, 1986). Thirty-five women, constituting 85% of the entire cohort, agreed to participate in the Gifted Follow-up Study and to provide, via questionnaires and interviews, detailed information about their background, their adult development, and their attitudes about such issues as work, competence, giftedness, relationships, and balance at midlife.

In light of the literature on gifted women that has pointed to the absence of longitudinal and phenomenological data on this population, my investigation was designed to obtain in-depth information about these women's lives. Accordingly, several questions were posed at the outset:

1. Who were these women? What was their background? What was their undergraduate experience like? What characterized their adult lives? And what were they "doing" now?

2. What could these women tell us about the experience of giftedness over the life cycle? Was giftedness important to them? Had it been a source of conflict in childhood, adolescence, or adulthood?

3. What had been the social experience of these women? Had giftedness affected their sense of social acceptability or social efficacy? Had they felt socially inhibited as a result of their superior abilities? How would they describe their relationships in adulthood?

4. What characterized the work lives of these gifted women? What kinds of careers had they pursued and what had mattered to them in their work endeavors?

5. What did these women have to say about "balance" at midlife?

The findings provided a broad overview of the lives of 35 gifted women at midlife and also raised some important questions about the needs and concerns of gifted women today.

Group Characteristics

The following group profile was drawn from questionnaires that the UCLA gifted women completed in 1984 (mean age: 45) prior to participating in personal interviews. The women came from a range of socioeconomic backgrounds, but nearly three quarters grew up in white, middle-class, stable families in which the fathers were fully employed and the mothers were homemakers. Of the 35 women, 32 were first-born or only children.

The women's descriptions of themselves as children were differentiated into three categories: a "shy" group (63%) who described themselves as having been quiet, obedient, "good" girls; an "outgoing" group (31%) who recalled having been gregarious, popular, and generally happy leaders during their school years; and a "socially uncomfortable" group (6%) who remembered themselves as anxious, insecure, or overly aggressive during childhood.

On the whole, the gifted women reported that they fared very well academically throughout their school years. None attended high schools that had special programs for gifted students. Although the majority knew from parents and teachers that they were intellectually talented, few recalled having received specific encouragement to plan for professional careers or to pursue rigorous academic programs.

Of the 35 women, 33 earned BA degrees (28 from UCLA). As undergraduates, 45% chose nontraditional majors in the sciences, mathematics, or business. Of the women, 60% earned advanced degrees, including six doctorates, five law degrees, and one medical degree.

Over half of the gifted women worked throughout adult life. In 1984, 83% were involved in professional work at least half time. Listed in Table 10.1 are the diverse career activities in which the UCLA gifted women were engaged at midlife.

Three quarters of the women were married within 3 years of college graduation, and in 1984 more than half had been married for 19 or more years. Of 14 women who divorced, 5 had remarried by midlife. One woman had not married.

Of these women, 80% had children, most during their 20s. At midlife only 11% of these women had children still in elementary school, and most were about to "empty the nest."

When surveyed in 1984, most of the gifted women were involved in both work and community activities. When asked about the impact of the major social or political movements of the 1960s and 1970s, only a handful indicated any longstanding interest, involvement or activism. As a group, these women described themselves as relatively conservative in terms of current lifestyle, but "unconventional" relative to the values with which they had been raised. While the married women more often than not rated themselves as dependent on their husbands for emotional support, none of the women viewed themselves as dependent in terms of earning potential or the capacity for self-sufficiency.

Overall, the women rated themselves as being in good-to-excellent physical, emotional, and spiritual health. The majority indicated that they felt they had lived up to their intellectual potential and rated themselves as relatively high in life satisfaction. The least satisfied women were those who were unemployed or underemployed, with divorced women demonstrating lower satisfaction than married women.

The Meaning of Giftedness in the Lives of Gifted Women

One of my objectives in studying gifted women was to find out what they had to say about giftedness. How did they experience their own giftedness? What was the impact on their development of having been told they were gifted?

In the interviews, I asked the women to elaborate on their "experience of being bright, gifted, intellectually able during childhood and adolescence"

TABLE 10.1
Current Activities of Gifted Follow-Up Study Women

Field	Position/Activity	n=35
Education	Secondary school teaching	4
	Community college teaching	2
	College teaching	2
	University administration	1
Social sciences	Community leader/organizer	2
	Social service administration	1
	Social science research	1
	Clinical psychologist	1
Science/engineering	Applied math research	1
	Scientific research	1
Medicine	Physician	1
	Nurse	1
	Medical technology	1
Business/government	Certified Public Accountant	2
	Management consultant	1
	Government administrator	1
	Home-based crafts manufacturer	1
	Administrative assistant	1
Law	Attorney	2
	Legal consultant	1
Art/music/literature	Artist	1
	Art collector/gallery owner	1
	Assistant film producer	1
	Piano teacher	1
	Writer/journalist	1
Religion	Minister	1
Homemaking	Homemaker	1

and to speculate about the overall impact of having been identified as gifted during their formative years. Fifteen of the women (43%) described the experience of giftedness in positive terms. For example, one woman stated:

Giftedness was positive. School was easy. My best friend was more gifted than I....My teachers encouraged me. I remember a high school philosophy teacher who told me I had an original mind.

Another commented:

Being bright made it easier in school. I never had to struggle like others did....I chose the smartest friends and always had a core group. My teachers would try to bring me out, teasing, "We know you're shy."

And a third said:

> I always knew I was smart in some areas. And I had a lot of reinforcement from
> my parents. I could memorize things, do recitations; I knew that others my age
> were not doing these things. I had a long interest span. I knew I was different.
> I didn't know many others who liked to be quiet, who had more fun being
> quiet. When we moved from the city to the affluent suburbs in junior high, it
> was the first time of being with lots of people who were smarter than I was. I
> met a girl the first day of school who said, "You are not one of the silly people."
> I always had a lot of close friends who were very bright.

The "positive" women generally mentioned having found a peer group of friends at least as bright as themselves. They indicated that they always had taken being bright for granted. They described giftedness as the ability to learn and perform quickly.

For the majority of the gifted women, however, feelings about giftedness were less sanguine. Reflecting on their childhood and adolescent experiences, 20 (57%) of the women recalled situations in which they felt ignored, discounted, embarrassed, or downright discouraged about their intellectual talents. In this group, few women felt that their apparent abilities had been prized by their families or their teachers, and many felt a lack of peer-group affirmation or support. Giftedness was, as one woman put it,

> no big deal. It functioned for me in high school, because I was socially inse-
> cure. I expected to get good grades. The teachers took it for granted. I knew
> what I wanted [to work in a medical field]....There was no intellectual environ-
> ment at home. I was able to know what the teachers expected. I was able to
> concentrate, I was a fast learner; but once the test was over, I'd forget it all.

Another observed:

> Prior to going to UCLA, I hadn't thought much about my having any gifted
> abilities. It was not a big factor in my life. I did the same normal things as ev-
> erybody else. Perhaps if my parents had been smarter....I was thought of as a
> dependable person who'd do no wrong. I missed an important part of grow-
> ing up; I was never turbulent; I was too responsible.

A third stated:

> I felt like I was an outsider in my family. I was different from them. I remember
> at age six, I wanted to be an expert in some area. I felt apart from my family,

from the people they associated with. I was bookish. My mother would say, "Go out and play, get more exercise"....I wish I had gotten personal, private strokes...between fifth grade and ninth grade I wasted so much time, I was so bored, I was treading water.

For these women, giftedness was alienating. During critical developmental years their intellectual identities lacked mooring or nurturance. Some of these women also expressed a general disregard for the concept of giftedness. For example, a woman who had earned a doctorate in the social sciences and now worked for a major university stated:

I didn't like UCLA's gifted label. Giftedness was the artifact of a test. This had happened to me in grade school too. I'm verbal, not gifted. I don't have any special talent....Teachers always told me that I wasn't living up to my potential, and I believed them, but I never took my intellect seriously. Doing that would have meant I could see myself as capable of "x" and thus would do "y." I never saw myself that way. I simply assumed I would earn a living—get by in life not using my hands.

This same woman mentioned that her mother had always told her that "it didn't do any good to be bright" and that it was too bad that the daughter was not "a nicer person." Similar sentiments were expressed by another academic who recalled her experience of giftedness with considerable contempt:

Shit! It was very uncomfortable. I had lots of negative reinforcement. I didn't think I was that bright. I always said the wrong things. I wasn't good in school. People always thought my [younger] brother was brighter. My mother would say, "What good are brains with that sarcastic mouth?" My Iowa test scores gave me the first clue, but...I used to lie about the scores, just like I'd cut out the cashmere labels from my sweaters. I was uncomfortable with it. I wanted boys to like me. Being bright wasn't something I thought was neat. I didn't know any bright women....I experienced myself as weird, not popular, loud, not brilliant. All I wanted to do was go to parties. I didn't expect to go to college. My peers were not intellectuals. I just wanted to be accepted.

The women for whom giftedness was essentially negative in adolescence did not, as a group, assert that being labeled as gifted had been detrimental during college or adulthood. In terms of long-term effects, both the positive and the negative groups concluded that the overall impact of the gifted label itself had been either insignificant or neutral. For the "positive" women, especially those who had always taken their intellect seriously, being told they were gifted was just one more affirmation of something they valued in themselves. Some of these women said that they had found the gifted label "comforting" or "reassuring," and the majority indicated that being selected for UCLA's Gifted Student Program had provided an extra boost to their self-image. Ultimately, however, these women found that actual work productivity and achievement were the most important contributors to their positive self-esteem.

For the women who had felt more "negative" about giftedness during adolescence, the discomfort of the gifted identity seemed to abate as they separated from their families or moved toward careers that utilized their interests and abilities. Selection for the Gifted Student Program was especially beneficial to a number of "negative" women who sought academic and personal counseling from the program staff; several women recalled specific statements made to them by a female counselor who encouraged them to value their talents and expand their professional goals. For the more negative women, participation in the program appeared to help undo the stigma of "difference" suffered in earlier years. A few of these women indicated that, as adults, the gifted label still caused them to feel pressured to "prove" themselves or "do more," but the great majority simply were happy to be in careers that allowed them to use their minds and feel effective professionally.

The Social Experience of Gifted Women

As the recent literature on the needs of gifted women has pointed out, the social and interpersonal experience of this population can be fraught with ambivalence, embarrassment, and self-consciousness. For the UCLA gifted women, feelings of social ease and efficacy did not come automatically. As noted earlier, about two thirds of these women reported that they had felt shy or socially uncomfortable as children. From questionnaire self-ratings, it appeared that there was a significant relationship between childhood social vulnerability and adult feelings of social discomfort ($X^2 = 4.08$, $df = 1$, p .05).

In my interviews with the UCLA gifted women I sought to probe more deeply those social circumstances that they described as problematic at home, in school settings, at work, and in close interpersonal relationships over the life cycle. In our discussions of the high school experience, I found that even some of the women who had described giftedness in positive terms recalled having been subjected to a certain amount of social rejection by high school classmates. These women attended high school at a time when most bright girls were stigmatized for their academic accomplishments. As one woman recalled:

> I was good in math in high school, was at the top of the class in algebra and geometry. As a senior, all of a sudden, the boys got better. I didn't want to com-

pete with the men; I wasn't about to go in and stand up for my rights in math class. It wasn't cool to outshine a man. I lost my confidence, thought they were smarter than I was.

Another woman mentioned that she had been "among the top four or five people" in her high school but had "had no real friends." A third woman said: "I had to hide my smartness to be lovable," and then quoted the familiar Dorothy Parker line, "Men seldom make passes at girls who wear glasses." The "hiding" theme was repeated by a woman who described her giftedness as "a secret between my teachers and me." Another recalled having had "two sets of friends"—those who knew her in academically oriented classes and those with whom she partied. Another said that her talents intimidated her peers and consequently she "played dumb, never showed my grades to anyone, and denied my intellect."

The social vulnerability experienced by the UCLA gifted women during high school was seldom mitigated by the interventions of teachers or counselors. Only eight of the women even mentioned having been explicitly encouraged by school personnel; most felt they had been ignored. A shift in social context occurred for many, however, with entry to college and selection for the Gifted Student Program. An administrator described the shift she experienced moving from high school to the university:

> In high school, the teachers never really paid any attention to my abilities. I expected myself to do well...but I didn't feel unique, I took it for granted. I had figured out what it took to "be smart," but a lot of others had caught on to that too. College was a turning point, though. I'll never forget how surprised I was to find out in college that everybody in the room was thinking that it was o.k. You didn't have to be cool about it, to be a thinker.

In a similar vein, an attorney said:

> I got one B all the time I was in high school. I was in the fast track. Then I flunked my first college midterm and was stunned. I learned from that professor how to analyze things—which was very tough—but I loved the notion that there were things to teach me.

For many of the gifted women, the UCLA environment provided both social acceptance and intellectual challenge. They discovered that their giftedness was not an interpersonal handicap and most developed successful social lives.

During the interviews, I asked the gifted women whether they had experienced any social alienation during adult life. Had being gifted, or intellectually competent, caused them any interpersonal conflicts in adulthood?

Had they found that "competence" and "close interpersonal attachments"
could co-exist?

As a group, these women indicated that as adults they indeed had found
ways to assert themselves and their abilities without threatening or jeop-
ardizing their connections with other people. A number of the women mentioned that they had found it helpful to surround themselves with other
competent people, especially with other women with whom they shared a
sense of intellectual equality. As one put it:

> My women friends are competent themselves. Some have less feelings of com-
> petence than they should, but it's voiced and we can encourage one another.
> And others need to be sat on. We all teach each other.

By tending to limit their adult social groups to like-minded peers, the
gifted women generally found they were able to avoid social conflict due to
giftedness. A few of the women did mention experiences in which they had
found that their abilities threatened others, but they also mentioned having
taken deliberate steps to appear less imposing; one observed that

> I don't use my competence against others, don't make others feel smaller. I try
> to make them feel better.

Another woman also mentioned making others comfortable:

> I can think of a couple of examples where relationships came to an end because
> another woman saw me as superwoman. Not that I was. It was their impres-
> sion. I don't now always let my competency come out to the full degree. I have
> been hurt by a close friend feeling inadequate due to my teaching, my manag-
> ing several roles. I set my abilities aside except with other teachers. I put my
> competency in the background so that the relationship is not affected. I hid my
> smarts in high school. At UCLA, I wanted to put smartness behind me, be care-
> free. I have the same role now: it's become a habit, trying to make others com-
> fortable—not to be uncomfortable due to my ability to do things.

From the interviews, it appeared that many of the women had spent their
late teens and early 20s overcoming earlier problems with social inhibition;
during their adult years they had focused more on the development of competence and the achievement of emotional independence. The process of integrating competence and relationships had not always gone smoothly. A
clinician commented:

> I used to believe that I was incomplete and the only way to be liked was to re-
> main incompetent. I believed if I were competent and able, then my relation-

ships would crumble. But they didn't. And my partner has encouraged me to be competent. As I become more competent, I am more "myself."

Another woman indicated that she was still seeking ways to combine the work and intimacy aspects of her life:

> I don't think I am [competent] yet. I'm just now exploring relationships in a new way....Rather than seek my career to the exclusion of relationships, I'm seeing that these two things go hand in hand....Relationships require my believing I am worthy of it, choosing someone who is my equal.

Overall, however, the majority of the women had moved from feelings of social discomfort with their intellectual abilities in high school to a more integrated, comfortable outlook at midlife. As they grew into their adult identities, their competence proved beneficial. As they sustained adult relationships, they felt more accepted. As they separated themselves from nonsupportive environments, they found healthy sources of affirmation and support. They saw positive changes in themselves and their surroundings. As a "new" professional observed?

> Things have gotten a lot better. I've changed the people I'm close to. My relationship with my husband is evolving. As I've changed, I have sought out different kinds of people—people who are very involved, doing things, making it. I used to have incredibly close relationships with mothers of young children. I don't have that kind of time now. I seek people who don't *need* to see me. And I find that men like me better now too, find me more attractive. I've moved to a different place.

Work in the Lives of Gifted Women

In addition to exploring themes about giftedness and competence, I asked the UCLA gifted women about the "experience and meaning of work" in their lives. Because as freshmen these women had demonstrated unusually high ego strength, strong theoretical and aesthetic interests, and preferences for nontraditional fields, I wondered whether they were pursuing careers that tapped their superior intellectual abilities and whether they were heavily career-oriented at midlife. At the same time, because these women had been reared in the 1940s and 1950s when women were expected to devote themselves primarily to family roles, I also wondered how they coped with multiple roles—whether they felt they had successfully integrated both work and intimate relationships.

When surveyed in 1984, the UCLA gifted women provided strong evidence of positive experiences both in the work force and in their personal lives. The majority of the women had worked outside the home throughout their adult lives, and at midlife only three women were not employed in at least some capacity. The criteria used to determine these women's employment history patterns (Table 10.2) were adapted from Ginzberg (1966); from the aggregate data about the women's work lives, several interesting patterns were identified.

First, the number of completed degrees and advanced degrees was unusually high for women who entered undergraduate programs in the late 1950s. The only women in the UCLA gifted group who did not complete bachelor's degrees were a woman who had been a re-entry student in 1957 and then had to drop out due to financial pressures, and a woman who had gotten married during her junior year and had become pregnant shortly thereafter. Both of these women had worked intermittently during adult life and had not felt handicapped by the lack of a bachelor's degree. In terms of advanced degrees, 60% of the women who had earned BAs went on for additional education. For women of this cohort, the proportion who earned advanced degrees—many of them in nontraditional fields such as chemistry, anthropology, medicine, and law—was remarkably high.

Second, nearly all of the women were involved in careers that, by the standards of the era in which they were raised, were "nontraditional." Of the 35 women, only 1 had become a nurse and only 1 worked in an essentially clerical role. None taught at the elementary school level. The piano

TABLE 10.2
Career Histories of 35 Gifted Follow-Up Study Women[*]

	%
Continuous (has held full-time jobs throughout adult life)	31
Minor breaks (has worked full time, but has interrupted her career for short intervals during which she may have worked part time)	23
Intermittent (has spent three or more short periods away from work, has worked part time only, or has re-entered school or the work force, and continues full time)	26
Periodic (has dropped out of full-time work one or more times, and each time for 3 or more years, now works part time)	11
Terminated, temporarily or permanently (has left the labor market after a substantial period of work and has not yet returned to work	6
Minor or none (has had less than 4 years in the labor force or has had no work experience at all)	3

[*]modified version of Ginzberg (1966)

teacher had received a law degree but preferred to teach adults and to pursue extensive musical interests. The range of career fields reflects both the diverse interests of the group and the expanding employment opportunities for women during the past 25 years.

Third, as a group, these women tended to be relatively high achievers, even if they had started careers after their child-rearing years. At midlife, 64% of the group provided evidence that they were utilizing their education and professional training and were earning more than the median income for American women of their age group (U.S. Bureau of the Census, 1984). In addition, several women who had recently begun professional employment anticipated making major career and salary gains within the next several years. Only five women (14%) appeared to be on an ongoing "low-achievement" course.

For the group as a whole, neither longevity in the work force nor current income correlated directly with the women's actual "level of achievement." For example, a university administrator who had earned only a BA had spent many years serving as a community volunteer; eventually she was elected mayor of her small city, and with that experience moved into a significant role of coordinating programs between a major university and political groups. Evaluating this woman's level of achievement could not be based solely on her employment rank or income; at midlife, diverse aspects of her complex "career" contributed to her high level of "success." Similarly, a woman who had worked first as an actress and then as a university administrator completed a law degree in her early 40s; at 46 she was just beginning to build a private law practice and also expressed interest in elective politics. Whatever this woman had attempted, she had been a popular leader. Her likely success as an attorney was easy to envision, and her "achievement level" had to be considered very high despite her limited income in 1984.

Imminent high achievement could also be imagined for a community college English instructor who had spent 10 years as a homemaker and then 7 years completing a doctorate; at midlife this woman described her activities as "teaching English, doing research, writing, giving papers, publishing, and having a ball." This woman brought very high energy and creativity to her work and, despite her relatively low status within her place of employment, her overall profile was one of high achievement.

These women's stories were not exceptional among the UCLA gifted group, and their experience reflected the consistent ability of this sample to move beyond the social conventions and constraints imposed on females of their generation. As adults, these women found ways to utilize their intellectual abilities, to enter and achieve upward professional mobility, and to sustain a strong sense of efficacy and well-being over time.

Fourth, given the accelerating divorce rate for this age cohort during recent years, the number of long-term marriages in the gifted group was disproportionately high. Although a few of the long-married women reported marital distress, the majority indicated that they felt supported emotionally by their husbands and that their marriages had grown richer over the years. Only one woman indicated that her husband had resisted the full development of her intellectual abilities. As a group, the UCLA gifted women appeared to have selected mates whose values and interests complemented their own.

Using even the most conventional measures of achievement for this cohort, therefore, the UCLA gifted women appeared to be an unusually successful, accomplished group at midlife. The majority expressed the belief that they were using their intellectual talents and living up to their potential. They were leading busy, complex lives that involved careers and relationships and community activities.

In my interviews with the women, I sought to determine what characterized the essence of work for them—what aspects of their careers gave meaning and value to their lives. For nearly all the gifted women—regardless of their technical competence, their creative ability, the nature of their work, their income, or their level of "success"—the issue of *interactive communication* stood out as the most salient characteristic of their work lives. In nearly three quarters of the interviews, the gifted women described themselves, their achievements, and their sense of professional well-being in terms of relationships. For example, when asked to describe when she was the most effective at work, a psychiatric nurse responded:

> Those situations where I've done the most and best I could....Breakthroughs at work, establishing a relationship with a patient. I'm lucky. I can do that. When I've really connected, get to the nitty gritty, had a breakthrough in communication.

And a lawyer who recently had begun to work as a consultant in the field of bio-ethics stated:

> I'm most effective when I'm teaching. Not just imparting information, but when I'm interacting. At [ ] Hospital where I work with a committee: when I have to explain medical ethics. I'm good at not provoking anger or irritation. I'm able to make them feel they're good. Reinforcing the other person's sense of competence, being able to bring out people's strengths, what they're excited about. I used to see it when I was working as a therapist. I facilitated people going out, doing; I got people thinking.

Again and again, when describing what they were "good at," the gifted women used such words as "teaching," "communication," "explaining," and "giving to others" in their responses. Frequently they spoke about their experiences as effective educators. A college instructor who had returned to teaching after 20 years as a full-time homemaker focused more on communication than on the mathematics content she was responsible for imparting; she said that she received the greatest work gratification from

> my relationship with others...my students, through them. I get a lot of satisfaction from students, out of being someone who is understanding, caring, will help them. The main thing now is to help kids grow, to be loving, kind, and to stimulate them intellectually. I am better at relating than before. I grew through parenting.

A journalist spoke of her enthusiasm for using magazine articles to broaden public understanding. Her greatest work pleasure derived from "finding out about a subject and doing something about it....I like to take something complicated and explain it to the 'little guy.'"

About one quarter of the gifted women described their work competencies in terms of organizational ability; in most of these instances the interactive aspects of the work again predominated. For example, the director of development of a large philanthropic organization perceived herself as

> really good at working with people, getting others to work on projects, getting them motivated toward goals I want, getting them to be open to thinking in new ways, bringing them along, knowing how to listen to them. I'm good at bringing ideas together making it mesh. And I'm good at taking on things I know little about, picking others' brains.

Another quarter of the gifted group identified their abilities in terms of being sensitive and responsive to other people. These women used phrases such as "sensing others' needs," "talking about feelings," "discussing my own experience," "making others comfortable," and "good listener." Some of these women reported that they were also very good organizers, but the primary thrust of their responses was that they used their interpersonal skills in ways they believed were especially effective. For example, one woman who worked as project leader on very high-powered engineering contracts with the military described herself as

> good at dealing with people, getting at roots of problems. People will tell me things they won't tell anyone else. Is it because I'm female? I'm obviously sensitive, so they will tell me things. And that makes me more effective. I become a storehouse of knowledge. I'm good at interpersonal relationships. I'm a good public speaker. A good organizer in my work. I like to take problems that are difficult, that are unconventional, that have not been done before.

The centrality of interpersonal communication thus dominated the gifted women's responses about the meaning and experience of work. Consistent with the professional women interviewed by Gilligan (1982), these women appeared to place the highest value on their abilities to interact effectively with others and to foster understanding. Their relationships within the workplace were of major importance.

The theme of relationships also surfaced when these gifted women discussed how they coped with multiple roles at midlife and their "zones of vulnerability" (Baruch et al., 1983). The majority of the women spoke with enthusiasm about juggling several "selves," but they frequently reported concern about the nature of their interpersonal interactions. Regardless of their work or domestic situations, when asked about those aspects of their lives in which they felt incompetent or especially vulnerable, the gifted women tended to describe interpersonal shortcomings or frustrations. In nearly half of the interviews the women described their discomforts in terms of poor social skills or unsatisfying interpersonal relationships. For example, despite considerable public acclaim for her creative work, one woman faulted herself for her social behavior when she said, "I have poor social graces. I don't live in the world of all that stuff. I forget about it."

And a doctor who had described her competence in terms of outstanding interactions with cancer patients and their families nonetheless judged her social skills harshly:

> I still feel socially incompetent....I can't say the right things, come up with the right answers. Put me with people who are intellectual and witty and I can't say anything.

Other women referred to feeling inadequate in parenting relationships, in supervisorial relationships, in casual social situations, in public speaking situations, and in general "people handling." Not all of these women had described themselves as shy or socially awkward as children, although women who had been shy more often reported adult social discomfort than women who had been outgoing. Some of the most intense reports of social self-consciousness came from those gifted women who had grown up in nonintellectual, relatively lower income families that had provided limited exposure to a broader world or little validation for intellectual achievement. These women in particular felt unprepared for the demands of multiple roles in adulthood and some wondered whether they had missed certain "lessons" while growing up. They mentioned the utter absence of role models in their lives. Regardless of background, however, it appeared that a significant proportion of the gifted women felt underdeveloped and undereducated socially. Despite their skills as communicators, their overall professional success, and their talent for coping with multiple roles, many of these women felt socially insecure. As one woman summed it up:

> Nobody teaches you how to relate. You can learn other things through a book or a course. Even a therapist can't do it. Building close interpersonal relationships is the single hardest thing I do, can do....It's the one area in which I feel totally incompetent.

Balance at Midlife

Throughout the Gifted Follow-up Study, a key question was: "What do gifted women have to say about balance at midlife?" A starting assumption was that, given their unusually high intellectual aptitudes, the gifted women in this sample might demonstrate superior insight about how to make the choices and evaluate the costs that are involved in "fine-tuning" balance among competing priorities in adult life. On the other hand, given the multiple barriers that tax the development of gifted girls and confound the achievement of gifted women, perhaps it would follow that gifted women might be especially prone to "imbalance" or even disequilibrium in their various adult pursuits.

From the questionnaires and interviews, I found that the UCLA gifted women had thought a great deal about the issue of balance in their lives. As a group, these women were very articulate, and their answers reflected considerable introspection and self-awareness. As already established, these were very busy, accomplished individuals who were trying to manage complex lives; they also tended to be highly self-critical about their self-perceived limitations. Of the gifted women, 89% said that they felt they had achieved a sense of balance, but most threw in "qualifiers." For example, a university administrator said that she felt she had achieved a comfortable balance "although I am probably destined to permanent frustration as I always want to do each thing more and better." Similarly, a nurse said, "Basically I feel I've done well. But I still have trouble with trying to do everything in all areas and depleting mental and physical resources." And a woman who returned to college after a 20-year hiatus and had just completed her BA degree said, "I have achieved a balance of sorts. I am in a post-academic holding pattern because I feel I could be doing more for myself."

In their responses, the UCLA gifted women tended to suggest that achieving balance was an ongoing process—and that imbalance always lurked nearby. Family demands tended to disrupt the flow of some lives; the absence of a partner caused disequilibrium in others. For example, an attorney replied that "It's easier now; there are not so many competing demands now that my children are grown. But I don't have an ongoing relationship with a man."

And another women wrote, "Yes, I have achieved a balance. I would definitely prefer an ongoing, stable relationship with a man to living alone, however."

Overall, the gifted women indicated that achieving a sense of balance had come only with the passage of time. Adulthood had afforded these women time to try out different roles, to discard dysfunctional behaviors, and to consolidate choices. Balance seemed to be more a function of life experience than superior intellectual insight. Achieving balance had required conscious effort for many of the gifted women. An accountant summed up the spirit of the group:

> I am truly comfortable with the choices I am currently making and the real balance that I have achieved. However, I feel it's important that you know that much of my adult life has been directed at learning to achieve the balance that I now have.

STUDYING GIFTED WOMEN AT MIDLIFE: SOME CONCLUSIONS

The present investigation of gifted women was designed to obtain a broad picture of the adult life experience of 35 gifted women. As such, it did not seek to provide an in-depth analysis of the socioemotional concerns of gifted women in contemporary American life. However, despite its relatively small sample size and the absence of a matched control group of "nongifted" women, this study yielded several important findings that inform our understanding of gifted women and point to issues for future research.

First, from the present analysis, it appears that gifted midlife women today *are* utilizing their intellectual abilities and finding professional outlets for their talents and interests. They are not falling as short of their potential as some forecasters predicted. In this regard, the UCLA women may have been "on time" for the positive roles for women afforded by the women's movement and the changing national economy. Few of these women reported major barriers to achievement in the work force. Although some of them had only recently re-entered the labor market, few were experiencing genuine "underemployment." As a group, the UCLA gifted women's experience confirmed Bardwick's (1980) prediction that the cohort of women in their 40s would be especially likely to participate in the work force in the 1980s with vitality and psychological well-being. Whether this experience will be replicated by later cohorts of gifted women requires future investigation.

Second, in and of itself, "giftedness" is but one of the important variables in women's personal or professional development. Although many of the women benefited from their intellectual talents, most felt that giftedness had not made a significant difference in their work lives. At the same time, there was evidence that the positive effects of giftedness frequently had been undermined during childhood and adolescence by mixed or negative messages from parents, teachers, and peers. Whether there are significant long-term consequences of such negative messages generally in the lives of gifted women—or whether these consequences are gradually mitigated by adult and career development—should be explored more fully.

Third, feelings of social vulnerability characterized the lives of many of the UCLA gifted women; at midlife, despite considerable achievement as communicators in the workplace, a substantial number still felt socially awkward or insecure. This phenomenon may have reflected the fact that the UCLA gifted women grew up at a time when the assertion of their talents was generally discouraged; as adults, when expected to promote themselves and their abilities, they may have suffered the continuing effects of childhood shyness or adolescent "hiding." Or it may be that these women were more inclined to develop their intellectual strengths rather than "learn" more ephemeral lessons about relationships. Or it could be that when asked about their vulnerabilities most women tend to cite interpersonal insecurities more than other concerns. Whether or not lifelong patterns of social vulnerability exist among other gifted groups remains to be seen. Certainly the dilemma of social inhibition among gifted women still remains an important area for research.

Fourth, interpersonal relationships appeared to lie at the center of the lives of the UCLA gifted women. Although these women may have been shy as children, may have hidden their talents, may have felt ambivalent about giftedness, and may have developed intellectually more comfortably than socially, as adults they found relationships, pursued careers, and developed a sense of balance in their lives. They prided themselves on their communication and teaching skills; perhaps because they had tended to be good students, they had come to understand what learning and the fostering of learning are about. They were self-critical about their interpersonal limitations; it may be that because they had encountered potential social rejection they had become unusually sensitive to the importance of healthy interpersonal skills. Future studies of gifted women should include specific inquiries about the nature of this population's interpersonal experiences.

Fifth, as midlife women, the UCLA gifted group demonstrated acquaintance with the issue of balance. These women had discovered that balance in life does not come automatically, and they demonstrated how they had made careful choices in order to effectively handle competing demands. At midlife, the majority of these women felt they had achieved a sense of balance, and they articulated the benefits of life experience and maturity. At the same time, their responses implied that they would have to remain vigilant in order to keep their lives "in tune." From these responses, it is clear that many questions remain about how competent, interpersonally responsible women can achieve and maintain balance in their lives.

Finally, in studying the work lives of gifted women, it is reasonable to expect that we will find women who are faring well, endeavoring (along with the rest of us) to find meaningful work and positive interpersonal relationships. As we study the lives of such women, we should not be too surprised to find genuine stories of "success." The current cohorts of gifted women are being afforded new and exciting opportunities, and many of them are capitalizing on their talents and strengths to truly "fulfill the promise." On the other hand, when we study gifted women, we must remain sensitive to the ongoing themes of personal insecurity and interpersonal vulnerability that continue to punctuate women's lives. We need to help gifted women to attend to both their intellectual development and their interpersonal needs. Only then will gifted women gain the personal and professional power of which they are fully capable.

REFERENCES

Abramson, J., & Franklin, B. (1986). *Where they are now: The story of the women of Harvard Law.* Garden City, NY: Doubleday.

Bardwick, J. M. (1980). The seasons of a woman's life. In D. G. McGuigan (Ed.), *Women's lives: New theory, research & policy* (pp. 35–57). Ann Arbor, MI: The University of Michigan.

Baruch, G., Barnett, R., & Rivers, C. (1983). *Lifeprints: New patterns of love and work for today's women.* New York: McGraw-Hill.

Birnbaum, J. A. (1975). Life patterns and self-esteem in gifted family-oriented and career-committed women. In M. Mednick, S. Tangri, & L. W. Hoffman (Eds.), *Women and achievement: Social and motivational analysis* (pp. 396–419). New York: Hemisphere-Halstead.

Faunce, P. S. (1967). Academic careers of gifted women. *Personnel and Guidance Journal, 46*(3), 252–257.

Gallese, L. R. (1985). *Women like us.* New York: William Morrow.

Gilligan, C. (1982). *In a different voice: Psychological theory and women's development.* Cambridge, MA: Harvard University Press.

Ginzberg, E. (1966). *Life styles of educated women.* New York: Columbia University Press.

Helson, R. (1967). Personality characteristics and developmental history of creative college women. *Genetic Psychology Monographs, 76,* 205–256.

Hollinger, C. L., & Fleming, E. S. (1984). Internal barriers to the realization of potential: Correlates and interrelationships among gifted and talented female adolescents. *Gifted Child Quarterly, 28*(3), 135–139.

Kerr, B.A. (1985). *Smart girls, gifted women.* Columbus, OH: Ohio Psychology Publishing.

Langland, L. E. (1961). *Some characteristics of gifted students.* Unpublished doctoral dissertation, University of California, Los Angeles, CA.

Morantz, R. M., Pomerleau, C. S., & Fenichel, C. H. (1982). *In her own words: Oral histories of women physicians.* New Haven, CT: Yale University Press.

Noble, K. D. (1987). The dilemma of the gifted woman. *Psychology of Women Quarterly, 11*, 367–378.

O'Connell, A. N., & Russo, N. F. (1983). *Models of achievement: Reflections of eminent women in psychology.* New York: Columbia University Press.

Oden, M. H. (1968). The fulfillment of promise: 40-year follow-up of the Terman gifted group. *Genetic Psychology Monographs, 77*, 3–93.

Reis, S. M. (1987). We can't change what we don't recognize: Understanding the special needs of gifted females. *Gifted Child Quarterly, 31*(2), 83–89.

Rodenstein, J., Pfleger, L., & Colangelo, N. (1977). Career development needs of the gifted: Special consideration for gifted women. *Gifted Child Quarterly, 20*, 340–347.

Schuster, D. T. (1986). *The interdependent mental stance: A study of gifted women at midlife.* Unpublished doctoral dissertation, The Claremont Graduate School, Claremont, CA.

Schwartz, L. L. (1980). Advocacy for the neglected gifted: Females. *Gifted Child Quarterly, 24*, 113–117.

Sternburg, J. (Ed.). (1980). *The writer on her work.* New York: Norton.

Terman, L. M. (1925). *Genetic studies of genius, volume I. Mental and physical traits of a thousand gifted children.* Stanford, CA: Stanford University Press.

Terman. L., & Oden, M. H. (1947). *Genetic studies of genius, volume IV. The gifted child grows up: Twenty-five years' follow-up of a superior group.* Stanford, CA: Stanford University Press.

Terman, L., & Oden, M. H. (1959). *Genetic studies of genius, volume V. The gifted group at mid-life: Thirty-five years' follow-up of the superior child.* Stanford, CA: Stanford University Press.

U. S. Bureau of the Census. (1984). *Statistical abstract of the United States: 1985* (105th ed.). Washington, DC: Author.

Yohalem, A. M. (1979). *The careers of professional women.* Montclair, NJ: Allanheld Osmun.

Chapter 11

The Working Lives of Terman's Gifted Women

Carol Tomlinson-Keasey
University of California—Riverside

This chapter examines the experience of work among a group of gifted women whose adult lives have been painstakingly researched. In order to understand that experience, it needs to be established from the outset that work must be defined in broader terms than work for pay. Women have always worked to help sustain themselves and their families (Midgley & Hughes, 1983). Whether or not women were paid for that work did not become an issue until recently. In an agrarian economy, for example, family farms were the rule and women worked alongside their spouses to sow and harvest their crops. The money the couple obtained from selling their products was used to meet the family's needs and to begin the cycle of planting and harvesting anew. As the United States industrialized and the economy shifted from agriculture to industry and then toward service, the monetary value of work assumed more importance in the society. In many ways, the emphasis put on salary has eroded the value society places on the varied responsibilities of women. Whether farming, taking care of the home, working as an executive, or performing some combination of these activities, women contribute their labor and skills. This research attempts to evaluate the women's experiences and the value they place on their working lives.

To examine the personal experience of work for women, one needs to follow women throughout their adult years and chart the multiple ways in which women contribute to the society, the family, and their own life satisfaction. Fortunately, a data set exists that allows us to trace the changing course of work for a sample of adult women.

The data presented are taken from a series of studies known collectively as the Terman Genetic Studies of Genius. This study began in the 1920s when Professor Terman from Stanford University recruited 1,528 gifted elementary students (672 girls and 856 boys) for the sample. The 672 women in this sample have been followed for 65 years, from approximately 11 years of age into their 70s. This longitudinal study is highly atypical in the annals of psychology because it provides the woman's own commentary on her life.

The present study focuses on five questionnaires sent to the Terman subjects in 1936, 1945, 1951, 1972, and 1977. Each questionnaire recorded the more objective aspects of adult life—husband, children, job, illnesses, deaths, and divorces. In addition, each survey asked more subtle questions about the woman's hopes and dreams, the value and satisfaction she derived from life (Terman & Oden, 1959). These two sorts of information, woven together, create a rich tapestry of each woman's life. For the purposes of this chapter, we can use this tapestry to evaluate the meaning that women who lived during this era derived from their work. The voices of these women, speaking to us across four decades, highlight the conflicts between personal and professional identity and describe, often in painful detail, the obstacles that prevented women from achieving their goals.

Although 672 women were initially identified, the number of women who filled out every questionnaire was significantly smaller. The information presented in this chapter was drawn from the responses of the 40 women who filled out all five of the questionnaires mailed to the Terman subjects in 1936, 1945, 1951, 1972, and 1977. These particular questionnaires provided the richest data about the women's adult lives. Furthermore, these questionnaires covered a period of 40 years, extending from young adulthood to the retirement years, approximately 25 to 65 years of age. It would have been possible to expand the sample to 250 women by including women who filled out four of the five questionnaires, but many of the women's life stories would have had significant gaps. In order to give full voice to the woman's personal assessment of her life and work, the smaller sample, with more complete data, was selected.

A comparison between the 40 women in this sample and the 672 women in the entire sample revealed several differences of note. The 40 women in this sample were 4 years older when they were initially located than the entire sample of 672. The women examined for this report had a mean IQ of 144, whereas the larger sample had a mean IQ of 148. The subsample and the full sample report similar views about whether they had lived up to their intellectual potential, even though the subsample expressed slightly more satisfaction with their occupational success (3.8 vs. 3.6).

The information in the questionnaires was occasionally augmented by correspondence between the women and Professor Terman, the Stanford researcher responsible for initiating the study. Letters, typically written in response to some crisis or change in the women's lives, add light and color to the picture drawn from reading the questionnaires.

These 40 women provide a glimpse of how intellectually talented women from this era viewed their work and how they integrated their work into the overall context of their lives. The problem, in terms of this chapter, is how to introduce these women. Although each file serves as a kind of diary of the life of a single human being, and hence could be presented separately, the diaries take on added power when the same patterns emerge across the lives of several women. I have chosen, therefore, to introduce a few of the Terman women, each of whom represents a particular solution to the problems of work and identity these women faced. The five patterns presented are easily recognized as work patterns still used by contemporary women. Hence, after describing these patterns, and presenting women who exemplify each approach to work, I turn to the stability of these patterns and their viability among contemporary samples.

PATTERNS OF WORK AND IDENTITY

The Woman Who Enables

The Terman women who served as "enablers" did not pursue a career of their own, nor did they share as a colleague in the work of their husbands. Instead, through their efforts, each woman enabled her husband to reach his potential. Enablers provided help to their husband in all areas except his particular career area. They entertained business associates; maintained correspondence; assumed the responsibility for home and children, often including financial decisions; and they provided emotional support, succorance, and nurturance to their spouses. The women in this group were devoted to their husbands and typically derived great satisfaction from the success their husbands achieved. These women felt actively involved in their husbands' success and derived real feelings of personal worth from the fact that they had been so helpful to their spouse. "I have been extremely happy in the measure of success and recognition which has come to my husband in the last few years. It is a wonderful thing to see a person grow, and of course, I feel part of that." Typically, the husband reinforced this feeling, letting his wife know that without her help, his career would have suffered enormously.

The following case history traces a woman, with an IQ of 144, whose primary "work" was to enable her husband to achieve. In 1936, Lorraine was 26 years old, married, and had two children. As she described her life, it revolved around her husband, Henry.

> I am deeply happy in my marriage and motherhood. Perhaps I would not be so enthusiastic if I did not feel that as a normal woman I am finding the finest expression of myself in creating a lovely home for my family. My greatest joy is in the knowledge that my husband is a man of outstanding talent who, at the age of 28, is considered one of America's outstanding sculptors. I feel that any slight abilities I may have are finding their greatest possible expression in the work of my husband. His record, if you are interested in it, is easy to find. It includes many prizes, invitations to all of the great exhibitions, purchases, etc. I feel embarrassed at reading this. Henry is a very modest person and would be chagrined if he knew I raved so.

As part of the 1936 questionnaire, Lorraine indicated that her ultimate goals were "to be, in the most complete sense, a good and helpful wife and mother, and to develop my own life as much as possible." Her responses in 1945 indicated that her husband had been involved in the war effort and had been overseas. She described her days as full "with the care of our four children and our home." But with her husband gone, the zest disappeared from Lorraine's comments.

In 1951, at the age of 41, Lorraine's enthusiasm for her position had not diminished.

> I think my life is integrated toward a definite goal. But since my husband is definitely the center of my life and since he is a vivid, forceful, creative person, his energies and ideas lead him into many ventures. Our life is often hectic and diverse; yet we always swerve back to our goal which is to live as richly and fully and creatively as possible. While our natures come into conflict now and then, and I am often disturbed by the way he drives himself and takes on too much for his strength; on the whole, our marriage has been an exciting and gratifying adventure. I have tremendous admiration for his creativity and his forceful mind, as well as his extremely high ideals and his delightful personality.

Although Lorraine defined success in life as the "ability to use one's self and one's special abilities to the fullest," her life was happily given to the goal of helping her husband use his special abilities. Her own career aspirations in college were to follow art in some form. "I was taking a teacher's course, but I never had a real desire to teach. My vocation was still nebulous. My parents were very happy to have me choose marriage as my career. My husband was *the* influence in my final choice."

Women in the role of "enabler" often followed their husbands to a variety of job locations. Although Lorraine and Henry did not move often, they did travel extensively, including a year-long stint on an island where Henry escaped the hectic pace of his busy life. "During the years, his accumulation of activities and responsibilities have reached unbearable proportions. The rich full life can become indigestible so we are investing in a year's diet to avoid what we feared might be fatal dyspepsia. I'm sure that all six of us will return to our home refreshed, rested, and with a far better perspective."

Lorraine's questionnaire in 1955 indicated that she was a housewife. She said, "as usual I do nothing startling or noteworthy, but my husband continues to do distinguished work and to challenge imaginations. Among other things he is creating a sculpture for a new building which has received a great deal of publicity. Two more sculptures of his design are underway, and he has been asked to create works for several clinics and churches."

In 1957, when Lorraine was 47 years old, she took some time for herself. "I am enjoying to the utmost a self-indulgence that I have coveted for years. I am auditing a freshman humanities class. I hope I can go on through the second and third courses."

The 1972 questionnaire asked women to evaluate their contribution to their husband's lives. Lorraine, now 62 years old, answered that her work contributed directly to her husband's. She said her husband made life challenging, exciting, and rewarding and she enjoyed her share in his doings. Her comments developing these answers give us a clear view of her "enabler" role.

> In filling out your questionnaire I'm forced to admit that on my own I have achieved nothing noteworthy or publishable, or even especially punishable in my long life, yet I'm not frustrated or disappointed, and I don't think that Dr. Terman would have completely disowned me as one of his failures. A person of Henry's talent and drive desperately needs a partner to take care of family, home, and all of the social needs and other involvements. Especially in the early years, I was deeply concerned in his work and his brilliant exhibitions. So my career has been and still is to supplement the other facets of his life. We entertain a great many friends and business associates here at our home, as well as in Southern California where we keep an apartment and Henry still has his studio and office. We travel often and we enjoy finding treasures for our quite exciting collections. My husband's multifaceted career has been the central factor in my life. Ours has been a partnership in many ways, as I have carried most of the home, family, and social responsibilities. This has enabled him to devote full time to his creative work, his teaching, etc. I wish I could have achieved creatively myself, but what small talent I might have had was absorbed in his great gifts.

It is not surprising that occupational success held less importance for

Lorraine than it did for many of the women. When asked to list the five most salient events in her life, she listed marriage to Henry as the most salient. "He and his demanding and rewarding career have been my life work. His crowded life has been my life too. It has been quite an adventure, often exhausting, sometimes overwhelming, but always challenging and rewarding."

The woman who enabled her husband to become a success often expressed the complete devotion seen in Lorraine's file. Lorraine's comments exemplify the feeling shared by these women that any abilities they have find their greatest possible expression in the work of their husbands.

Did Lorraine live up to her intellectual abilities? Maybe not, if you use today's standards of individual achievement; yet in her own mind, she did. When asked in 1950 and 1960 to evaluate the degree to which she lived up to her intellectual abilities, Lorraine gave very positive responses.

What kind of satisfaction did she derive from her chosen role as an "enabler"? The professional woman of the 1980s might suggest that Lorraine's life lacked personal satisfaction; but Lorraine's own comments charted a life of fulfillment, adventure, and happiness. When asked in 1950, 1960, and 1972, to rate her degree of satisfaction with her life, she reported being moderately pleased with her work, thereby indicating that she regarded her activities as work. Her greatest satisfaction, not surprisingly, came from her marriage, her family, and her social contacts. Overall, in 1972, she characterized herself as having enjoyed life to an exceptional degree.

The "enabler" role is critical to our understanding of how the 40 women from the Terman sample viewed work. Approximately half of them devoted their lives primarily to enabling their husbands to succeed. As early as 1936 these women indicated that being a wife and mother was their ultimate goal. Four years later, two thirds of the women in this group indicated a desire to spend their lives supporting and caring for their husbands and children. Their success in achieving their goals can be evaluated by looking at the sources of satisfaction they cite 20 years later. In 1960 over half of the women who functioned as "enablers" saw their marriages as a source of particular satisfaction. Only one of these women listed their own work as a particular source of satisfaction. These women achieved the goal they set in 1936 and, for the most part, they expressed satisfaction with their lives and their role as "enablers."

The Woman As a Mother

The woman whose life work concentrated on her children's activities was aptly characterized as a "mother." Women in this category emulated in many ways the enablers already described, but the objects of their efforts were their children, not their husbands. A woman who saw her life's work as being a mother commented "I consider my children quite enough of a masterpiece for me."

These women volunteered in organizations that served their children. They served on PTAs, were den mothers, and so on. Because men were seldom free to serve in these organizations, women often were put in posts that required them to exercise real leadership.

Sarah's career goals, listed when she was 21, were in physics. She wanted to pursue a research career. Her tested IQ of 160 indicated that she had the requisite intellectual skills. She noted, without bitterness, that practically no opportunities existed for women in physics, but she thought she could get a general teaching credential. She swerved from her goal when she married and began her family. Her career intentions were further derailed by a mild bout with polio in the early 1940s. After this, she seemed to focus her energies squarely on her children. For several years she concentrated on the care of her infants and preschool children. As the children reached school age, her work shifted to the children's organized activities.

On her 1955 questionnaire, Sarah reported that she was a summer day camp director for a national youth organization. In addition she served on the PTA, had a group of 15 girls in Brownies and 9 lively scouts. As such, her days were "filled with training sessions, board meetings, PTA chores, and other activities pertaining to her children's school." She commented "there are times when I begin to think it is foolish to become so involved. But, then, the youngsters are growing up so fast, we'd better belong to their activities while we can. Besides, we enjoy the adults whom we meet in these organizations."

Perhaps the most intriguing question concerning women who make a career of being a mother, is what happens to them when their children leave the home. Sarah chose to continue the volunteer skills she had developed. Without missing a beat, she began working as a volunteer in a local art gallery.

How did this woman, with an IQ of 160 and educated as a physicist, feel about her life? As she approached middle age she felt she had lived up to her intellectual skills reasonably well. Her primary sources of satisfaction were her husband and her children. She reported that she derived little satisfaction from her work, primarily because she did not regard her activities as work.

At age 57, when a new era for women was breaking in the United States, Sarah acknowledged that her life had not worked out the way she planned. But when asked how she would live her life if given a second chance, she decided that she would choose to be a homemaker. As she approached retirement, she reported a full measure of satisfaction with her life.

Being a "mother" leads to a natural hiatus in a woman's "work." As the children grow and leave home, the mother must turn her energies in another direction. The 40 women in the present study handled this midlife shift in very different ways. Some women, like Sarah, volunteered in adult organizations or pursued independent careers when their children left home. Some became "partners" or "enablers," thereby effectively switching the focus of their efforts from their children to their husbands. Other women began to cautiously survey other options when the meaning that their children had supplied was no longer a part of their lives. One wrote "in midlife, with the family grown and away from home, I feel the need for more constructive activity, which at times causes discontentment."

Women who chose a primary career as a mother faced other problems if they wanted a secondary career option. If these women wanted to stay home with their children for some period of time, their ability to compete in a professional arena was likely to be compromised. Professional jobs that require many years of training, and similar long years building a reputation, do not typically retain the kind of flexibility women need in order to pursue their work as a mother and then rejoin their career. This realization prompted women to select paid work that offered a maximum degree of flexibility. In practice, this meant that many women focused on teaching or jobs in the clerical area, not so much because of their abiding interest in these fields, but because they could pursue their primary career as a mother and maintain some career orientation in these areas. The need to maintain a flexible stance so that they could be with their children may also explain some of the serendipity that shaped these women's careers. These women could not focus their attention on a single career goal, so they pursued their job as mothers and let the turn of events in their lives lead them to a secondary career. Perhaps it was this recognition that provoked one woman who adopted the "mother" role to say "I'll never be great, maybe my children will."

The Woman As a Partner

A third pattern to emerge from the files of the 40 Terman women involved being a "partner." Women who saw their adult working lives as a partnership with their husband differed from the "enabler" in that the woman was employed with her husband in the actual work. The husband and wife, for example, may have owned a business, a car shop, a grocery store, or a farm. Although the husband and wife often had separate duties, each contributed to the financial success of the venture. The woman was an equal in the partnership in that her contribution was made directly rather than indirectly, as was the case with the woman who enabled her husband to achieve.

At the age of 24, Julie's goals were clear. Despite the fact that she had a tested IQ of 150, she said "quite frankly, anything other than marriage is a secondary choice. I, myself, am not an outstanding person. I've never been particularly outstanding, nor have I achieved a great deal in a professional way, but I do feel that I have a fairly level head, am sympathetic with other people and want most of all to live honestly. After all, it is these qualities that bring contentment, and that's all I'm asking in life." Julie succeeded in finding a husband and in 1945 they were operating a local weekly newspaper and printing plant. Their business was not yet financially successful so, to help out, Julie kept books for several small firms. On the side, she pursued a job as a medical technician. In 1955, their income was still derived primarily from the publication of their weekly newspaper. The picture she painted indicated that she and her husband were trying to protect their capital investment in a small business that was struggling to survive. "We feel this is wiser than selling out."

When her husband died, Julie was 52. She carried on the newspaper, and over the years, achieved some recognition for her work on the paper. Still she noted that "I was always more a home and family type than a seeker after glory, so I may foul up your scores on what gifted children are supposed to achieve. But the truth is the truth, and some of us are happy and content to sit and chew our cuds like so many contented cows. When circumstances demand it, our ability to face up to situations and our capability of handling emergencies appears."

Julie described her marriage as a joyous one and felt that after her husband died in 1964, she had to live up to the faith he expressed in her. When Julie was asked whether she felt she had lived up to her intellectual abilities, she answered "reasonably well," suggesting that she felt she had used her cognitive skills to good advantage. As she approached her retirement, Julie characterized her work history as involving steady, satisfying work throughout her life. She had planned to be a homemaker, had been forced by the family's financial situation to pursue a career, and looking back, decided that she would now choose a career at the outset of her adult life. When asked about the satisfaction she has experienced in her life, she reported that her marriage and two children were her primary sources of satisfaction, and her work, while an important source of satisfaction, did not provide the same high levels of contentment. Looking back over her life in 1972, she characterized her adult years as being full of work, "usually team work with my husband." At 60 years of age, she reported that overall she had experienced excellent fortune in her life.

The difference between a "partner" and an "enabler" is evident when one of the partners dies. In this case, Julie continued their partnership. An enabler would not have had that choice, as her contribution to the couple's success was indirect. Women who served as "partners" were not as common as "enablers" among the Terman sample investigated for this study. Approximately 15% of the sample reported being a full collaborator with their husbands. In 1960, when these women were asked to evaluate the sources of satisfaction in their lives, they listed their marriages as a primary source of satisfaction. Their work, although providing some satisfaction, was not as important.

Although both the "enabler" Lorraine and the "partner" Sarah had children, the children appear only briefly in the questionnaires. These women devoted time to their children and both expressed occasional pride in their children's accomplishments, but their lives were entwined with their husbands, and their identity was placed more centrally in that arena.

The Woman As an Independent Worker

About half of the 40 women in the present sample of Terman women reported that they had engaged in steady, paid work for a period of several years during their adult lives. Perhaps their intellectual skill prompted them to enter the labor force; perhaps these women sought work outside the home because others recognized their talent and tried to tap it. It was not the case that only single or childless women pursued paid work. Only 16% of the women in the current sample were single. Another 9% of those who married did not have children. Together these women could have accounted for 25% of the women who worked outside the home. An additional 25% were employed during some of the 40-year span investigated.

Examining these working women as a single group would be a mistake because four different subgroups were evident (Warr & Parry, 1982). The first subgroup were those women who saw their life's work as evolving from their husband's work, then taking an independent course. A second group pursued independent employment because their relationships with their husbands were somehow severed, either through war, death, or divorce. A third group of employed women were those who never married. A fourth group consisted of women who had been trained for and pursued an independent career. Two case histories bring the independent paid work of these women into view. The first woman is married, the second is not.

In 1936, Denise was 27, married and had a child. Her husband was a minister. Many minister's wives were "enablers," devoting themselves to helping their husbands succeed. Denise's career, although it got its impetus from her husband's position, evolved into an independent life's work. In an early questionnaire, Denise indicated that she would like to write, but her marriage in 1930 mandated a move to a large metropolitan city where she was drafted as the organizing president of a Women's Auxiliary project. The auxiliary group, consisting of more than 500 people, would aid a newly established Christian Home for the Aged. Denise organized this auxiliary and sheparded the project to completion. Despite this detour from her goals, in 1940 Denise reiterated her intention to write.

Denise's success in the Women's Auxiliary led quickly to a regional presidency. Part of her new position involved writing about the region for a nationally distributed educational magazine. Her presidency continued through three terms and saw her become heavily involved in religious education programs. Her "work" at the regional level attracted national attention and she was selected as one of 12 women to prepare a study topic for the church. "This was a major writing assignment in our church and I was very thrilled, though it meant considerable research and hard work. My editor estimates that the program I write will be used by approximately 90,000 women."

By 1972, Denise indicated that her main accomplishments came from her positions of leadership among the women of the church. Her work in these areas carried her to the national level. Many of Denise's jobs involved significant financial, educational, and managerial responsibilities. In these positions, she was able to actualize her early desire to write. On many occasions she was honored for her skill, and as she approached retirement, she reported that her accomplishments over the previous 35 years were highly rewarding personally.

Denise joined the church organization as a result of her marriage. She seemed to function in an "enabler" role for a year or two, but then took a rather independent direction for a minister's wife and rose to great heights in her field. Some of her positions were paid, she was given continuing training as she reached higher levels in the church, and her expertise was prized just as companies today might prize a highly trained and effective executive.

When asked at the age of 40 whether she had used her intellectual skills (IQ = 145), Denise indicated that she had fallen considerably short of living up to her abilities. By 50, her accomplishments warranted revising her position and she felt that she had given a reasonable account of herself. It is a commentary on our cultural definition of work that Denise discounted her earlier efforts by reporting that she had rarely or never worked. In 1961, as a result of her paid positions in the church, she began to see herself as being steadily employed. Although she reported a harmonious marriage and rated it as a primary source of satisfaction, she decided that, given a chance to live her life again, she would give concerted attention to a career of her choice, rather than backing into a career as she had. Still, her evaluation of her life, as she looked back over it, gave her great joy.

A less enthusiastic picture was often painted by single women who were pursuing a career independently. When Cecilia was 25, she could not decide what to do. She tried teaching for a year, but didn't like it. By 1945, she had become a buyer for a department store, traveling frequently to the fashion capitals of the World. She started work as a trainee and retired 35 years later in the highest possible position available at that time to women in her firm. Despite this obvious achievement, Cecilia did not report being particularly satisfied with her career. In 1960, at the age of 49, Cecilia reported receiving some satisfaction from her musical avocation, but none from her paid work.

After 25 years with her company, Cecilia decided to take a year's leave of absence just for pleasure. She used this year to travel and, after many years as a single woman, she married. Looking back in 1972, she indicated that if she had it to do over again, she would probably choose to be a homemaker. Cecilia had succeeded in an independent career, and she felt that she lived up to her intellectual abilities reasonably well; nevertheless, she derived little pleasure from her paid work.

The Terman women who pursued independent careers were a heterogeneous group (Sears & Barbee, 1977). Some never married and devoted their lives to their careers. Many were married and joined the labor force because they needed the extra income. Some were newly divorced or widowed when they entered the job market. As the decades flowed by, women moved in and out of this group, until ultimately, approximately half of them had been steadily employed outside the home for some period of their adult lives.

Women Whose Avocations Become Work

Many of the Terman women were interested in the arts. These women seldom pursued a career in that direction, but rather married and developed their interest in the arts into an avocation that gradually took on more and more of the characteristics of paid work.

Mary's life work as a musician took many forms and seemed to founder periodically, but despite the ebbs and surges, she continued to make music a part of her life. Mary first commented on her identity and how it was tied into her musical talent in a 1936 letter to Dr. Terman.

> I hope that if you repeat your inquiry you will try to counter the tendency in mentally superior children to exert as little effort as necessary, and persuade them that their gifts should be considered a rather solemn responsibility and they should put forth as much effort as they can. Having done a great deal of self-probing in the last few months it has become clear to me that this characteristic is a serious and long-standing character fault. With the exception of a few intensive years, musically speaking, at college, my adult life has been one long journey down the path of least resistance; punctuated frequently with noble enthusiasms which peter out as soon as I satisfy myself that I have conquered the first goal. Since my marriage, it has been a growing temptation to identify myself increasingly with my husband and his interests, and to become completely absorbed in his stronger character and personality. At times

I rationalize my doubts by telling myself I am being a good and loving wife, thus submerging my own life in his, but in saner moments I am perfectly sure that if such identification were anything but easy and pleasant, I should have remained the rugged individualist.

The goals Mary outlined in 1936 included "a normal home life with children and music. But, I dare say, when children have come and gone, I shall join the ranks of discontented women."

By 1945, Mary was coaching a women's chorus at a state college. She had returned to school to qualify for a teaching credential and hoped to find a full-time teaching job. She still played the piano, but found the most pleasure in ensemble work. Although she wished fervently for children, she was unable to become pregnant.

Ten years later, she still had not found a full-time job.

Keeping house and caring for my husband and adopted child and doing a limited number of musical things is no longer enough. Now I want a full-time teaching job. In retrospect, I now see that I've spent too many years of my life wishing and waiting for the children that never came. I wish that I had gone ahead professionally with my music or public school teaching. From the very beginning I never let the music slip too much, but I am finding that it is hard to break into the teaching field at my age with so little experience. However, I am plowing along now doing what teaching I can, and preparing myself for better things when openings occur.

Although she eventually found a teaching job, Mary decided to give it up to enable her to spend more time with her music. "My extra-curricular musical life continues to absorb our leisure time and enthusiasm. We sing in a madrigal group which I direct. We perform publicly twice a year. I play in several chamber ensembles for my own pleasure. I'm on the verge of buying a harpsichord." One year, she played in four chamber concerts, three for piano, and a baroque recital for harpsichord, strings, and flute.

Mary's musical career really began to flower when she was offered a faculty position at the local university. In this setting, she enjoyed a great deal of public recognition as a performing musician. "In our community I have probably played more concerts than any other member of the musical fraternity. This has been a continuing source of satisfaction and pleasure to me. I have also continued my teaching; this year my students are better than ever."

The question, "Do you feel you have lived up to your intellectual abilities?" had special significance in relation to Mary, as her tested IQ of 175 was one of the highest in the Terman sample. Toward the end of her career, after joining a university faculty, she reported that she had used her intellectual skills reasonably well.

Mary's musical avocation became her life's work and was always a source of pleasure to her. Many of the Terman women who were similarly gifted in the arts put their dreams for a career on hold for many years while they dealt with family responsibilities. Although some, like Mary, were then able to develop their artistic interest into a career, most yielded to the demands of their families and pursued their artistic and musical gifts as a diversion, rather than as a career.

Isolating these five work patterns and focusing on particular case histories can distort the overall view these women held of their work history. To regain a general view, we need to consider the women as a group. The 40 files investigated in the current study indicated that 66% of the women were content with the "work" patterns that they followed over four decades. These work patterns included being a homemaker. In other words, from their vantage point, in 1972, the work pattern they would now choose agreed with the work pattern they followed. Sears and Barbee (1977) evaluated 430 of the Terman women on the same index and reported that 68% of this larger sample would again choose the work pattern they had followed through life. In their sample, the women who were most likely to now choose a different pattern were those who spent their lives as homemakers or those who worked but had no career direction. These women would now explicitly pursue a career. In fact, two thirds of Sears and Barbee's sample, speaking in 1972, would pursue a career if they were given a second chance at life.

The desire for a career, expressed in 1972, after the society had opened up to women, should not be construed to mean that women who did not have careers were unhappy with their lives. Rather the opposite was true. Looking at the overall life satisfaction of the Terman women at the age of 70, Holahan (1981, 1984) found that the women who were homemakers were slightly more satisfied with their lives than women who pursued occupations. Holahan also reported that the Terman women were as satisfied and happy with their lives as the men in the Terman sample. This was true despite the fact that the men were much more likely to have reached the goals they set early in life. Career satisfaction, then, should not be confused with life satisfaction for the women.

THE STABILITY OF WORK PATTERNS

The five patterns presented here are by no means mutually exclusive, nor do they pretend to be all encompassing. Each case history was selected because it provided as clear an example of each work pattern as could be found in the files. The single-mindedness of many of these women should not be taken as an indicator that the Terman women remained in a single pattern throughout their lives. Many of the women in the sample changed work patterns, especially as the study moved into its third and fourth decade. Work patterns were most likely to change if the women had been in an "enabling" relationship and something occurred to alter that relationship. Hence, women whose life work was that of "enabler," or "partner," may have moved into an independent career if their husband died or the couple divorced. When divorce became a reality for Marsha, she wrote that "The sudden necessity to quit school and get a job forced a quick choice. I had to get any kind of job. I would have preferred to be an aeronautical engineer or to do aerodynamics. This is good old hindsight or what I would do if I could do it over." The urgency of Marsha's life situation did not allow her time to plan or prepare. She was forced to leave the role of "enabler" and pursue an independent career as a clerical worker.

"Mothers" in the Terman sample were forced to reevaluate their lives when their children left home. Often this reevaluation led to the woman assuming a different work pattern. Occasionally a woman who had pursued an independent career embraced the role of "enabler" after she married. Although women altered their work pattern in response to several kinds of events, the most common impetus for change was a modification in the relationship between husband and wife. One woman married as a young woman, lived happily in an enabling role for many years, and was devastated when her husband died at an early age. She was forced into an independent career. When she married again, she left a prestigious doctoral program at Berkeley without a second glance and began to assist her second husband.

The stability of the work patterns followed by the Terman women was also a function of the opportunities available to these women (Holahan, 1984). American society during the 1930s, 1940s, and 1950s placed severe limits on the work patterns that women might follow. The social climate surrounding the Terman women encouraged them to become "enablers." Thus, parents, husbands, children, and the extended culture all acted to funnel women into this role. Still, the very bright women in this sample found several ways of expanding their work patterns which allowed them to go beyond the expected role.

Women could enter a field and compete more easily if they were in a partnership with their husband. Once the societal door was opened for them by their husbands, they could exercise their considerable intellectual skills and contribute to most enterprises in an equal way.

Women were welcomed in the arts. Music, art, and some of the literary arts were areas where many talented women found personal expression. The difficulty in earning a living in these areas extended to both sexes. For this reason, few women earned a livelihood from their gifts in these areas.

Women sought success in careers defined as feminine. In the present study, the women were asked what careers their parents had suggested. Of the parents who expressed a preference, 65% indicated that they wanted their daughters to teach. This was a safe occupation, one open to women in which women were accepted. Teaching remains a field congenial to women. In 1967, teaching was still perceived as a preferred field for women (Jenkins, 1987). Over half of the women in Jenkins' sample pursued teaching as a career.

The woman volunteer, whether she was working in her church, her child's school, or in other social organizations was welcomed by the larger society. As a result, over one third of the Terman women spent significant amounts of time during their adult lives working as volunteers. Both "mothers" and "enablers" became involved in volunteer organizations that complemented their children's lives or their spouses' work. Occasionally, as the case history of the minister's wife indicated, a woman pursuing an independent career started on that path through volunteer work. Although few psychologists have examined women's volunteer activities, the Terman data indicate that women made substantial contributions to the society through these organizations. Recently, Shulamit Reinharz from Brandeis University recognized the importance of women's contributions in these areas. She argued that society has overlooked an arena where female role models predominate, where women are active, persistent, problem oriented, and decisive. Her brief review (Reinharz, 1984) documents the fact that women have worked hard and been effective in neighborhood activism, political activism, religious activities, and as social service volunteers. This was true of the Terman women and remains true of contemporary women.

The five work patterns described earlier were not followed rigidly by the Terman women. In fact, between the ages of 21 and 60, approximately two thirds of the women in the study changed from one work pattern to another. The patterns should also not be conceived as a comprehensive description of any woman's activities. Even though a woman's primary identity might have been as a "partner" for her husband, typically she was also raising children. The patterns presented, then, should be construed as descriptions of the woman's primary work pattern and her primary source of identity during a particular period of her life.

RECURRING THEMES IN THE FILES
OF THE TERMAN WOMEN

The work patterns just outlined pertain to a woman's search for a meaningful identity in a rather direct, but work related, way. An overall assessment of the meaning of work in woman's lives, however, requires that we go beyond the patterns described to a discussion of other forces that shaped a woman's identity. Several such forces or themes recurred in the lives of the 40 women investigated in the present study.

Lack of Confidence

One startling finding, given that these women had an average IQ of 143, was their lack of confidence in their abilities and the belief that their intellectual skills were ephemeral or were not developed. The depth of this feeling was repeated in file after file.

"You might be interested to know that if ever I had a good mind, it has been lost in the shuffle. I seem to have stagnated and I am aware that I'm not using any capacity that I have to the fullest, however, don't give up hope, maybe I'll make you proud yet."

"I'm afraid I'm surely one of these stupid people who didn't avail themselves of the opportunities afforded them by their natural mental endowments."

"I'm sending back my questionnaire with the usual feeling of being the "black sheep" of the group. Scholastically and civicly, my contributions are always huge blanks."

"I feel that in regard to scholastic achievements, I have been a failure. I never developed work habits because things were too easy. Still, I find life vital and challenging."

"I have been unproductive, however, I have been very happy because my intelligence has made me aware of things, which is wonderful."

"I know, in myself, I am not a mental giant, but I feel that I have a good mind and try to make use of it. I am often ashamed for not developing my mind more, and yet, I feel that if I live my life the way it should be done, I can be very happy."

"Frankly, the thought of myself as a gifted child seems very funny to me, for I can seriously claim no particular distinction at present."

"As I grow older, I am more and more surprised at the thought that I was ever considered a gifted child. I realize that I am slightly more intelligent than the average, but only slightly."

"I am afraid I am one of your failures."

"I have always been able to gather facts, but unfortunately, I don't seem to go very deep."

"I know I shall always be a marginal person."

"I have not used my gifts and regret this very much. Also I believe IQs change and mine dropped considerably. I'm no longer very competent in any area. My children all turned out well but not due to me, rather to a strict father who allowed no nonsense."

When reading the Terman files, one expects an occasional aside indicating that an isolated woman or two lacked faith in her abilities. But the number of comments, the repetition of those comments over the years, and the contrast between the women and men on this dimension suggest that the women were sorely lacking in confidence.

The 40 women in the present sample encountered a series of obstacles that would have daunted the most career-minded woman. The Depression of 1929 hit as they were entering adulthood. Thus, some of the women could not attend college because their family's financial fortunes took a sudden downward turn. Even when these women were able to complete their education, they emerged from the ivory towers into an economy struggling to break the grip of the depression. When men could not find jobs, the likelihood of a woman being hired, especially a married woman, was slim. Several women reported being fired when they married, despite the fact that they were in feminine fields. The Second World War had a similar disrupting effect on the lives of these women. Given these obstacles to a career, women who were going to succeed in the world of paid work needed a generous dose of confidence as well as unflagging support. The comments of many of these women indicated that they were not sure of their abilities. Some of these very bright women were able to overcome their lack of confidence because they received encouragement from their husbands and families. Such support was especially likely to be forthcoming if the woman's energies were funneled into accepted areas, such as feminine fields, volunteer organizations, or serving as social facilitators for their husbands. Several women openly credited their husbands for the success that they felt as they pursued opportunities outside the home. "I know that whatever stability, maturity and balance I may have achieved, I owe to my husband's influence."

The lack of confidence these women expressed was part of a cycle that included the women being unsure of their skills as young adults, then being rebuffed by society or having their talents funneled into limited areas. Women were able to surmount these obstacles if they chose a feminine field or had the support of their husbands or families.

Serendipity in Career Choices

A second theme running through these women's lives is a certain randomness surrounding their work experiences outside of the home. Like leaves carried along by a stream, these women were buffeted by social forces— their husbands, their children, even their parents. Because they often put their husband's and children's needs ahead of their own, their work histories seemed to defy planning. The most extreme example of this aimless wandering into a career involved a woman who went to her child's school to ask what the school intended to do to replace her daughter's teacher who had quit abruptly. Within minutes the mother was conscripted to teach, within days the mother had been awarded an emergency wartime teaching certificate.

Examples like this suggest that these women's careers were not purposefully orchestrated. In 1940, 63% of the women in this small sample listed their life goal as being a wife and mother. Thirty-two years later, in 1972, only 29% saw themselves as having spent their lives as homemakers. Economic exigencies, divorces, and a world war were only a few of the factors that conspired to pull these women into the work force. Unfortunately, their paid work was often in response to a crisis and hence lacked any overall plan or direction. If these women were able to relive their lives with the knowledge and experience they had amassed by 1972, 45% would now choose a lifetime career and another 20% would embark on a career, taking time off to raise their family. These women, looking back on their lives in 1972, recognized that they had often worked outside the home because they needed the additional income, but their work lacked a focus or a continuing direction. In this respect, their choices were not viewed as optimal. Thus, with hindsight, if these women had known that they were going to work outside of the home, they would have planned and pursued a specific career.

The Importance of the Social Context

A third theme running through these women's files was the critical importance of the social context surrounding them. These women's lives, their plans, and their desire to pursue work outside the home all depended on the social context in which they found themselves. A woman with a husband was subject to certain expectations. The presence of children brought an additional set of expectations about the acceptable roles a woman could play. The women in the present sample were bound by their primary commitment to their families, thus they were limited in the extent to which they could involve themselves in independent activities. As a result, their career aspirations were often put aside to meet their family's needs and demands.

"You will notice that we have twins, a very convenient excuse. I blame everything I fail to do or be on them."

"In 1961, after 12 years of intermittent work and work done in my home, I took a half-day position and it worked fine. I got the children off to school and returned home before they did."

"I have picked being a housewife because I always liked to cook and still do. I still think I'm going to write something sometime."

"I was awarded a scholarship to study music, but I decided to get married instead. During the last 6 months, I decided my little boy was old enough to allow me to start teaching again. I started with 2 pupils and have built my class up to 10. However, we are going to have another blessed event, so I will probably give my class up."

"I should mention the state of my art work at present. I've kept at it a little at a time through the years, but I've often chosen to give my time to things more of immediate benefit to my family. I still have the urge to someday do some art work that will be recognized by others."

Although the press of family expectations was subtle, these women felt the restraints strongly enough to put their own career aspirations on hold until the needs of their families had been satisfied. Holahan (1984) reported that approximately half of the Terman women changed their life goals after young adulthood. Only one quarter of the Terman men reported similar changes in their goal directions. Holahan concluded that the career environment of these women "had been subject to circumstances outside their direct control. Sex role norms for this cohort of women strongly encouraged them to place their roles as wife and mother before that of employed persons. This, in combination with lesser career opportunities, made sustained involvement in careers difficult" (pp. 25–26).

The Attenuation of Intellectual Growth

A fourth theme recurring in the files suggests that the intellectual potential of these women has not been realized. Only 1 of these 40 women felt unequivocally that she had lived up to her intellectual potential. The majority of the women in this sample thought they had used their intellectual gifts "reasonably well." After reading the files, this response can be taken to mean that when given an opportunity or asked to function intelligently, these women always did. Typically, their intelligence was used to direct and control opportunities for their husbands and children. Perhaps because they had so little opportunity to use their intelligence to direct their own career success, 40% of these women responded that they had not lived up to their intellectual potential.

SIMILAR PATTERNS AND THEMES AMONG CONTEMPORARY WOMEN

The 40 women in the present sample belonged to a cohort that is 25 years older than today's middle-aged professional woman and two generations older than young college-aged women who are just entering their adult, working years. What, if anything, do the patterns and themes identified among these women have to say about contemporary women? What are the similarities and differences that soften or exacerbate the patterns expressed by these women? A few contemporary women may choose one of the work patterns described earlier and follow it throughout her adult life. A larger number of contemporary women pursue the work patterns described earlier sequentially (Waite, 1980). For example, a woman might aspire to an independent career until she has children, then define her work as being a mother, and ultimately, decide to go into partnership with her husband. However, the majority of women who embark on a professional career in the 1980s find that they are simultaneously pursuing several of the work patterns outlined earlier.

During the late 1960s, the 1970s, and the 1980s, occupational discrimination against women plummeted in the United States. As a result, women expanded their occupational horizons, and many pursued an independent career while they simultaneously tried to be an "enabler" and a "mother." Although the wider occupational choices now available to women are important to their work patterns and identities, it does not necessarily follow that career women reduce their responsibilities as "enabler" or "mother" (Haw, 1982). Instead, it seems that contemporary college women express interest in careers and also expect to get married and have children (Bridges, 1987).

The 1970s and 1980s will surely be characterized as the era of the "superwoman," meaning that women pursued multiple work patterns and several identities with a vengeance. The toll this has taken on contemporary professional women has only recently been recognized (Shehan, 1984). Professional women who work and have children often feel that they are not meeting either set of responsibilities adequately (Gray, 1983), and leisure time is a luxury these women cannot afford (House, 1986). Perhaps this explains why women's attitudes from 1978 to 1984 tended to shift back toward more traditional role expectations (Weeks & Botkin, 1987).

If the dual or triple work pattern pursued by contemporary women is to be successful, women need the kind of help typically provided by an "enabler." For some women, this has been achieved by having a member of the extended family help with child care. Other women have bought the help of a surrogate "enabler" in the form of a nanny, a babysitter, a social secretary, and/or a housekeeper. Women trying to balance their roles as career women, "enablers" and "mothers" have scaled down their activities in the latter two areas (Tangri & Jenkins, 1986). Reduced and delayed childbearing, and a streamlining of cooking and homemaking duties have helped the woman pursuing multiple paths.

The 40 Terman women provided us with clear examples of life patterns women followed during the 1930s, 1940s, and 1950s. Similar patterns exist among contemporary women, but these patterns are mixed and matched in a seemingly endless set of combinations as women try to forge their own identity and their own life paths (Hirsch & Rapkin, 1986; Warr & Parry, 1982).

The collage of work patterns among contemporary women and the seeming frantic quality of many of their lives prompts another question. Are contemporary women deriving satisfaction from their careers? The answer according to a 1983 survey by *The New York Times* is "yes." Being a mother and pursuing a career were mentioned equally often as the most enjoyable aspect of being a woman (Dowd, 1983). The 40 women from the Terman group had responded to a similar question in 1951. They reported, by a ratio of 2:1 that they derived greater satisfaction from their children than their work outside the home.

In comparison to the Terman women, then, contemporary women seem to be garnering a sense of identity and self-worth from their work outside as well as inside their homes. Whether or not this will continue to be the case seems to depend on a woman's career orientation as well as her current career status. Pietromonaco, Manis, and Markus (1987) report that being employed is not valued by all women. In order for employment to enhance a woman's feeling of well-being, it must be an activity that she defines as a significant source of self-fulfillment.

Changes in the marital relationships of the Terman women typically signaled a change in work patterns. A sharp upswing in divorce, such as occurred over the last 20 years, has had a similar rippling effect on the work patterns of contemporary women. Between 1962 and 1981, the number of divorces in the United States tripled (National Center of Health Statistics, 1983). The alternative family patterns that followed the flood of divorces meant that many women were thrust into independent careers in order to make ends meet.

Single-parent families, stepfamilies, and families headed by fathers have increased dramatically. These societal as well as economic changes have significant ramifications for the work patterns the contemporary woman chooses and the identity she constructs. In comparison to the 40 women described earlier, it is reasonable to expect that fewer contemporary women would select the role of "enabler." Instead, these women might be expected to choose the role of "partner" or to follow an independent career. Although 90% of all women will eventually have at least one child (Westoff, 1986), and this figure has not changed dramatically during the last half century, fewer contemporary women devote their energy solely to their work as "mother." Instead, contemporary women combine and juxtapose these different patterns in ways that fit comfortably with their lives and the lives of their families. The five patterns of work—the enablers, the partners, the mothers, the independent career, and the woman who turns her avocation into her work—all continue to exist for contemporary women, but the sharp contours of the work patterns have been blurred by the desire to embark on two or more simultaneously.

In addition to the work patterns, the files of the 40 Terman women revealed four recurring themes that shaped the work identities of these women: a lack of self-confidence, a serendipity in career choice, a respect for social relationships, and an attenuation of their intellectual growth. Three of the recurring themes which shaped the identities of the 40 women in the Terman sample seem to have traveled across the generations relatively unchanged.

A lack of self-confidence played prominently in the 40 files of the Terman women. Unfortunately, this issue continues to dominate the psychological literature on women (Sleeper & Nigro, 1987). Widom and Burke (1978) report on junior faculty at two major universities. Both men and women were asked about their publications. The men were able to accurately appraise their scholarship as above average in comparison to their colleagues. The women saw themselves inaccurately as having fewer publications than their colleagues.

The lack of confidence among contemporary women is not limited to the halls of academia. Deaux (1979) found that women in entry level management positions evaluated their performance more negatively than men. Furthermore, women are more likely than men to question their ability and their intelligence. When asked to perform in achievement settings, women's pretask self-confidence was often lower than men's. Interestingly, in spite of their low initial self-confidence, women often outperformed men (Sleeper & Nigro, 1987).

These studies show that low levels of self-confidence still impinge on the contemporary woman's expectancy of success. "Women either (a) believe that they cannot be as successful or as competent as men in certain areas or (b) feel that they are performing less well than their male peers, even when they are, in fact, performing as well, if not better" (Gilbert, 1984, p. 12). Moreover, similar phenomena are observed in children, meaning that our culture continues to transmit a message to girls and women that they remain inferior to men.

One of the themes identified as important among the 40 Terman women was a lack of career direction in their lives. The need to maintain flexibility so as to be most useful to their families in a variety of contexts often meant that no career direction could be pursued. Career goals were quickly set aside as the woman's social context changed. Even when the women had set career goals, the social context often interfered, meaning that many of these women spent years marking time, hoping that they would be able to move into their chosen field. A similar ambivalence often afflicts contemporary women. Women continue to value and preserve relationships and thus try to integrate personal goals with family needs (Gilligan, 1982). Therefore, women are not as likely as men to plan for a career or to examine the specific steps necessary to pursue a particular career. Setting career goals is just one area where men and women show marked differences (Locke, Shaw, Saari, & Latham, 1981). Having a specific career goal leads to better performance, directs an individual's attention, mobilizes effort, increases persistence, and motivates the development of strategies. Yet women are reluctant to set specific, individualistic goals and strive to meet them without considering their families (Gilbert, 1984).

Female valedictorians from high school fall behind their male counterparts quickly. Take the cases of Nancy and Mike who were both valedictorians in 1981. Both wanted to be lawyers. By 1985, when they were both seniors in college, Nancy was engaged and was planning to accompany her fiancé to the midwest. Mike continued toward his original goal. This example, reported by Ornstein (1987), illustrates the more general finding that although the women valedictorians outperformed their male counterparts in college, they veered from their goals when they began seriously considering marriage and raising a family.

A central variable pervading the adult lives of the 40 Terman women was the social context that limited their horizons. Chodorow (1978) and Gilligan (1982) have cited the importance of the social context to contemporary women. They described the greater imbeddedness of women in social contexts and contrast the woman's imbeddedness with the more individualistic and controlled career activities of men. The social context, so central to the Terman women, and so important to maintaining the social order of the society, is still apparent among contemporary women and works to the detriment of their careers, although perhaps not to their detriment as human beings. Gilbert (1984) wrote that women in contemporary society cannot be meaningfully understood if they are isolated from the larger social context in which they live. Women in dual-career marriages continue to assume the major responsibility for their families and children (Baruch & Barnett, 1986). Because women value relationships, they funnel more time and energy into the preservation of meaningful relationships. Women work diligently at integrating their personal goals with their family's needs. This sense of the importance of relationships and the need for a balance between personal goals and family needs means that women are less likely than men to devote their time solely to a career.

The study of high school valedictorians referred to earlier provides some sense of the importance of the social context for contemporary women. Even spectacular achievement in college did not guarantee professional success for women because women faced a set of relationship issues that men did not have to address. In essence, the adult identity for the women valedictorians was more complexly constructed than for academically talented men (Ornstein, 1987).

The final theme, so discouragingly apparent in the files of the Terman women, was the attenuation of their intellectual growth. The increased openness of the society to the success of women has countered this tendency. In fact, a 1985 study of 95 gifted women who were approximately 30 years old indicated that many more of these women feel that they are living up to their intellectual abilities (Tomlinson-Keasy, in preparation). Among the contemporary sample of intellectually gifted women, 10% feel that they have fully realized their potential. This compares to less than 3% of the Terman sample. Over three quarters of today's gifted women feel that their intellectual skills are at least being used "reasonably well." Only 60% of the Terman women shared this feeling.

Another indicator that women are being allowed to develop their potential comes from a survey of student skills over several decades (Feingold, 1988). Gender differences in a variety of cognitive skills have declined precipitously over the years. On dimension after dimension, differences between the men and women that were evident in 1947 and 1962 had decreased substantially by 1980 (Feingold, 1988).

Despite these hopeful signs, a variety of subtle and not so subtle statistics suggest that the society is not yet fully committed to women reaching their intellectual potential. Differential pay status continues to exist for men and women in similar positions (Bergmann, 1987). A limited number of women have made it to managerial and leadership positions in business, universities, and government (Morrison, White, & Velsor, 1987). Furthermore, although affirmative action policies have assured that jobs are advertised widely, women are often not competitive for the best positions because of geographical limitations that impinge on their mobility or because they must balance the responsibilities of their children with their desire to pursue a career.

Terman's sample of gifted women reached adulthood in the 1930s and retired in the late 1960s. The patterns of work they followed during their adult years were uniquely configured by the Zeitgeist surrounding the culture and their lives. Despite the unique era, the work patterns so prominent among 40 of these women can still be found among contemporary women, albeit in somewhat altered form. The themes that recurred as important factors shaping the adult identities of the 40 Terman women have changed less. Contemporary women still lack confidence in their skills and look to or seek the direction and support of a mentor, husband, or manager in order to realize their career potential. Contemporary women continue to shy away from setting specific, individualistic career goals. Contemporary women continue to be pulled in several directions by the social context surrounding them. This means career goals and aspirations are often modified by personal exigencies. The bright note is that American society in the 1980s recognizes the intellectual potential of many women and has taken some initial steps to cultivate that potential.

ACKNOWLEDGMENTS

This chapter was made possible by an intramural research grant from the University of California—Riverside. The study owes a special debt to Robert Sears and Albert Hastorf of Stanford University for helping us gain access to the data from the Genetic Studies of Genius.

REFERENCES

Baruch, G. K., & Barnett, R. C. (1986). Fathers' participation in family work and children's sex-role attitudes. *Child Development, 57,* 1210–1223.

Bergmann, B. R. (1987, September 20). The wage gap between the sexes. *Los Angeles Times,* Section V, p. 5.

Bridges, J. S. (1987). College females' perceptions of adult roles and occupational fields for women. *Sex Roles, 16,* 591–604.

Chodorow, N. (1978). *The reproduction of mothering: Psychoanalysis and the sociology of gender.* Berkeley, CA: University of California Press.

Deaux, K. (1979). Self-evaluations of male and female managers. *Sex Roles, 5,* 571–580.

Dowd, M. (1983, December 4). Many women in poll value jobs as much as family life. *The New York Times,* pp. 1, 66.

Feingold, A. (1988). Cognitive gender differences are disappearing. *American Psychologist, 43,* 95–104.

Gilbert, L. A. (1984). Female development and achievement. In A. U. Rickel, M. Gerrard, & I. Iscoe (Eds.), *Social and psychological problems of women: Prevention and crisis intervention* (pp. 5–17). New York: Hemisphere.

Gilligan, C. (1982). *In a different voice.* Cambridge, MA: Harvard University Press.

Gray, J. D. (1983). The married professional woman: An examination of her role conflicts and coping strategies. *Psychology of Women Quarterly, 7,* 235–243.

Haw, M. (1982). Women, work and stress: A review and agenda for the future. *Journal of Health and Social Behavior, 23,* 132–144.

Hirsch, B. J., & Rapkin, B. D. (1986). Multiple roles, social networks, and women's well-being. *Journal of Personality and Social Psychology, 51,* 1237–1247.

Holahan, C. K. (1981). Lifetime achievement patterns, retirement and life satisfaction of gifted aged women. *Journal of Gerontology, 36,* 741–749.

Holahan, C. K. (1984). The relationship between life goals at thirty and perceptions of goal attainment and life satisfaction at seventy for gifted men and women. *International Journal of Aging and Human Development, 20,* 21–31.

House, E. A. (1986). Sex role orientation and marital satisfaction in dual-role and one-provider couples. *Sex Roles, 14,* 2245–2259.

Jenkins, S. R. (1987). Need for achievement and women's careers over 14 years: Evidence for occupational structure effects. *Journal of Personality and Social Psychology, 53,* 922–932.

Locke, E. A., Shaw, K. A., Saari, L. M., & Latham, G. P. (1981). Goal setting and task performance: 1969–1980. *Psychological Bulletin, 90,* 125–152.

Midgley, M., & Hughes, J. (1983). *Women's Choices: Philosophical problems facing feminism.* New York: St. Martin's Press.

Morrison, A. M., White, R. P., & Velsor, E. V. (1987). *Breaking the glass ceiling.* New York: Addison-Wesley.

National Center for Health Statistics (1983, October 5). Annual summary of births, deaths, marriages, and divorces. *Monthly Vital Health Statistics, 31*(No. 13).

Ornstein, H. (1987, November 8). In career goals, female valedictorians fall behind. *The New York Times,* Education Life Section, p. 7.

Pietromonaco, P. R., Manis, J., & Markus, H. (1987). The relationship of employment to self-perception and well-being in women: A cognitive analysis. *Sex Roles, 17,* 467–477.

Reinharz, S. (1984). Women as competent community builders: The other side of the coin. In A. U. Rickel, M. Gerrard, & I. Iscoe (Eds.), *Social and psychological problems of women: Prevention and crisis intervention* (pp. 19–44). New York: Hemisphere.

Sears, P. S., & Barbee, A. H. (1977). Career and life satisfactions among Terman's gifted women. In J. C. Stanley, W. C. George, & C. H. Solano (Eds.), *The gifted and the creative: A 50 year perspective* (pp. 28–65). Baltimore, MD: Johns Hopkins University Press.

Shehan, C. L. (1984). Wives' work and psychological well-being: An extension of Gove's social role theory of depression. *Sex Roles, 11,* 881–899.

Sleeper, L. A., & Nigro, G. N. (1987). It's not who you are but who you're with: Self confidence in achievement settings. *Sex Roles, 16,* 57–70.

Tangri, S. S., & Jenkins, S. R. (1986). Stability and change in role innovation and life plans. *Sex Roles, 14,* 647–662.

Terman, L. M., & Oden, M. (1959). *Genetic studies of genius: The gifted group at midlife.* (Vol. 5). Stanford, CA: Stanford University Press.

Tomlinson-Keasey, C. (in preparation). *Predicting life outcomes of gifted women.* Stanford, CA: Stanford University Press.

Waite, L. J. (1980). working wives and the family life cycle. *American Journal of Sociology, 86,* 272–294.

Warr, P., & Parry, G. (1982). Paid employment and women's psychological well-being. *Psychological Bulletin, 91,* 498–516.

Weeks, M. O., & Botkin, D. R. (1987). A longitudinal study of the marriage role expectations of college women: 1961–1984. *Sex Roles, 17,* 49–59.

Westoff, C. G. (1986). Fertility in the United States. *Science, 234,* 554–559.

Widom, C. S., & Burke, B. W. (1978). Performance, attitudes, and professional socialization of women in academia. *Sex Roles, 4,* 549–563.

Chapter 12

Blue-Collar Women: Paying the Price at Home and on the Job

Jean Reith Schroedel
Massachusetts Institute of Technology

As a result of affirmative action laws, women in the last 15 years have been entering into occupations that in the past were almost exclusively held by men. The most significant progress has been made by women breaking into management and the professions. Their success has generated an interest in both the popular press and academic circles on the problems and prospects of female pioneers in traditionally male work environments. Although most of the initial attention has focused on professional women (Epstein, 1972; Fernandez, 1981; Harlan & Weiss, 1982; Hennig & Jardim, 1977; Kanter, 1977a), there also has been a growing interest in the experiences of women entering into traditionally male blue-collar occupations.

Literature Review

Even though the literature on women in the trades is relatively small, its most notable feature is its sheer diversity. It is difficult to summarize the literature because the authors come from a variety of academic disciplines and are trying to accomplish very different aims. Some of the early research by oral historians (Schroedel, 1985; Wetherby, 1977) and vocational counselors (Lange, 1982; Lederer, 1979) was primarily designed to make women aware of the expanded opportunities available to them in the trades. These efforts performed an important function of providing basic information,

241

such as how one goes about getting a nontraditional blue-collar job, what clothing is appropriate, the tools that one must know how to use, and the types of discrimination that one might encounter.

Another group of research looks at the problem of women entering into traditionally male blue-collar occupations from the perspective of the firm employing the women. Their concern is how to successfully integrate women while maintaining productivity. The earliest of this research (anonymous, 1942; Baker, 1942) dates back to the Second World War. This and more recent research such as that of Brunner (1981) emphasize management support of women as being crucial to their success in blue-collar occupations.

In contrast, the works of Yoder (1983), Yoder and Adams (1984), and Yoder, Adams, Grove, and Priest (1985) have as their major aim influencing public policy. The authors use the case of women at West Point to show that women in the military are capable of performing as well as their male counterparts. They find that most of the difficulties encountered by the women are the result of stereotypical sex-role expectations on the part of male cadets and officers.

The studies of women at West Point make a valuable contribution to academic research on the conflicts between expectations about work roles and sex roles. Sociologists (Enarson, 1984), organization theorists (Schreiber, 1979), and psychologists (Adams, Lawrence, & Cook, 1979; Gutek & Morasch, 1982; Nieva & Gutek, 1981) have studied the interaction between women's sex roles and work roles. Although each of the scholars describe the phenomenon somewhat differently, what basically occurs is that women employed in a predominantly male workplace are seen as women first and only secondly as workers. To survive in this environment, the women behave in ways that are in keeping with the male expectations about women, but that are inappropriate to the work environment. Nieva and Gutek called this phenomenon "sex-role spillover."

Understanding to what extent a woman stands out in her work environment is also important because that has a significant impact on how she interacts with her supervisor and co-workers. There is evidence that token women and minorities face discrimination in hiring and advancement (Shaw, 1972) and have difficulties in successfully interacting with the dominant group. Kanter (1977b) found that the relative numbers of culturally and socially different people in a group affected the group dynamics. Tokens often end up taking on roles that are defined by and acceptable to the dominant group. According to Kanter, the roles available to token women are mother, seductress, and pet. None of these stereotypical roles are appropriate to the workplace. The previously cited literature on sex-role spillover, as well as parts of Enarson's study (1984) of women in the forest service build off this analysis. Enarson found that women in the forest service tried to accommodate themselves to an all-male environment by taking on the roles of little sister, pet, and ladylike buddy.

Walshok (1981) tried to identify the factors that successful tradeswomen have in common. Her research primarily focuses on the personal characteristics of the women in her sample, but does mention external factors such as helpful co-workers and supportive families. Other authors (Gruber & Bjorn, 1982; Lembright & Riemer, 1982; O'Farrell & Harlan, 1982) emphasized the importance of co-workers in determining whether the job experience is positive or not. Harlan and O'Farrell (1982) and Deaux (1984) drew upon internal labor market theory to explain why tradeswomen encounter difficulties in advancing within their firms. McIlwee (1982) found that as women stay in a trade that their sources of satisfaction and dissatisfaction come to resemble those of their male co-workers. The concern in Lillydahl's (1986) research is whether rural women prefer traditionally female jobs or if given an opportunity would take blue-collar jobs traditionally reserved for men.

As is evident from this chapter, research on women doing nontraditional blue-collar occupations is currently at the exploratory phase. Scholars are still trying to explain which women are interested in these jobs, how they get hired, and what are the impediments to their success. Even though there is not unanimity among scholars on their approach to the question, there are few debates within the literature. That will inevitably come as our understanding grows.

In this chapter I hope to contribute to that growth by exploring the extent to which women in nontraditional blue-collar jobs feel able to shape their work experiences and, in turn, to examine to what extent that work experience shapes the rest of their lives. This research is based on in-depth interviews with tradeswomen, who discuss factors that can affect their efficacy such as the importance of outside support networks, prior job preparation, and job-related variables such as unionization and management attitudes, as well as the women's own attitudes and background.

This research differs from most prior research in the field in two major ways. First, the research is based on the experiences of women who have held jobs in the trades for a long time. Most of the prior research involves women who have been in the trades for 2 years or less. This is significant because many trades have formal or informal training periods lasting up to 4 years. During that time, the woman is in an explicitly subordinate position vis-à-vis the majority of her co-workers. Second, most of the previous research is based on the experiences of women in a single trade or industry. The women I interviewed came from a wide range of industries and crafts. Thus, this study is the first in-depth examination of nontraditional blue-collar work from the perspective of long-time women workers from a variety of occupations.

RESEARCH METHODOLOGY

The data for this study came from intensive interviews conducted in 1981 and 1982 with 25 women working in nontraditional blue-collar trades. "Intensive interviewing" (Williamson, Karp, & Dalphin, 1977) is a research methodology that is particularly useful in eliciting information about sensitive issues. The researcher goes into the interview with prepared questions, but the exact use of each specific question is determined by the progress of the interview. The order in which the questions are asked may vary from interview to interview. If the person being interviewed has a lot to say about a particular question, that area is probed with additional questions. If a question gets minimal response, it can be restated in different terms. The aim is to get an in-depth understanding, which is impossible in a more structured interview.

I chose this approach because I wanted the women to feel comfortable talking about some of the most personal and painful aspects of their lives. For example, not only did I want them to tell me whether incidents of sexual harassment occurred, but also to describe what happened and what feelings they experienced. Most people are understandably reluctant to discuss these difficult areas, especially with a stranger. It was this depth of discussion that I felt was missing in the previous studies on women in the trades.

Williamson et al. (1977) stressed the importance of rapport between the interviewer and the person being interviewed. "We have stated more than once that the quality of the incipient or emerging relationship between interviewer and interviewee is the key to how productive the intensive interview will be" (p. 182). Clearly, my own background played an important part in gaining their trust. As someone who had spent over 8 years working at nontraditional blue-collar jobs, I was accepted as "one of us." Several of the women told me that I was the first person they had ever really talked to about their work.

Each of the interviews lasted from 2 to 5 hours and covered the woman's background, personal characteristics, training, on-the-job experiences, and family life. I was particularly interested in the impact that the work had on their self-esteem and personal relationships.

Because I was interested in studying the experiences of a wide range of women active in the trades for a long time, the sample could not be random. To find the women I ruthlessly exploited every contact that I had in the various unions, trade schools, and industries. If the person I contacted knew of a woman doing nontraditional work, I would have that person contact her first and if she was interested in the project I would then set up a time for a meeting. It was very helpful to have someone acquainted with the woman vouch for me. The loss of rigor brought about by having a nonrandom sample is more than made up for by the richness of the sample.

The length of time that the women had been employed in a nontraditional job at the time of the interview ranged from 2 to 40 years. The mean length of time was 7.5 years. When the extreme outlier (a woman who got into the trades during the Second World War) was removed the mean was still 6.17 years. The median length of employment was 7 years.

The women were employed in some of the area's most important industries. Twelve were involved in manufacturing industries, such as aerospace, shipbuilding, paper products, steel, and truckbuilding. The construction, maritime, and transportation industries each employed three women. Another three women worked at nontraditional jobs at public utilities. The last woman was employed in forestry. A number of the women had experience with more than one nontraditional trade. As they gained knowledge about different trades, they moved into more skilled and preferable positions.

The women ranged in age from 24 to 68 years old. Most were between the ages of 25 and 40 years old. The mean was 34 years old. When the outlier was left out, the mean age was still 33 years old.

The women were also diverse as to race, marital status, and whether or not they were parents. Twenty women in the sample were White. The racial breakdown of the remainder is as follows: one Asian-American, two Blacks, one Hispanic, and one Alaska native. At the time of the interview, 10 were married, 5 were divorced, and 10 were single. Fifteen of the women had children and 10 did not.

FINDINGS

There are three major questions that are addressed in this chapter. The first asks what effect does one's background have on success in the trades? The focus is on women's socialization and training prior to their first nontraditional job. The second considers characteristics of the actual work. This question explores what attracted women to nontraditional work, how they got their first jobs, and relations with co-workers and supervisors. In addition, the role of unions in helping or hindering women is analyzed. Finally, the issues of sex discrimination and sexual harassment are explored in some depth. The third question considers what affect nontraditional work has on the rest of one's life? The emphasis is to discover whether nontraditional work leads to changes in one's self-esteem, health, and personal relation-ships. The impact on family is looked at in some detail.

The Effect of Personal and Educational
Background on Success

There are two major controversies within the literature on nontraditional work that deal with the women's background. The first is the question of whether women who have succeeded in nontraditional blue-collar work can be distinguished from other women in terms of their socialization. The second area needing to be explored is how well trade schools prepare women for what they are likely to encounter on the job.

In most ways the women in the sample were indistinguishable from other women of their generation. The majority came from traditional families, where the father worked outside of the home and the mother was a housewife. Only 24% of the fathers were employed in white-collar oc-cupations. One woman did not know who her father was, but the rest had fathers employed in trades, fishing, or agriculture. Fourteen of the mothers were housewives who did not work outside of the home while the children were growing up. One woman's mother worked in a blue-collar job and three mothers worked in fishing or agriculture. One woman was raised by a grandmother, who was on welfare.

Although the Northwest has a relatively small Catholic population, nine of the women came from Catholic backgrounds, with an equal number coming from Protestant families. One woman came from a mixed Jewish/Methodist family and another from an entirely Jewish family. The rest had no particular religious upbringing, although one woman espoused a pantheistic faith.

When asked to discuss their childhoods, the women were fairly evenly split between those preferring fairly traditional sex-role pastimes and those favoring nontraditional pursuits. Although most mentioned a fondness for sports, such as bicycle riding, only a few described themselves as tomboys.

Their job aspirations while growing up were also fairly evenly divided between traditionally female roles, most notably growing up to be mom-mies, and more nontraditional pursuits. Only three of the nontraditional pursuits mentioned could be classified as blue collar. One woman had wanted to be a fireman, another wanted to be a cowboy, and one always wanted to go to sea. Only the last woman fulfilled her childhood ambition.

As a group, the women were probably better educated than men pursu-ing the same type of work. Of the women, 20% had college degrees and one even had an advanced degree. Another 11 had attended but not graduated from college. Only three of the women had not graduated from high school. The remainder had high school educations, but no college.

Of the women, 88% had prior job experience before entering into nontraditional blue-collar occupations. Two of these women had gone into nontraditional work immediately after leaving school. The other woman had been a housewife for a number of years before going to work on a truck assembly line. Of those with prior job experience, 11 of the women had worked at both blue-collar and white/pink-collar occupations. Nine had worked exclusively at blue-collar jobs and two of the women had only held white-collar jobs prior to going into a nontraditional blue-collar occupation. It can be concluded that the women had accumulated quite a bit of knowledge about female job prospects prior to choosing a trade. They had not grown up planning to go into a trade, but had weighed the different options and chosen nontraditional blue-collar work as being the best prospect.

Only 28% of the women attended some type of trade school before getting their first nontraditional job, so one does not want to generalize too much on the basis of their experiences. Those who attended trade school did so to obtain entry-level skills necessary to do deck work on an oil tanker, truck driving, carpentry, plumbing, machining, electrical wiring, and to be a mate on a tug boat. Although it is true that most men going into these trades do not attend trade school, the women felt they needed training prior to getting a nontraditional blue-collar job. Some of the women mentioned the need for women to learn skills that boys naturally learn growing up. The machinist described the problem as follows:

> I think women have a disadvantage, not as soon as they walk in that door and start working on the men's job, but they have a disadvantage from the moment they're born because somebody's gonna raise them to be a woman...There are little things that men take for granted, like when they're growing up their fathers teach them how to fix their cars, they learn what a feeler gauge is, how to set spark plugs, and how to understand mechanical levers.

Next to learning necessary entry-level skills, confidence was the most important thing the women gained by the schooling experience. By learning the vocabulary, the use of tools, and to read diagrams, these women felt they had a head start on some men starting out in a trade. This foothold gave them the confidence to compete with the men on the job. A cement truck driver said that the men in her truck driving school had a natural confidence that they could shift gears, but that she and another woman had to keep shifting over and over until they were convinced that they could do it.

The final thing that women got out of their trade schooling was experience with sex discrimination and sexual harassment. For most of the women the discrimination in trade school was relatively mild. This was especially true for those attending special programs for training women and racial minorities. The most important determinant of the degree of discrimination faced in trade school seems to be the attitude of instructors. When the instructors were supportive, the women did very well. When the instructors were hostile, the women had a very rough time. One of the women in the sample had an instructor who made a pass at her and then gave her a very low grade when she turned him down. Another recalled a teacher making numerous comments about her body in front of the rest of the class.

Even though they had some difficulties in school, the women generally considered it to be a positive experience. Schooling provided them with the skills necessary to be taken seriously when they applied for nontraditional blue-collar jobs. Often it meant they had greater skills than similarly placed men. This boosted their self-confidence and heightened their sense of efficacy. It is, however, important to remember that most of the women in this sample, like most males working in the trades, learned their skills on the job. In the next section I examine some of the reasons why it is more difficult for women than men to pick up the skills as they work.

In terms of their background, there is nothing that would predict that these women were likely to be successful in the trades. They came from traditional nuclear families and had typical childhood hobbies. Prior to entering into trades they were indistinguishable from other women of their age. Once they made the decision to go into a nontraditional blue-collar work, attending trade school helped prepare them for successful careers.

Characteristics of Blue-Collar Job Experiences

In analyzing the women's experiences with non-traditional blue-collar work, I was most interested in discovering what attracted women to this type of work, how they found their jobs, and what their relationships with their co-workers and supervisors were like.

Because there did not appear to be anything in the women's socialization that indicated they were destined for nontraditional work from an early age, the attraction probably appeared later as a result of life experiences. This supposition is supported by the fact that virtually all of the sample had extensive work histories prior to switching to nontraditional blue-collar jobs.

When asked an open-ended question about what attracted them to these occupations, 18 said it was primarily the money. That is not surprising because the average wage of the women in the sample at the time of the interviews was $9.84 an hour. That was almost twice the national average wage of women workers at the time of the interviews (Bureau of the Census 1986). Six of the women indicated that they were primarily attracted to the work itself. They mentioned liking to work with their hands, preferring to work outdoors, and the satisfaction they got from actually creating a product. One woman, an Alaskan native, said that she liked the lifestyle and sense of community that she had in her fishing village.

When asked how they got their jobs, a majority said that a family member or friend suggested that they apply at the place they got hired. Prior to the suggestion, they had not thought of doing nontraditional work. Three of the women were already working for a company when trades jobs were made available to women. Two women got work through trade school referrals and one used an employment service.

Most of the women also mentioned at some point in their interviews that affirmative action laws played a role in their getting jobs. A few, such as a transit supervisor, said that companies had been desperate to get women to fill a quota. Others felt affirmative action laws helped them only to the extent that it meant that good paying blue-collar jobs were no longer automatically reserved for men.

Most of the women in the sample felt they had been able to develop decent relationships with their male co-workers. However, 25% of the women did not believe they had acceptable work relations. Seventeen of the women said they had developed friendships with men at work. This is borne out by the fact that most of these women also said they usually ate lunch with the men. For women who are not accepted as part of a work group, lunch can be the worst part of the day. The women have different ways of coping with the ostracism at lunchtime. A construction worker buried her head in a book to avoid the awkwardness of having no one to talk with at lunch. One printer quit taking lunch breaks. "Nobody would associate with me or talk with me. I ate my lunch in my car by myself until I told the boss I preferred working a straight 8 hours and then just go home."

There were some indications that women working in racially mixed work places had better work relations than did those working with all or virtually all White men. Perhaps tolerance developed through working with nonWhite men carried over to women, who have minority status in the workplace because of their sex.

Relations with supervisors were more problematic. Only about half of the women have developed acceptable work relationships with their supervisors. Of the women, 76% reported that their supervisors discriminated against them because of their sex and 20% said their supervisors sexually harassed them.

There also appears to be support for Kanter's (1977b) and Enarson's (1984) findings that women in sex-skewed work environments assimilate by taking on roles appropriate to their sex. Even though the women were never specifically asked a question about sex roles, 10 of them described their relations with co-workers and/or supervisors in terms of sex roles rather than work roles.

The most common sex role taken on by women in the sample was that of daughter to an older man, which is very similar to Enarson's "little sister" role. The interactions between the parties are similar with the major difference being a larger age gap. A fourth-year plumbing apprentice described the dynamics of the relationship as follows:

> I think it's easy for a White man especially to put a White woman like in the role of their kid. Even if they don't think it's good for you to be doing this, a lot of their kids are doing things they didn't plan or want them to do. Even though there might be a lot of animosity, I think it sometimes makes it easier when they do have a kind of family feeling for you and they'll kind of take you under their wing.

This pseudo-adoption of a younger woman by an older man is not that dissimilar to the more traditional mentor relationships that exist between older and younger men. Those often have the character of a father–son relationship. Although there is some tendency for the older man to be more protective of the younger woman than he is of a younger man, these pseudo-adoptions are a good way for a woman to learn trade secrets. It also may have the effect of desexualizing the relationship.

In contrast to older men, young men were usually seen as the most hostile to women co-workers. This is in keeping with Riemer's (1979) hypothesis about construction workers. Riemer postulated that young male apprentices are most threatened by women because they are unclear about both their male identity and work status.

One older woman in the sample clearly took on the mother role at her work site. She listened to their problems, brought them cookies, and hugged them when they were down.

> I'd usually pick out two or three older drivers that had been there 30 years— they were the drivers that would come to work, sign in, not talk to anybody, and they'd go to work, and then all of a sudden they retired, and nobody knew who they were. It was sad to me so I started hugging them every day. I just felt they probably needed it and then they would start talking to people. They'd come in the morning and smile.

Several other womens' identities on the job were tied to the sex role of wife/girlfriend. This only occurred, however, when their spouse or boyfriend also worked at the same place. One woman in the sample reported filling the role of a pet when she was younger. As she got older and began competing with the other fishermen, that role disappeared.

It is very difficult for minority women to fill these types of roles unless they happen to be working with some minority men. One Asian-American woman developed a father–daughter relationship with an older Asian-

American man in her plant. White men may be less likely to think of non-White women as daughters, which is the most common way for younger women to be assimilated.

The effect of women having to take on sex roles as a means to workplace assimilation is that they are made to feel they cannot be accepted simply on the basis of their work performance. Thus, they experience the additional pressure to adhere to behavior that is appropriate to the sex-role, but irrelevant and possibly antithetical to the work role.

Sex Discrimination As a Source of Stress. Even though most of the women in the sample claimed to have developed acceptable working relations, every one of them reported that they had personally suffered from sex discrimination. When asked a general question about sex discrimination, the women listed nine different types of discrimination that they had experienced. Most of the women reported being discriminated against in a variety of ways.

One of the common complaints was that men continually questioned the woman's competence. Male co-workers can undermine a woman's competence by either broadcasting every mistake that she makes or by acting as though routine job performance is a major accomplishment. In both situations the assumption is that the woman cannot do her work as well as men. Of the women, 48% reported having this occur to them.

Half of the women also reported facing more difficult job requirements than men of the same level. Conversely, nine women said they were not allowed to do all of the things that their male co-workers were expected to do.

Forty-four percent of the women said they were either denied jobs or advancement because of their sex. One woman had to sue the Plumber's Union to get into the apprenticeship program. At that time there were no women plumbers in the union and this woman had successfully completed a training program and worked as a plumber for several years.

Another common complaint was that male co-workers and supervisors would withhold necessary job information from the women. This is a real problem because virtually all of the women had to learn the basics of their trade through some sort of formal or informal apprenticeship program. A woman electrician, for example, reported spending 6 months of her training period sitting at a bench repairing fluorescent light bulbs while male trainees were sent out to troubleshoot machinery and learn wiring. Other less common complaints included being paid less, having different dress or language standards, inferior bathrooms, less job security, and poor job evaluations.

When faced with discrimination, most of the women took some kind of action to resolve the situation. Fifty-six percent of them complained to the person doing the discriminating or to their supervisor. An additional 16%

filed a formal complaint with the company's equal employment opportunity office or a government agency. The remainder felt the best way to survive was to keep quiet about the discrimination.

In most of the cases, the supervisors and male workers were not supportive of the women. Seventy-six percent of the women reported that their supervisors supported the discrimination. Only 3 of the 25 reported their supervisors were supportive. The rest either did not know of the incidents or showed no reaction. Among co-workers the reactions were: 11 supported discrimination, 9 had mixed reactions, 2 supported the woman, and 3 did not know or showed no reaction.

Husbands or lovers were only slightly more supportive of the women. Most of the women did not tell their partners of the discrimination they faced on the job because many of the men were not in favor of them working at nontraditional occupations. As one woman said:

> I don't think my husband liked me working there so I couldn't tell him about all of the things that went on. He would have gotten too mad if I'd told him about the sex stuff. It would have been nice if I could have talked about things that were bothering me, but he would have started throwing things.

Several women had men in their lives who were supportive, however, one reported a partner, who explicitly agreed with the discrimination. Of the women, 28% said they had no husbands or lovers.

When asked about how the sex discrimination made them feel, a majority of the sample (72%) said it made them angry. Twenty-four percent described it as making them feel incompetent. Another 8% seemed to accept discrimination as just being part of life and not worth getting upset about.

Even though most of the women were quite angry about the sex discrimination, few of them were able to gain support from co-workers and supervisors about changing conditions. Often even their husbands and lovers did not back them up. This led to enormous frustration and a lowered sense of efficacy.

Sexual Harassment. Sexual harassment was defined as occurring when a person is subjected to sexually explicit derogatory comments, unwanted physical contact, or sexual advances. The seriousness of the sexual harassment experienced by these women ranged from relatively mild forms to quite serious incidents. The most common complaints involved the more mild forms of harassment, such as sexually explicit comments about one's body and exposure to pornography. Eighty-eight percent of the women said they had been verbally harassed. Twenty-eight percent said they were the victims of unwanted physical contact, such as pinching or fondling. The most serious complaints came from two women, who reported that they had been physically assaulted. In addition, two of the women told me "off the record" of women they knew who had been raped.

As was the case with sex discrimination, the women got very little support from their supervisors in dealing with the sexual harassment. In fact, 20% of the supervisors were the actual perpetrators of the harassment. Another 28% of the supervisors actually seemed to support the harassment. Only one supervisor sided with a woman against sexual harassment. The remaining supervisors either did not know of the harassment or had no reaction to it.

It was particularly striking that no woman had male co-workers who supported her against harassers. They reported an even split between those having no reaction and those supporting the harasser.

Husbands' and lovers' reactions to the sexual harassment of their wives and girlfriends were similar to their reactions to the sex discrimination. Forty-four percent of the partners either did not know or had no reaction. Twenty percent were supportive of the woman and one supported the harassment. The remaining women did not have a male partner.

The most common strategy for handling the harassment employed by this sample of blue-collar workers was to ignore it. A cement truck driver described why she ignores the sexual innuendoes of her supervisor:

> The dispatcher is your immediate supervisor. He has a lot of power over a driver. There's a real difference in the jobs you're sent out on and he can really play havoc with that. As a woman it's even harder. The dispatcher is the big cheese and you're the new girl. So it kind of makes you fair game according to male thinking. You put up with a lot of sexual innuendo, like this dispatcher's standard, "Should I call you in the morning or should I just nudge you?" And you can't take it seriously.

The technique of ignoring the harassment was mentioned by 28% of the women. Other strategies were telling the harasser to stop (24%), making a joke out of the harassment (16%), complaining to supervisors (12%), filing an equal opportunity complaint (4%), and filing a union grievance (4%). The latter two approaches were used in the most serious situations.

When asked about their emotional reaction to the sexual harassment, women reported feeling anger (32%) and fear (12%). Another six respondents said they had no particular emotional reactions. The remainder described their emotional reactions in terms like "trampy," "numb," "stressed out," "defensive," and "hurt."

These findings imply that sexual harassment is a very real and serious problem for women doing nontraditional work. It is important to understand that even relatively mild forms of harassment can make a job unpleasant. The situation is exacerbated by the lack of support from male supervisors, co-workers, and partners, which could be why many women chose to be silent about their experiences of harassment on the job.

Racial Discrimination of Women Workers. For the nonWhite women, racial discrimination was combined with the sexual harassment and sex discrimination. Derogatory stereotypes about Black and Asian-American women's sexual practices were common. A Black sheet metal worker described how that made her feel as follows:

> When I first started working there, they gave me a hard time and wrote dirty words on the ladies room walls about what they would like me to do for them—sex and all that. After a while I just got tired of looking at it so I spoke to my supervisor, who finally got the walls cleaned off. And when I would walk up the aisles they would make wise cracks about what they would like to do. I just kept on walkin' and pretended like I didn't hear 'em. It made me feel trampy. That's because I was a Black girl...The White men think that they can take advantage of a Black woman. They think that she'd be proud to be with a White man. That's true. But I don't want no White man. I love my own Black people.

The nonWhite women and a White woman married to a Black man reported that they also encountered extensive racial discrimination that was unrelated to their sex. A couple of the women said the racial discrimination was much worse than the sex discrimination.

Sources of Support. Given that their jobs were often stressful, I asked the women to describe their sources of support for job-related problems. A majority looked to other women for support primarily from women friends (40%), but also from a women's trade group (8%), a woman counselor (4%), and from her mother (4%). Four women turned primarily to their husbands and one got help from a male co-worker. Another got assistance from friends of both sexes. The remaining women either felt they did not need support or could not identify any particular source of support.

Even though 21 of the women were union members, none of them listed the union as a source of help for job-related problems. When probed about the role of unions in helping women, only 8% of the sample had unabashedly pro-union comments. Twenty percent of the women described their unions as hostile to women within their ranks. One woman said:

> The union didn't want me in and the big-wigs haven't given me support since I got in. One time I ripped some porno off the wall, a poster size crotch shot of a woman, and the apprenticeship coordinator said I should have called him, but that I had to understand I was in a man's trade, and that men shouldn't have to live by my rules.

The remainder felt their unions had a mixed record as far as women went. Some in this last group reported that their unions were getting better as the number of women members increased.

Impact of Nontraditional Work on Personal Life

The focus of this section is on how doing nontraditional blue-collar work changes women's self-images, health, and personal relationships. The last topic is dealt with more extensively than the other two.

Self-Image. Most of the women in the sample experienced positive changes in their self-images as a function of being blue-collar workers. One of the women said that doing nontraditional work made her feel special. Forty-eight percent of the sample reported increased self-confidence, whereas only 8% said they had lost confidence in themselves as a result of the work. The following comments from a machinist expressed how many of the women felt about themselves. "I've gained a lot more self-confidence. I feel like I've conquered the world. I feel like I can do anything if I set my mind to it."

There was some concern about body image as is indicated by the three women voicing concerns about having big muscles. "I used to be afraid I was going to look like this big-shouldered broad. I didn't want to look like a broad. I wanted to look pretty. Now it's fun having more muscles." Three others mentioned that they and other people felt they had lost their femininity by working in a trade.

Health. The impact of the work on their health was more divided. Thirty-six percent reported positive changes tied to growing physically stronger. An equal number, however, voiced fears about their bodies wearing out or said they had been injured on the job. At the time of the interviews, three of the women were at least partially disabled due to injuries suffered at work. Only one woman felt there had been no significant changes in her health since going to work.

Personal Relationships. When asked to describe how their lives were different since going into a trade, the most commonly cited response was that it had hurt their marriages or relations with men. Fifty-six percent of the women said this had happened to them. Forty percent of the married women went through divorces while working in the trades. A woman working in a truck factory matter of factly describes the break up of her marriage. "With me working the whole family had to pitch in and help. My husband pitched in for awhile. Then he just stopped coming home. He found another lady that didn't work, had four kids, and was on welfare." Another woman said that she had decided to give up a job that she loved as a telephone frameman to save her marriage.

Almost half of the women cited their inability to keep up with household chores as a source of conflict in their marriages. In some cases, children, and rarely husbands, pitched in to do more. Another source of stress in marriages could be the increased independence that six women said they had gained by doing nontraditional work.

> Last year my husband was on a 4-day work week so I made only $800 less than he did for the whole year. I was in seventh heaven. I was equal to him. I wasn't below him. I think that's been hard for him. Traditional people have been brought up that a woman isn't in the same classification as her husband. Now I feel that I'm just as good as he is. Maybe I'm even better.

Some of these strains probably would exist in any marriage when the woman took on a difficult job. Pleck (1984) discovered that men find working wives to be psychologically threatening because they take away a major source of male identity (breadwinner). When the wife does work outside of the home, this threat to the male identity can be limited by the wife taking a job that does not have greater prestige or earnings than the husband's.

There is some evidence that indicates that working-class families are more traditional than are middle-class families. Mortimer and London (1984) found that traditional sex roles of husband as breadwinner and wife as homemaker are central to conceptions of the "good life" in working-class families. Duncan and Duncan (1978) found auto workers in Detroit were more likely to limit the type of work that women could do than were other workers in their survey.

Four other women cited strained social relations as being a result of doing nontraditional work. Much of this strain also dealt with difficulties in reconciling work roles and sex roles. A papermaker described her dilemma as follows.

> I'm not a macho person but I don't lean too far to the left because I'm not a real feminine person. You know, I'm not a really frilly, squeaky, high-voice, "Oooo, poor little me" and I'm not a real "Boy, let's get out there and cut another cord of wood" person. I'm right in the gap...It's hard. I haven't found anybody that fits into that area that I can talk with, you know, intimately, yet be accepted for what I do...Men don't want a woman that goes out there, cleans her sledgehammer, and hits a plastic wedge to break wood apart. And a lot of women don't see me as being feminine. They can't talk to me because of the work I do.

Fifteen of the women in the sample were parents. Even though Mortimer and London (1984) had found that children in working-class families had much more rigid notions of appropriate sex roles than did middle-class children, the parents in my sample said that their children were in favor of their working a nontraditional blue-collar job. One woman reported that her children were actually disappointed when she was promoted from a bus driver to a transit supervisor. Her children had enjoyed telling people that their mother was a bus driver. Only two reported that their children were opposed to their choice of work. Given that most working-class families are more traditional about sex roles and that women doing non-traditional work put greater demands on their children as far as housework is concerned, it is surprising that the children were fairly supportive. It bodes well for future generations.

Yet when asked if they wanted their children (real or hypothetical) to do this type of work, only the fisherwoman was unabashedly in favor of them following in their mothers' footsteps. Most reported that it was up to the children, but 28% were strongly opposed to their children doing the same work. These women wanted a better life for their children than they had.

In contrast to their aspirations for their children, most of the women would definitely encourage other women to pursue opportunities in the trades. A plausible explanation for this divergence is that these women are aware of the current options available for women. Given those options most of them consider trades to be a good choice for themselves and other women toady. That, however, does not mean it will be the best option tomorrow when their children grow up.

CONCLUSION

Even though the backgrounds of the women in the sample varied in terms of religion, childhood aspirations, age, race, marital status, and parenthood, most of the women were united in their belief that for themselves nontraditional blue-collar work was the best option. This agreement is quite remarkable when one looks at the actual cost the women have paid and are continuing to pay in their personal and work lives.

The most notable cost of their choice of career was the deep estrangement from men. This estrangement occurred at work, where the women could only gain acceptance by taking on sex roles that were inappropriate to the workplace, and where they had to confront sex discrimination and sexual harassment. It was not that any one of these incidents in and of itself was that bad. Instead it was the effects of continually being treated as less equal, that wore away at these women.

The lack of support by men for the women confronting sex discrimination and sexual harassment was stark. Co-workers, supervisors, and sometimes even partners were unwilling to break from their fellow men to support the women. Given this, it is actually a bit surprising that the women felt that they had acceptable working relations with the men on their jobs.

The implication of this finding is that researchers cannot take statements about workplace relationships at face value. The researcher must explore the meaning of those statements by asking more detailed questions about what constitutes an acceptable relationship with male co-workers. For example, because women might have low expectations about male behavior, even quite discriminatory relationships may be deemed acceptable. In addition, there were enormous strains in the women's personal relationships. They were continually juggling home and work responsibilities. The men in their lives were uncomfortable with the increased independence that comes from their earning a good living. They were also not willing to help pick up the slack on the home front by doing additional household chores.

Often in their internal life the women faced difficulties deciding who they actually were. They expressed difficulty in reconciling their work roles with images of themselves as feminine. This concern was expressed in their worries about developing too many muscles and an uneasiness about being around more traditional women.

Yet even with all of the difficulties, most of the women were satisfied with their choice of nontraditional blue-collar work. Obviously the money was a big factor in this satisfaction, but there were other benefits. The most positive change in their lives was increased self-confidence. These women felt good about themselves. They knew they were capable of performing very difficult jobs and surviving under a lot of stress. The mere fact that some women are capable of performing blue-collar jobs under very trying conditions does not, however, mean that people should be forced to work in these circumstances. There needs to be an increased awareness that sex discrimination and sexual harassment are still very real problems for women in blue-collar jobs. Even though many firms have stated policies against these practices, their concern often is not implemented at the level of the frontline supervisors. There needs to be a major effort to change the attitudes and practices of the men in direct authority over the women blue-collar workers, since they set the tone for all workplace interactions. Perhaps of greater importance is the need for more effort to attract women into blue-collar work. As more women enter these occupations, there will be greater opportunities for women to advance into supervisory positions, and thus gain some control over how women experience blue-collar work.

REFERENCES

Adams, J. R., Lawrence, F. P., & Cook. S. (1979). Analyzing stereotypes of women in the work forces. *Sex Roles, 5,* 581–594.

Anonymous. (1942). *Supervising the woman war worker.* Deep River, CT: National Foremen's Institute.

Baker, H. (1942). *Women in war industries.* Princeton, NJ: Princeton University Press.

Brunner, N. R. (1981, April). Blue-collar women. *Personnel Journal,* 279–282.

Bureau of the Census. (1986). *Statistical abstract of the United States 1987.* Washington, DC: U.S. Government Printing Office.

Deaux, K. (1984). Blue-collar barriers. *American Behavioral Scientist, 27,* 287–300.

Duncan, B. & Duncan, O. D. (1978). *Sex typing and social roles.* New York: Academic Press.

Enarson, E. P. (1984). *Woods-working women.* University, AL: University of Alabama Press.

Epstein, C. F. (1972). Encountering the male establishment: Sex status limits on women's careers in the professions. In R. M. Pavalko (Ed.), *Sociological perspectives on occupations.* Itasca, IL: Peacock Press.

Fernandez, J. P. (1981). *Racism and sexism in corporate life.* Lexington, MA: D.C. Heath.

Gruber, J. E., & Bjorn, L. (1982). Blue-collar blues. *Work and Occupations, 9,* 271–298.

Gutek, B. A., & Morasch, B. (1982). Sex-ratios, sex-role spillover, and sexual harassment of women at work. *Journal of Social Issues, 38,* 55–74.

Harlan, S. L., & O'Farrell, B. (1982). After the pioneers: Prospects for women in nontraditional blue-collar jobs. *Work and Occupations, 9,* 363–386.

Harlan, A., & Weiss, C. (1982). Sex differences in factors affecting managerial career advancement. In P. A. Wallace (Ed.), *Women in the workplace.* Boston: Auburn House.

Hennig, M., & Jardim, A. (1977). *The managerial woman.* New York: Pocket Books.

Kanter, R. M. (1977a). *Men and women of the corporation.* New York: Basic.

Kanter, R. M. (1977b). Some effects of proportions on group life: Skewed sex ratios and responses to token women. *American Journal of Sociology, 82,* 965–990.

Lange, S. (1982, December). Ten-hut! Careers for women in the military. *Vocational Guidance Quarterly,* 118–122.

Lederer, M. (1979). *Blue-collar jobs for women.* New York: Dutton.

Lembright, M. F., & Riemer, J. W. (1982). Women truckers' problems and the impact of sponsorship. *Work and Occupations, 9,* 457–474.

Lillydahl, J. H. (1986). Women and traditionally male blue-collar jobs. *Work and Occupations, 13,* 307–323.

McIlwee, J. S. (1982). Work satisfaction among women in non-traditional occupations. *Work and Occupations, 9,* 299–335.

Mortimer, J. T., & London, J. (1984). The varying linkages of work and family. In P. Voydanoff (Ed.), *Work and Family* (pp.). Palo Alto: Mayfield.

Nieva, V. F., & Gutek, B. A. (1981) *Women and work.* New York: Praeger.

O'Farrell, B., & Harlan, S. L. (1982). Craftworkers and clerks: The effect of male coworker hostility on women's satisfaction with non-traditional jobs. *Social Problems, 29,* 252–265.

Pleck, J. H. (1984). Men's family work: Three perspectives and some new data. In P. Voydanoff (Ed.), *Work and family* (pp. .) Palo Alto: Mayfield.

Riemer, J. W. (1979). *Hard hats: The work world of construction workers.* Beverly Hills: Sage.

Schreiber, C. T. (1979). *Changing places: Men and women in transitional occupations.* Cambridge, MA: MIT Press.

Schroedel, J. R. (1985). *Alone in a crowd: Women in the trades tell their stories.* Philadelphia: Temple University Press.

Shaw, E. A. (1972). Differential impact of negative stereotyping in employee selection. *Personnel Psychology, 25,* 333–338.

Walshok, M. L. (1981). *Blue-collar women: Pioneers on the male frontier.* Garden City: Anchor Press.

Wetherby, T. (1977). *Conversations: Working women talk about doing a "man's job".* Millbrae, CA: Les Femmes.

Williamson, J. B., Karp, D. A., & Dalphin, J. R. (1977). *The research craft: An introduction to social science methods.* Boston: Little, Brown.

Yoder, J. D. (1983). Another look at women in the United States Army: A comment on Woelfel's article. *Sex Roles, 9,* 285–288.

Yoder, J. D., & Adams, J. (1984). Women entering non-traditional roles: When work demands and sex roles conflict. The case of West Point. *International Journal of Women's Studies, 7,* 260–272.

Yoder, J. D., Adams, J., Grove, S., & Priest, R. F. (1985). To teach is to learn: Overcoming tokenism with mentors. *Psychology of Women Quarterly, 9,* 119–131.

Chapter 13

Discovering the Meanings of Work

Abigail J. Stewart
University of Michigan

The starting point for this book is the notion that it is not clear what "work" means to women. To begin here is to assume that the "meaning" of work for an individual is not simply a function of the prestige or economic value attached to it by the wider culture. Considerable evidence shows that many variables, in addition to prestige and income, contribute to occupational satisfaction and productivity for both men and women (see, e.g., Crosby, 1982; Veroff, Douvan, & Kulka, 1981). This book assumes further, however, that the meaning of work for *women* is complicated by the different meanings attached to women and *women's* work by the wider culture. Again, there is considerable evidence that women's work is viewed by both men and women through complex filters including broad sex-role expectations, work- and family-role ideologies and occupational stereotypes (see, e.g., Nieva & Gutek, 1982; Reskin, 1984). The assumptions behind this volume, then, seem amply justified by reasonable extrapolations from existing research evidence in the social sciences.

Even if we grant these two assumptions, however, a question remains: Is the meaning of women's work—indeed of anyone's work—really of consequence to anyone but the individual? Clearly one can justify the study of the subjective meaning of any aspect of human experience by noting that individuals themselves attach importance to their subjective experience; that is, the meaning of their work feels important and interesting to them. In the case of women's work, however, the problem's significance goes well beyond this sort of justification.

Feminist theorists from Mary Wollstonecraft (1792/1978) to Virginia
Woolf (1929/1974, 1938/1977) and Betty Friedan (1963) have repeatedly
pointed to the meaning of women's work as a central element both in understanding sexist social arrangements and in facilitating women's equal
social status and power. These arguments often have addressed the importance of socially valued work as a source of control over economic resources
(food, property, capital, etc., depending on the nature of the economy; see,
e.g., Engels, 1842/1972; Gilman, 1898/1966); this dimension of work's
"meaning" both for the observer and the subject of it cannot be minimized.
Many other aspects of work (derivative from this economic power, and perhaps from other sources as well) have been identified as crucial to women's
liberation, including a sense of personal worth and value; a sense of purpose and achievement; a capacity to contribute to the wider society; experience with and control over social arrangements outside the household;
and independence from the control of others (see, e.g., Brittain, 1953;
Friedan, 1963; Mill, 1869/1970; Schreiner, 1911/1985; Woolf, 1929/1974,
1938/1977). Feminist theories, then, have tied the meanings of work for
women very closely indeed to the position of women in the culture at large,
and women's consequent experience of many aspects of the culture and
especially of themselves.

Most often these theorists have grounded their arguments about the
general meaning of work for women in their own personal experience. For
example, Woolf (1938/1977) drew heavily on her personal experience of social devaluation as a woman without a college education in advocating for
women's education in *Three Guineas.* In fact, Rose (1978) has argued that "It
was written from her own rage and from the only point of her identity that
had not been shaken in her thirties, her femaleness and her identification
with other women" (p. 222). Similarly, Brittain (1953) argued that, in the
end, work was the only reliable source of personal satisfaction for women;
she based this argument on her own experience of disastrous losses and disappointments in relationships, coupled with a lifetime of deeply rewarding
work on social problems (see e.g., Berry, 1979; Brittain 1933/1980; Spender,
1982). Similar evidence for close links between personal experience of the
rich inner rewards associated with socially valued work and arguments for
the centrality of work in the liberation of all women may be found in the
lives of Mary Wollstonecraft (Tomalin, 1974), Charlotte Perkins Gilman
(Degler, 1966; Hill, 1980), and Olive Schreiner (Graves, 1978; Winkler, 1980).

Observing the connection between feminist theorists' experience of
work and their theoretical arguments should not be thought to imply that
the theorists' arguments cannot be valid. The validity of the arguments is
entirely independent of their source. Moreover, it is part of the epistemol-
ogy of much of feminist theory to value the role of subjective experience as
a source of knowledge (see Harding, 1986, 1987). However, if the subjective

experience on which feminist theories have been based is limited—to relatively educated, White, middle-class women raised in Western European cultures, for example—then feminist theory itself may be quite limited in its capacity to articulate the meaning of work for "women." Indeed, in recent years feminist theorists have increasingly recognized the futility of attempting to define "women's experience," and have learned to think more plurally about the experience of women in different sorts of situations (Harding, 1987). This volume fits in well with the recent cries for a feminist theory which can encompass *diverse* meanings of all of women's experiences (e.g., Hooks, 1984; Mohanty, 1982; Ong, 1988).

It is a relatively simple matter to call for such a theory; it is, however, not so simple to develop a broad base of information about the true range of meanings that women's work can have (more difficult still to combine this with the meanings of that work for their friends and relatives, and for social institutions). The strategy adopted in this book involves several elements: inclusion of studies of women engaged in a wide range of jobs and work settings (within the framework of contemporary U.S. society); emphasis on qualitative or open-ended data as providing the least "processed" or packaged version of the meanings of women's experience; valuing of detail and "richness" from each individual over large numbers of individuals. Each of these elements reflects a choice between defensible alternatives. Thus, it can be argued that it is valuable to study women in the few fields dominated by women rather than in a wide range of fields in which few women are working; that quantitative data would permit greater standardization and generalizability; and that less data from more individuals would produce findings that could be more directly translated into social policy.

This book is not, then, and cannot be, the last word on the meanings of work for women. It cannot address issues that demand quantification and generalizability. What it does do, however, is document some of the diversity in the meanings of work for women by presenting detailed, relatively less-processed accounts of some meanings of work for women in a wide range of work situations. This documentation, in turn, can and should be broadly generative both of richer, more adequate theorizing (within both feminist theory and psychological theory) and of more meaningful hypotheses. These hypotheses can now be tested using data collected on the basis of better understanding of the range of meanings of work for women. Most importantly, this documentation permits us to learn about some of the meanings that work has for women that may not be visible with the lenses of existing feminist and social science theory. For example, we have discovered in this volume how central the experience of relationships at work is to many women's experience of work (see, e.g., chapters by Crosby; Grossman; O'Leary & Ickovics), and now much the meaning of one's own talents and work achievements depends on one's life stage (see, e.g., chapters by Chester; James; Schuster; Tomlinson-Keasey) and the social context (see e.g., Gilkes and Tomlinson-Keasey).

The research presented in this book also permits us to learn about potential consequences of some work experiences for women. Thus, for example, we understand better why the positive experience of relationships at work might be tied to a high proportion of women in the work setting (as with Ickovics & O'Leary), in contrast with settings in which women are often "solo" or rare (as with Schroedel's blue-collar workers). Similarly, we can begin to see how the various tensions and complexities associated with work/home "boundaries" for women workers are affected by marital and parental situations, as well as work settings (compare Crosby's divorcees in a corporate setting, Grossman's pregnant therapists, and Richter's older mother managers in two-career marriages). We cannot know, from this book, how broadly the mechanisms displayed apply, but we can see—perhaps for the first time—their operation in a single woman or in a group of women and then consider how to assess the generality of the mechanism.

This book, in sum, presents a series of explorations, or voyages of discovery. In their travels, the researchers represented here employed many different navigational skills and instruments—tools for identifying where they were and what they could see. Social science researchers have little documentation of the skills and instruments we use in this kind of process. Although we have an elaborate canon of rules and procedures for hypothesis testing, we rarely expose the process of discovery to analysis or observation. In this book, however, we can find a rich assortment of examples of techniques available to social scientists working on problems of discovery.

Perhaps the simplest tool used by many of the researchers in this volume is the use of *small, purposive samples.* When the goal is discovery, rather than hypothesis testing, there is almost no premium on large, representative samples. If the researchers' goal is to identify the important dimensions of a phenomenon, they must find individuals who have experienced or display the phenomenon (e.g., contribution to the Black community, giftedness, blue-collar work, pregnancy during therapy, etc.), and who are willing and able to reflect on it. It is not important that identified individuals typify a much larger group, only that they discuss experiences common to a group which is clearly defined. Moreover, if the researchers hope to learn from the participants about their lives, they will need to choose individuals who can articulate their experience and to limit the number of individuals whose experience they can explore in detail.

Nevertheless, there is still relatively wide variation in terms of the numbers of individuals employed in these studies. Grossman and Stewart interviewed only six individuals; other researchers drew upon relatively large samples, but interviewed only a handful of women for their studies

(Chester and James). Most others interviewed larger, but still small samples (16–40 women). In some cases researchers presented a few individuals who served as "typical" examples (e.g., Tomlinson-Keasey), and in other cases they presented themes cutting across cases (e.g., Gilkes; Crosby; Grossman; O'Leary & Ickovics; Richter, Schuster; Schroedel). In general, the guiding principle was not so much how *many* individuals were included, but how clearly a meaningful informant or group of informants could be defined. Thus, Grossman and Stewart relied on the professional expertise they shared with their small number of "key informants," whereas James and Chester relied on the position of an individual as an interesting representative of a subgroup within their larger sample. Pragmatic considerations—how many individual cases can be understood by a single processing intellect—limited the collection of the larger samples in terms of number of cases, but not in terms of amount of information obtained from each woman.

Second, nearly all of the studies relied on a technique involving *focused comparison and contrast.* Sometimes the comparison was to an assumed or known other standard; thus, Gilkes compared her community workers with known or hypothesized characteristics of White women workers. O'-Leary and Ickovics compared the reports of their clerical employees of female bosses both with findings about clerical employees of male bosses, and other literature about women workers. Similarly, Schuster compared the experiences of the gifted women she studied with characteristics of gifted women identified in previous research. And Tomlinson-Keasey compared the experiences of her sample of older gifted women with findings from studies of contemporary women. Finally, Grossman and Stewart compared the power themes they identified in their interviews with women therapists and professors with those identified on a theoretical and clinical basis by Jean Baker Miller (1982).

Even more often, the comparison and contrast was internal to the sample of women, and involved comparing different types of experiences represented within the sample. Thus, Grossman and Stewart compared professors and therapists to each other in their experience of power in the work role. Tomlinson-Keasey compared five different "types" of life patterns of gifted women. Chester selected individual cases that reflected different personality patterns, and James selected individual cases that reflected different career patterns. Then both compared the different cases with each other. Grossman considered her pregnant therapists' experience before and after the birth of their babies.

Finally, the experience of women in a small sample was sometimes compared with the experience of men in a precise comparison sample. Thus, Crosby compared her divorcing female workers' experience with that of divorcing male workers in the same settings. Similarly, Richter compared the work/home boundary experiences of women and men in dual-career couples working in the same kinds of positions in the same companies.

A third methodological feature of these chapters is the *reliance on interview techniques.* Although a number of the studies used additional techniques (e.g., Grossman used group interviews; Chester, Richter and James referred to other quantitative data, etc.), all but one of these chapters depended on relatively open-ended interview procedures (and the one exception, Tomlinson-Keasey, drew upon open-ended questionnaire responses from a highly literate and articulate group). To the extent that researchers aim to identify the nature of a phenomenon as it is experienced and named by the subjects of that experience, they must rely on first-person reports. A number of the chapters in this volume discussed steps taken to ensure that researchers did not define their experience "for" their informants. Thus, for example, Schroedel discussed the importance to her of a flexible interview schedule, whereby the interviewer can ask questions in a sequence that flows naturally from the interviewee's responses. Grossman and Stewart began their interview with a request for women to "tell their own story" and not to worry about answering particular questions. Crosby relied on a repeated interviewing procedure, because "repeated interviews helped build trust" between interviewers and interviewees.

A fourth characteristic of the methods employed in this volume is the willingness to try out *innovative procedures.* Thus, Grossman employed a group interview format with the pregnant therapists, arguing that in this way group participants "were able to use their mutual experiences to clarify, intensity and illustrate the complex situation of being a pregnant therapist." Crosby contacted participants' supervisors and co-workers to gain an additional perspective on her divorcing workers' experience. Richter devised techniques to measure "planned" and "interposed" transitions between work and home. Grossman and Stewart asked their therapist and professor interviewees to react to their interpretations. Crosby used her team of interviewers as a check on her interpretations. All of these innovations were creations of individual researchers struggling to develop procedures which would enhance the likelihood that the data they obtained would be meaningful and trustworthy. Because there is no preexisting set of rules and procedures consensually accepted as conferring "reliability and validity" on qualitative data, researchers devised their own techniques for increasing their own faith in the data.

A related characteristic of much of the research reported in this volume is the *collaborative stance* many of the researchers took toward study participants. This collaborative stance is most obvious in instances where researcher and participant shared aspects of their work identity (Grossman; Grossman & Stewart; Schroedel). This stance is apparent, too, in the common technique of asking participants very direct questions about the meaning of their experience, and assuming that they are able to reflect intelligently on it. Thus, for example, James took seriously her interviewees' own judgments about the aspects of their own lives that had been important prods to personal growth and development. Similarly, Chester took seriously the self-reports of a concern with personal achievement from women in her sample who scored "low" on the "need-for-achievement" measure. By doing so, she was able to clarify the much narrower, but precise significance of the "need for achievement," as well as the many ways in which achievement and competence matter in *different* ways (not less) to women low in the "need."

Perhaps also as a derivative of the collaborative stance, many of the studies reported here depended on *multiple interactions with research participants.* Crosby, Grossman and Stewart, and Grossman all conducted multiple interviews with each participant. In addition, Chester, James, Tomlinson-Keasey, and Schuster relied on longitudinal data, or data collected on several occasions over time. When the research participant is defined as a collaborator in the research process, the desirability of several occasions for contact becomes clearer. Moreover, when conventional techniques for establishing reliability and validity of measurement cannot be used, researchers rely on multiple contacts to increase their sense that participants are comfortable telling what they know, and that they (the interviewer) have understood what they have been told.

Both as a result of the effort to take research participants' own understanding seriously, and as a result of the focus of this volume on *meaning*, researchers' methods depended very heavily on techniques of *interpretation.* Often these interpretations took the form of fairly standard content analyses, or analyses of themes that recurred within and across informants. Often themes were identified by assessing frequent responses to particular questions. Thus, for example, O'Leary and Ickovics described the "common complaints" of their sample of clerical workers. Alternatively, many researchers identified themes that commonly recurred across different respondents, but in different places in the interviews. For example, Schroedel reported that "most of the women also mentioned at some point in their interviews that affirmative action law played a role in their getting jobs." Crosby used different responses in the interview to identify women's various ways of using work as a device for coping with the pain involved in their divorce (e.g., work provided structure, time out, self-esteem, etc.). Grossman and Stewart identified thematic consistencies in the experiences of power across both therapists and professors (e.g., the centrality of nurturance, empowerment, and legitimate authority to the pleasures involved in power), as well as a few themes which were frequent only in one group or the other (e.g., feelings of inadequacy, which were stronger among professors).

In these different examples, the themes identified vary in the degree to which they involve abstractions from the women's own descriptions. Some authors identified themes representing direct counts of frequently expressed concerns in interviews; other themes represent inferences or categorizations from the directly expressed concerns. In all cases, researchers relied heavily on their own capacity to interpret the interviewee's account. Because all of the accounts in this volume include detailed verbatim quotations from the interviews it is quite possible for the reader to assess the plausibility of the interpretations. Thus, "interrater reliability," far from being absent or problematic, can actually be evaluated by the reader directly (see Runyan, 1982, on evaluating the validity of accounts of lives).

Moreover, in some cases, authors described other efforts they made to assess the interrater reliability of their content analyses. Thus, Grossman and Stewart required agreement with each other's independent derivations, and requested feedback from the participants; Crosby required a high degree of frequency of occurrence, and checked categories with interviewers; and Grossman held followup discussions with group members and one individual interviewee to discuss her analyses.

It is the individual case studies, however, that illustrate the heavy reliance on interpretation most clearly. Here the researcher, in describing the experience of her exemplar, must bring her powers of interpretation to bear on a vast sea of words, and then present them in a way which seems to reflect the interpretation as well as the voice of the individual woman. In describing Sandy, for example (the woman high in need for achievement and with consistent employment), Chester showed us with Sandy's words how she arrived at the notion that Sandy views the juggling of roles itself as an achievement task. She quoted Sandy as saying that she was "the *only* person in the history of this organization to come back after having a baby" and "I see myself as a mother, which is very important to me, but I also know I can manage and juggle a lot more than I ever thought" and also "As my experience grows, so does my capacity for problem solving." Chester convinces us by her judicious selection of quotations from Sandy that role combination is itself a source of achievement gratification for Sandy.

The contrast with Janet was very instructive. Janet had low scores on the need for achievement, but also showed a continuous employment pattern. Chester showed, again by presenting critical evidence from the interview, that Janet views her involvement in her work very differently. She sees herself as returning to work "to help out with the finances" and because it gave her "something extra to do." She enjoys her work, but the reasons she gives are very different: "The people are great; it's only a few miles away from our house. The hours are convenient. Also, I like a little variety in my life."

All of the studies in this book, then, depend both on the presentation of women's own accounts of their experiences at work, and on the researchers' interpretations of those accounts. By presenting the women's own words in such volume the authors have put before us a tremendous amount of raw material interpretable by others. In offering their own interpretations of the narratives, the researchers have drawn upon psychological theory, empirical research and their own personal understanding of the women they studied and offered their viewpoint to us, most often documented in sufficient detail for us to accept or reject it for ourselves.

It is clear that the authors represented here are quite self-conscious about the dependence of this research on reflective, sensitive interpretation by the researcher. As a result, these papers include many thoughtful discussions of the *researchers' personal relationship both with the participants in the research and with the research process itself.* Schroedel, for example, pointed out that "As someone who had spent over 8 years working at nontraditional blue-collar jobs, I was accepted as 'one of us.' Several of the women told me that I was the first person they had ever really talked to about their work." She indicated that she wanted

> the women to feel comfortable talking about some of the most personal and painful aspects of their lives. For example, not only did I want them to tell me whether incidents of sexual harassment occurred, but also to describe what happened and what feelings they experienced.

She concluded, at the end of the chapter, that the evidence of discriminatory and harassing relationships at work was at variance with the women's descriptions of their work relationships as acceptable. She suggested that:

> The implication of this finding is that researchers cannot take statements about work place relationships at face value. The researcher must explore the meaning of those statements by asking more detailed questions about what constitutes an acceptable relationship with male co-workers. For example, because women might have low expectations about male behavior, even quite discriminatory relationships may be deemed acceptable.

This kind of lead—about when to take individuals' account at face value, and when we may be misled if we do—is invaluable for the future researcher hoping to contextualize Schroedel's findings, or to assess their generalizability.

The methods employed in this volume are not without limitations. In some cases the lack of a focused comparison may have diffused the findings; in some cases interpretations may seem too hesitant and in others too bold; in some cases accounts may seem well-justified and in others less convincing. This is to be expected. Moreover, for many purposes the research reported here can only be a beginning. No one would expect policy recommendations to flow from a study of the impact of pregnancy in a small sample of pregnant psychotherapists; or blue-collar workers drawn from many different trades; or clerical workers working in a single feminist institution. For these purposes we do need large-scale studies involving "representative samples." But the policy and other "basic research" studies—whatever methods they adopt—waiting to be designed will be better ones if the rich detail and insight about the many meanings of women's work presented in this volume are set in juxtaposition to each other, and used as a source of better, clearer questions than those we would have been able to ask before.

REFERENCES

Berry, P. (1979). Introduction. In V. Brittain (Ed.), *Testament of experience* (pp. 7–13). London: Fontana.

Brittain, V. (1953). *Lady into woman: A history of women from Victoria to Elizabeth II.* London: Andrew Dakers.

Brittain, V. (1980). *Testament of youth.* New York: Wideview. (Originally published 1933)

Crosby, F. (1982). *Relative deprivation and working women.* New York: Oxford.

Degler, C. (1966). Introduction. In C.P. Gilman, *Women and economics* (pp. vi–xxxv). New York: Harper.

Engels, F. (1972). *The origin of the family, private property and the state.* New York: International Publishers. (Originally published 1842)

Friedan, B. (1963). *The feminine mystique.* New York: Dell.

Gilman, C.P. (1966). *Women and economics.* New York: Harper. (Originally published 1898)

Graves, J. (1978). Preface. In O. Schreiner, *Women and labour* (pp. 3–10). London: Virago.

Harding, S. (1986). *The science question in feminism.* Bloomington, IN: Indiana University Press.

Harding, S. (1987). *Feminism and methodology.* Bloomington, IN: Indiana University Press.

Hill, M.A. (1980). *Charlotte Perkins Gilman: The making of a radical feminist.* Philadelphia, PA: Temple University Press.

Hooks, B. (1984). *Feminist theory: From margin to center.* Boston, MA: South End Press.

Mill, J.S. (1970). *The subjection of women.* Cambridge, MA: MIT Press. (Originally published 1869)

Miller, J. B. (1982). *Women in power.* (Work in progress No. 82-01). Wellesley, MA: Wellesley College, Stone Center for Developmental Services and Studies.

Mohanty, C. (1982). Under western eyes: Feminist scholarship and colonial discourses. *Boundary 2, 12,* 333–358.

Nieva, V.F., & Gutek, B.A. (1982). *Women and work: A psychological perspective.* New York: Praeger.

Ong, A. (1988). Colonialism and modernity: Feminist re-presentations of women in non-western societies. *Inscriptions, 3/4,* 79–93.

Reskin, B. (1984). *Sex segregation in the workplace: Trends, explanations, remedies.* Washington, DC: National Academy Press.

Rose, P. (1978). *Woman of letters: A life of Virginia Woolf.* New York: Oxford.

Runyan, W.M. (1982). *Life histories and psychobiography.* New York: Oxford.

Schreiner, O. (1985). *Women and labour.* London: Virago. (Originally published 1911)

Spender, D. (1982). *Women of ideas.* London: Ark.

Tomalin, C. (1974). *The life and death of Mary Wollstonecraft.* New York: New American Library.

Veroff, J., Douvan, E., & Kulka, R. (1981). *The inner American.* New York: Basic.

Winkler, B.S. (1980, Winter). Victorian daughters: The lives and feminism of Charlotte Perkins Gilman and Olive Schreiner. *Michigan Occasional Papers in Women's Studies,* XIII.

Wollstonecraft, M. (1978). *Vindication of the rights of women.* Harmondsworth, Middlesex, England: Penguin. (Originally published 1792)

Woolf, V. (1974). *A room of one's own.* Harmondsworth: Penguin. (Originally published 1929)

Woolf, V. (1977). *Three guineas.* Harmondsworth: Penguin. (Originally published 1938)

Author Index

A

Aaronson, E., 160
Abramson, J., 190
Adams, D.M., 116
Adams, J.R., 240
Agins, T., 54
Aldous, T., 149
Anderson, K., 2, 3
Andolsen, B.H., 167, 176
Antonucci, T.C., 105, 107
Asher, S.J., 134
Astin, L., 1
Atkinson, J.W., 84, 86, 98

B

Baer, J., 4
Bailyn, L., 157, 160
Baker, H., 240
Ballou, J., 57
Balsam, R., 57
Barbanel, L., 57, 58
Barbee, A.H., 224, 226
Bardwick, J.M., 47, 190, 208
Barenbaum, N.B., 12

Barnett, I.B.W., 179
Barnett, R., 4, 99, 105, 107, 236
Bartolome, F., 144, 149
Baruch, G., 4, 99, 107, 236
Bass, B.M., 12
Baum, E., 57, 58, 79
Becker, H.S., 166, 170
Bell, J.H.,
Benedek, T., 57, 58, 79
Bergman, B.R., 107, 237
Berk, R.A., 11
Bern, P., 35
Bernard, J., 6
Berry, P., 260
Betz, N.E., 109
Bhrolchain, M.N., 105
Birnbaum, J., 105, 190, 191
Bjorn, L., 241
Bloom, B.L., 134
Bond, J.C., 175
Botkin, D.R., 233
Bowman, G., 35, 54
Breen, D., 57
Brewer, M.B., 11
Bridges, J.S., 233
Briles, J., 35
Brittain, V., 260

Brown, G.W., 105
Brunner, N.R., 242
Bureau of National Afairs, 54
Bureau of the Census, 248
Burke, B.W., 235
Burris, B.H., 36
Butts, N., 57, 58

C

Cade, T., 167, 182
Caldwell, B.E., 54
Cancian, F.M., 130
Cardoza, A., 106
Carson, J., 182
Cavenar, J., 57, 58
Chester, N.L., 6, 7, 8, 12, 84, 85, 264–268
Chodorow, N., 13, 77, 236
Christian, B., 175, 177
Coleman, L.M., 105, 107
Contratto, S., 13, 77
Corcoran, M., 103
Cott, N., 3
Cox, O.C., 178
Crites, J.D., 1
Crosby, F., 2, 6, 12, 13, 35, 36, 261, 263–267

D

Daniels, P., 5, 11
Dash, L., 53
Davids, A., 57
Davies, M.W., 4
Davis, A., 165, 176
Davis, E.L., 179
Deaux, K., 235, 243
Degler, C., 262
Delano, M., 43
Devault, S., 57
Dietz, J., 116
Dill, B.T., 169, 178
Dinnerstein, D., 13, 14
Doering, S., 57
Donovan, M.E., 117
Douvan, E., 11, 107, 108, 261
Dowd, M., 234
DuBois, W.E.B., 177, 178, 180
Duncan, B., 256

Duncan, O.D., 11

E

Eccles, J., 83, 84
Enarson, E.P., 242, 249
Engles, F., 262
Entwisle, D., 57
Epstein, C.F., 241
Erikson, E., 104
Erlich, E., 6
Etzion, D., 160
Evans, P.A.L., 144, 149
Exum, P.C., 182

F

Falbo, T., 11
Faunce, P.S., 191
Feagin, J.R., 178
Featherman, D.L., 11
Feingold, A., 237
Feinleib, M., 36
Fenster, S., 57, 77, 79
Ferber, M., 35, 54
Fernandez, J.P., 241
Field, H.S., 54
Fields, E.L., 179
Fitzgerald, L.F., 1, 109
Fleming, E.S., 189, 191
Fox, M., 2, 11
Franklin, B., 190
Franz, C., 104
Frazier, E.F., 178
French, J.R.P., 12
Freud, S., 13, 121
Freudenberger, H.J., 160
Friedan, B., 117, 262

G

Gallese, L.R., 190
Gardner, S., 57
Genovese, E., 175, 176
Gerson, K., 2, 83, 84, 103, 106
Gerstel, N., 127, 134
Giddings, P., 179
Gilbert, L.A., 236

Gilkes, C.T., 6, 168, 264, 265
Gilligan, C., 7, 144, 155, 158, 206, 236
Gilman, C.P., 262
Ginzberg, E., 109, 190, 191, 202
Gofman, E., 147, 166
Goldberg, P., 40
Golding, J., 36
Goode, W., 12
Gora, J.G., 105
Gordon, S.L., 12
Gould, R.C., 149
Graves, J., 262
Gray, J.D., 233
Greenwald, M., 4
Grossman, H.Y., 4, 6–8, 47, 59, 60, 61, 77,
   263, 265–268
Gruber, J.E., 243
Guba, E.G., 59
Gupta, N., 36, 52
Gutek, B.A., 36, 40, 45, 52, 83, 242, 261

H

Hall, D.T., 145, 149, 150
Hall, F.S., 145
Hansen, R.D., 48
Hardesty, S., 35, 117
Harding, S., 262, 263
Harlan, A., 241, 243
Harlan, S.L., 4, 243
Haw, M., 233
Haynes, S.G., 36
Heller, D., 14
Helson, R., 191
Henning, M, 46, 241
Herman, A., 5
Herring, C., 57, 58, 79
Hill, M.A., 262
Hirsch, B.J., 234
Hoffman, L.W., 105
Holahan, C.K., 226, 227, 232
Hollander, E.P., 36
Hollinger, C.L., 189, 192
Hollingshead, A.B., 108
Holt, R., 106
Hooks, B., 179
House, E.A., 233
Huber, J., 35, 54
Hughes, E.C., 177
Hughes, J., 213

I, J

Ickovics, J.R., 7, 8, 35, 36, 40, 44–45, 54, 264,
   267
Jackson, J.J., 167, 181
Jacobs, N., 35, 117
Jacques, E., 103
James, J., 6, 7, 264–267
Janeway, E., 14, 17, 61
Jardim, A., 46, 241
Jenkins, D., 36
Jenkins, S., 84, 228, 233
Jerdee, T.H., 54
Johnson, C., 6
Johnson, F., 6
Josselson, R., 105, 113, 117
Jung, C., 103

K

Kafry, D., 160
Kagan, J., 38, 54
Kahn, E.D., 11
Kahn, R.L., 144
Kahn, W.A., 35
Kanter, R., 2, 13, 36, 43, 46, 52, 144, 149, 241,
   242, 249
Kariv-Agnon, E., 57, 58, 79
Karp, D.A., 244
Karschak, E., 13
Katz, D., 144
Kayden, Z., 47
Kelly, J.B., 134
Kerr, B.A., 189, 191
Kessler, R.C., 106
Kessler–Harris, A., 3, 4
King, M.C., 167, 183
Kranichfeld, M.L., 13, 78

L

Lange, S., 241
Langland, L.E., 192
LaRue, L.J.M., 167, 174
Laslett, B., 59
Lawrence, F.P., 242
Lax, R.F., 57, 58, 79
Lazarus, R.D., 135

Lederer, M., 241
Lembright, M.F., 243
Lerner, G., 167, 175, 179, 180
Levinson, D.S., 124, 145
Lewin, K., 143, 151
Lewis, T.L., 167, 184
Liefer, M., 77
Lillydahl, J.H., 243
Lincoln, Y.S., 59
Lipman–Blumen, J., 40, 46
Locke, E.A., 236
Loevinger, J., 108
London, J.T., 256
Long, J., 106
Lopatta, H.A., 150
Lorr, M., 108
Lubin, B., 57

M

Madden, T.R., 35
Majchrzak, A., 36
Malveau, J., 38, 54
Manis, J., 234
Marcia, J.E., 104, 105, 117
Matthaei, J., 2, 4
Mauri, N., 57
McAdams, D., 12
McClelland, D., 13, 84, 98
Mcliwee, J.S., 243
McNair, D.M., 108
McRae, J.A., 106
Midgley, M., 213
Milkman, R., 4
Mill, J.S., 262
Miller, J.B., 7, 12–15, 17, 19, 21, 78, 265
Miller, K., 178
Mishler, E., 16, 59
Mohanty, C., 263
Moore, K.K., 35, 54
Morantz, R.M., 190
Morasch, B., 242
Morrison, A.M., 237
Mortimer, J.T., 256
Murray, A., 166
Murray, H., 84
Murray, P., 182

N

Nadelson, C., 57, 58, 79
Nagy, S., 56
Naparstek, B., 57, 58
National Center for Health Statistics, 234
Nelson, B.J., 4
Nemerowicz, G.M., 105
Nieva, V.F., 40, 52, 183, 242, 261
Nigro, G.N., 235
Noble, J., 167, 177, 191
Noble, K.D., 189, 192
North, G., 160
Notman, M., 57, 58
Nye, F.I., 105

O

Oakley, A., 16, 59
O'Connell, A.N., 190
Oden, M.H., 190, 191, 214
O'Farrell, B., 4, 243
O'Leary, V.E., 7, 8, 35, 36, 40, 41, 44, 45, 48, 52, 54, 264, 267
Ong, A., 263
Oppenheimer, V.K., 1
Ornstein, H., 236, 237
Osherson, S., 11
Osipow, S.H., 1

P

Paluszny, M., 57, 58, 79
Parkhurst, J., 175
Parry, G., 222, 234
Patton, G.C., 183
Peery, P., 175
Peplau, L.A., 12
Peterson, K.S., 40
Pfleger, L., 192
Phillips, S., 57, 58, 79
Pietromonaco, P.R., 234
Pines, A., 160
Pines, D., 57
Pleck, J., 155, 156, 256

Pomerleau, C.S., 190
Powell, B., 105
Pozanski, E., 57, 58, 79

R

Rainwater, L., 175
Rapkin, B.D., 234
Rapoport, R., 11, 59
Raven, B., 12
Reid, I.S., 167, 182
Reinharz, S., 228
Reis, S.M., 189, 190, 191
Reissman, C.K., 127, 134, 140
Repetti, R., 121
Reskin, B., 261
Richter, J., 6, 150, 266
Riemer, J.W., 243, 250
Robbins, L., 11
Rodenstein, J., 192
Rollins, J., 169
Rose, P., 262
Rosen, B., 54
Rosenwald, G.C., 15, 60
Rossiter, M., 4
Rubin, C., 57, 58
Rubin, L., 130
Rubington, E., 165
Ruddick, S., 2, 11
Runyan, W.M., 268
Russo, N.F., 190
Ryan, W., 175

S

Salmon, M., 3
Salt, P., 4
Samson, R.V., 13
Sanford, L.T., 117
Sawin, L.L., 13
Scheff, T.J., 166
Schein, E.H., 149
Schein, V.E., 40, 53
Schenkel, S., 105
Schreiber, C.T., 242

Schreiner, O., 262
Schrodel, J.R., 8, 241, 264, 266, 267, 269
Schur, E.M., 165, 166
Schuster, D.T., 7, 8, 192, 264, 267
Schwartz, F., 6
Schwartz, L.L., 189
Schwartz, M., 57, 58
Sears, P.S., 224, 226
Sekeran, U., 150
Shaw, E.A., 242
Shaw, K.L., 236
Shaw, L., 83, 103, 106
Shehan, C.L., 233
Sheldon, E., 106
Slade, M., 53
Sleeper, L.A., 235
Sorenson, A., 103
Spence, J.T., 13
Spencer, D., 262
Stainles, G., 40, 156
Staples, R., 175
Sternburg, J., 190
Stewart, A., 12, 83, 84
Stiver, I.P., 117
Stratham, A., 2, 35, 36, 44, 54
Sutton, S.D., 35

T

Tangri, S.S., 233
Tennov, D., 13
Terman, L.M., 190, 191, 214, 215, 222
Terrell, M.C., 179
Tesch, S., 105
Tiger, L., 130
Tomalin, C., 262
Tomlinson–Keasey, C., 6, 7, 8, 236, 264, 265, 267
Travis, C., 40
Trebilcot, J., 13
Treiman, D.J., 11

U

Ulrich, L.T., 3

U.S. Bureau of the Census, 203
U.S. Department of Labor, 1

V

VanDusen, R., 106
Vaughan, D., 127, 134
Verbrugge, L., 105
Veroff, J., 11, 12, 84, 85, 107, 108, 261
Voydanoff, P., 11

W

Waite, L.J., 233
Walker, A., 168, 181
Wallace, M., 167
Wallerstein, J., 134
Walshok, M.L., 242
Warr, P., 222, 234
Weeks, M.D., 233
Weinberg, M.S., 165
Weiss, C., 241
Weiss, R.S., 127, 132, 133
Weitzman, L.J., 132
Wertheimer, B., 4

West, C., 179
Westoff, C.F., 234
Wetherby, T., 241
Whitbourne, S., 105
White, D.G., 175, 176
White, K., 104
White, R.P., 237
Williams, D., 167
Williamson, J.B., 244
Winkler, B.S., 262
Winnicott, D., 77
Winter, D., 12, 17, 61, 83, 86
Wollstonecraft, M., 262
Woolf, V., 262
Wortney, B.N., 35

Y

Yancy, W.C., 175
Yoder, J.D., 242
Yohalem, A.M., 191

Z

Zajonc, R.B., 135
Zellman, G., 103

Subject Index

A

Abandonment, 88, 90, 94, 96, 98, 223, 251
Accomplishment, 18–20, 26, 28, 30, 62, 63, 69, 71, 78
Achievement, 189, 191, 203, 204, 207, 209, 216, 218, 224, 229, 236, 263, 267, 268 (see motivation)
Activists, 6
Adjustment, 107, 114, 146, 170
Adolescence, 45, 53, 88, 104, 115, 116, 191, 193, 196, 197, 198, 209
Advancement, 39, 41, 106, 251
Affirmative Action, 122, 166
Age (Aging), 42, 43, 123, 159, 160
Aggression, 26, 27, 193
Agrarian economy, 213
Agricultural work, 4
Alienation, 51, 197
Ambivalence, 14
Anger, 16, 17, 20, 26, 31, 63, 67, 68, 134, 137, 204
Anxiety, 14, 15, 26, 29, 31, 65, 67, 69, 70, 77, 90

Assertive, 172
Attitude, 40, 83, 84, 98, 100, 170, 243, 258
Authority, 23, 26, 31, 48
Autonomy, 84, 92, 106, 109, 185

B

Baby (also see infant), 57, 58, 61, 62, 66, 67, 69, 70, 71–80, 90, 91, 93, 95, 97, 98, 268
Babysitter (see childcare, daycare), 62, 90, 96, 156
Balancing (career and personal life), 6, 158, 160, 206–210
Bias, 53, 125
Black history, 169, 173, 175
Black men, 172, 173, 181–184
Black women, 3, 4, 6, 165–185, 245, 254
Blue collar, 241–258, 264, 269
Boss, 7, 35–54, 66, 89, 137, 265
Boundaries, 5, 6, 28, 75, 76, 79, 143–162, 263, 266
Bureaucracy, 43
Burnout, 56, 149, 160, 161, 162

C

Career, 104, 106, 107, 109, 111–113, 115–117, 125, 131, 138–141, 144, 149, 160, 203, 215, 217, 219–222, 233, 234, 236
  aspirations, 162, 216, 232
  choices, 1, 6, 7, 78, 111, 113, 116
  development, 72, 83
  goals, 219
  path, 124, 149
  pattern, 108, 109, 111
  stage, 159, 160
Case study, 15
Census bureau, 5
Challenge, 39, 40, 50, 52, 68, 84, 88–90, 99, 115, 140, 215, 218
Childbearing (see pregnancy), 3
Childcare (see babysitter, daycare), 4, 69, 75, 115, 129, 177, 233
Childhood, 45, 70, 195, 196, 209
Children, 59, 67, 69, 74, 75, 77, 114, 123, 124, 127, 129, 130, 138–141, 150, 152, 154, 156, 158–160, 176, 182, 183, 191–194, 201, 207, 218, 220, 221, 225–228, 231
Civil Rights, 4, 175
Clerical workers, 4, 139, 171, 202, 220, 227, 264, 267, 269
Colleague, 24, 75, 79, 147, 157
Committment, 31, 43, 51, 77, 96, 103, 104, 140, 141, 149
Communication, 47, 48, 52
Community, 42, 51, 52, 167–170, 174, 175, 181, 183, 194
Community workers, 171–173, 175, 176, 178, 180–185
Compartmentalization, 7
Competence, 26, 31, 37, 43, 44, 52, 68, 84, 89, 92, 99, 135, 138, 177, 190, 192, 193, 200, 201, 204–206, 210, 230, 236, 251, 267
Competition, 36, 40, 41, 69, 237
Confidence, 47, 85, 89, 113, 115, 116, 189, 229, 230, 235, 237, 247, 248, 255, 258
Conflict, 14, 89, 93, 96, 144, 145, 146, 158, 200
Control, 78
Cooperation, 37, 40, 42, 52
Coping 35, 57, 71, 132, 135, 137, 150, 153, 154, 156, 158–160, 162, 206, 249, 268

Co–workers, 36, 37, 39, 41–43, 50–52, 68, 125, 128, 242, 243, 245, 248–253, 257, 266
Culture, 77
Custody, 138

D

Daycare (see babysitter, childcare), 85, 88, 91, 99
Decision Making, 104
Dependency, 31, 93
Depression, 66, 89, 95, 105, 127, 135, 136
Destructiveness, 18–20, 24, 26, 28, 30, 67, 79
Devalued, 78
Development, 15, 57, 59, 60, 79, 90, 104, 107, 109, 111, 114, 116, 190, 193, 207
Deviance, 166, 170, 175, 176, 177, 178, 183, 185
Discrimination, 6, 7, 8, 11, 123, 166, 185, 242, 245, 247, 249, 251–254, 257, 258, 269
Divorce, 66, 106, 107, 111, 121–141, 194, 203, 222, 224, 226, 231, 234, 245, 266, 267
Domestic work, 3, 4, 107, 167, 171, 172
Dual Career, 148, 150, 157, 236, 265

E

Earnings (see fees, income, pay, salary, wages), 117, 248
Efficacy, 7, 18, 69, 191, 192, 193, 198, 203, 252
Empathy, 25, 63
Employment, 103, 104, 107, 108, 111–113, 116, 117, 121, 128, 129, 131, 141, 234, 268
  Opportunities, 105
  Patterns, 103, 106, 108, 109, 116, 117
Empowering, 30, 31, 63, 77
Enablers, 215–235
Envy, 19, 26, 67, 69, 70, 78
Expectations, 77, 85

F

Family, 4, 62, 64, 66, 69, 70, 78, 83–100, 139, 140, 150, 154, 156, 158, 160–162, 170, 213, 217–219, 226, 231, 246

Farming, 213
Father, 110, 115, 127, 158, 159, 193, 229, 246, 250
Fees (see earnings, income, pay, salary, wages), 23
Feminine, 106, 176, 178, 192, 227, 230, 231
Feminism, 106, 167, 170, 179, 181
Feminist, 5, 15, 16, 50, 51, 53, 174, 175, 182, 184, 185, 189, 261–263, 270
Financial, 106–111, 116, 129, 132, 202, 221, 223, 230
Friend (Friendship), 37, 42, 130, 249, 263
Frustration, 81, 91, 92, 207, 252

G

Gender, 123, 137, 140, 141, 148, 153, 155, 157, 237
Gifted women, 189–238, 264, 265
Guilt, 17, 20, 61, 69–72, 76–78, 111, 115

H

Harassment, 8, 11, 245–258, 270
Health, 105, 115, 116, 127
Helping Professions, 13, 14
Helplessness, 21
Hispanic women, 4
Home chores, 152, 161
Homemaker (see housewife), 107, 109, 112, 113, 114, 116, 174, 193, 203, 205, 219, 221, 224, 225, 226, 231, 256
Housewife (see homemaker), 141, 217, 246
Husband (see spouse), 62, 69, 72, 73, 83, 88, 91–93, 95, 97, 98, 107, 110, 112, 113, 115–117, 125, 129, 132, 133, 135, 156–158, 182, 201, 204, 215–228, 230, 231, 237

I, J

Identity, 2, 6, 14, 15, 18, 22, 28, 29, 59, 61, 72, 73, 76, 78, 79, 104–106, 110, 112, 113, 116, 117, 170, 198, 201, 214, 215, 228, 234, 236, 250, 256, 262, 266
 Professional identity, 72, 78, 79, 214
Inadequacy, 18, 20, 21, 28, 191, 206
Income (see earnings, fees, pay, salary, wages), 83, 106–108, 131, 203–204, 206
Independence, 63, 78, 91, 95, 200

Infant (also see baby), 85, 93
Infertility, 69, 70
Interview, Interviewing, 15–24, 28, 37, 53, 58–61, 75, 79, 84, 86, 89, 93, 108, 109, 123–125, 136, 137, 150, 151, 168, 190, 198, 200, 207, 244, 249, 264, 265, 267, 268
Intimacy, 37, 42, 45, 104
Isolation, 170, 171, 183, 184
Job environment (see work environment), 51

L

Labeling, 165–185, 189
Labor force, 108, 115
Leader (leadership), 46, 52, 219, 223, 237
Lesbians, 50, 51
Life stage, 149, 150, 159
Limits, Limit setting, 30, 75, 76, 79
Longitudinal, 84, 105, 190, 193, 214, 267

M

Male dominated professions, 4
Management, 123, 132, 148, 150
 Skills, 44, 46, 223, 237
 Style, 35, 37, 46, 53, 241, 242, 243
Managers, 4, 35, 46, 52, 122, 124, 129, 130, 132, 134–136, 139, 149, 237, 264
Marriage, 66, 86, 88, 92, 103, 106, 107, 121–133, 144, 145, 196, 203, 204, 216–224, 229, 235
Maternity leave, 60, 62, 69, 71, 73, 77, 95, 96, 98, 99
 leave of absence, 90
Matriarch, 169, 172, 174, 175, 181–183
Medical students, 4
Mental health, 28, 107
Mentoring, 40, 237
Middle age, 104, 106
Midlife, 103, 107–118, 190–194, 200–209, 220
Minority (minority women), 5, 166, 173, 250
"Mommy– Track," 6
Money, 40, 97, 108, 114, 117, 131, 132, 140, 213, 248
Mother, 58–80, 83–100, 107–109, 112, 114, 115, 158–161, 170, 175, 193, 218–221, 226, 228, 233, 235, 242

Motherhood, 6, 13, 14, 42, 57–59, 64, 73, 74, 77, 79, 103, 177, 216
Motivation (also see achievement), 83–100, 109, 266, 268
Motives (for work), 5, 11, 12, 31

N

NAACP, 173
Nurse, 86, 90–92
Nurturance 23–26, 30, 31, 60–64, 75–77, 176, 197, 215, 267

O

Old age, 106
Overcompensate, 77
Overqualified, 36, 39

P

Parent (see single parent), 77, 83–100, 113, 206, 209
Parental status, 42
P.T.A., 219
Partner, 220–222, 226, 228, 234
Patients, 26, 57–80
Pay (see earnings, fees, income, salary, wages), 50, 52, 106, 115, 191, 213
Personal growth, 91
Personality, 84, 85, 149
Personal life/experiences, 16, 42, 44, 57, 67, 70
Policy making, 4, 5
Poor women, 5
Postpartum, 57, 60, 67, 72, 76–78
Poverty, 106
Power (power holders), 4, 5, 7, 11–32, 35, 46–49, 60, 61, 64, 76–78, 109, 173, 177, 210, 262, 265, 267
Pregnancy, 7, 53, 57–80, 224, 264, 266, 269
Prestige, 4, 11, 12, 39, 64, 77, 78
Priorities, 57
Professional
  careers, 4, 6, 7, 13, 15, 107
  development, 91
  growth, 91

professionalism, 58
self, 75
Professors, 11–31, 265, 268
Promotion, 52, 90, 98, 132
Psychotherapy, 28, 29

Q

Qualitative
  analyses, 151
  data, 190
  methodology, 5, 124
  research, 125, 263

R

Race, 123, 244
Racism, 4, 170, 172, 178, 184, 185
Relationships, 5, 7, 14, 15, 26, 28, 31, 36, 39, 40, 42–46, 48, 51, 54, 57, 59, 66, 74–78, 85, 113, 117, 133, 143, 148, 149, 174, 192, 193, 200–209, 227, 236, 244, 245, 249, 250, 254, 258, 262, 263, 269
  hierarchical, 7, 23, 26, 30
  non–hierarchical, 7
Respect, 38, 40, 49, 52, 54, 78
Responsibilty, 21, 46, 47, 54, 69, 71, 78, 88, 90, 91, 95, 157, 161, 215, 218, 223, 224, 233, 258
Retail work, 4
Retirement, 107, 123, 128, 220, 221, 223
Role (see sex role), 28–31, 41, 43, 44, 54, 57, 63, 64, 77, 78, 84, 85, 92, 99, 109, 141, 145, 147, 148, 149, 152, 155, 166, 167, 176, 190, 200, 201, 207, 208, 218, 227, 231, 233, 242, 249, 268
  combination, 85, 88, 92, 99
  conflict, 153
  distinction, 46
  model, 25, 44, 51, 170, 206, 228
  overload, 161
  strain, 105

S

Sadness, 16, 17
Salary (see earnings, fees, income, salary, wages), 140, 213

Satisfaction, 23, 24, 30, 36, 39, 40, 84, 86, 87, 89, 90, 94, 95, 98, 99, 108, 117, 131, 150, 161, 191, 195, 213–227, 234, 243, 248, 258, 261, 262
Schedule, 149, 150, 161
  flexible schedule, 110, 129
Secretary, 35–54, 86, 95, 97, 103, 106, 178
Self, 75, 78, 89, 91, 101, 105, 112, 117, 135, 137, 144, 146–148, 165, 206, 225
  awareness, 207
  concept, 189
  definition, 72
  esteem, 7, 18, 20, 72, 78, 107, 108, 111, 113, 116, 117, 129, 130, 131, 138, 141, 198, 244, 246
  image, 18, 20, 21, 131, 148, 198, 255
  worth, 72, 138, 234
Selfishness, 18–21, 26, 28, 69, 71, 78
Selfless, 25
Sensitivity, 37, 43, 44, 46, 48, 49, 52, 58, 61, 68, 205
Sexism, 6, 7, 185
Sexist, 262
Sex role, 6, 45, 242, 247, 250, 256, 257, 261
  female sex role, 12, 13
  gender role, 84
Sexual, 16, 17, 26, 36, 67, 78
Single
  parents (see parents), 5, 134, 139, 234
  women, 106, 123, 129, 222, 224, 245
Slave, 167, 169–178
Social class
  middle, 36, 86, 87, 171, 174, 182, 184, 193, 256, 262
  upper, 177
  working, 87, 256
Socialization, 45, 103
Social Security, 106
Spouse (see husband, wife), 78, 85, 127, 130, 132–134, 137, 138, 149, 150, 161, 191, 213, 215
Status, 4, 12, 35, 36, 52, 77, 84, 91, 99, 117
Step family, 234
Sterotypes, 13, 51, 54, 166–169, 172, 173, 175, 176, 178, 179, 181, 261
Stress, 22, 24, 85, 99, 126, 134, 137–139, 144, 160–162, 185, 256, 258
Subordinates, 36, 133

Success, 215, 218
Supervisors, 36, 39, 43, 44, 46, 89, 91, 95, 125, 132, 133, 137, 206, 242, 245, 248, 249, 251–258, 263
Superwoman, 233
Support, 52, 89, 96, 131, 143

T

Teaching, 84, 86, 103, 205, 218, 220, 223, 224, 225, 227
Theory, 14, 37, 72, 73, 263, 264
  Theoretical constructs, 61
  Theoretical model, 104
  Theoretical orientation, 73
  Theoretical perspectives, 75
  Theoretical stance, 74
Therapists, 7, 11–32, 57–80, 204, 264, 265, 269
Trades, 241–249
Transitions, 143–162

U

Underpaid, 160
Unemployment, 106
Unions, 4, 253, 254

V

Values, 57, 73, 78, 84, 100, 114, 213, 214
Violence, 67
Volunteer work, 111–117, 203, 219, 227, 228, 230
Vulnerability (see economic vulnerabilities), 57, 63–69, 78, 107, 111, 115, 116, 189, 191, 192, 199, 206, 209, 210

W

Wage differential, 4
Wages (see earnings, fees, income, salary, wages), 117, 248

Well–being, 103–118, 192, 203, 208
Wife, 89, 107, 156–158, 175, 216, 217, 227
"Womanist," 168, 181, 184
Women's Movement, 165, 168, 170, 174,
    183, 184, 208
Work
    Dead End, 39
    Definition, 5, 6
    Environment (see job environment), 44,
        149, 160
    Models, 1
    Part–time, 79, 83, 88, 90, 92, 96, 97, 99

Patterns, 215, 225–228, 233–235
Performance, 44
Skills, 39
Unpaid, homework, 1–3, 5, 6, 107
visibility, 3
Women's work history in the U.S., 3–5,
    171
Work and family
    Blending, 4, 6, 117
    conflicts, 156, 160
    lives, 136, 149